Mrs Ingma
Bless you
ongoing su
Jackie R

A time to live, a time to die

by
Jackie Ryalls

Published by the
Holy Ground Mission Society
P.O. Box No. 275.
Barnsley,
S75 - 3YE,
England.

A time to live, a time to die.

1. To everything there is a season,
   A time for every purpose under heaven:

2. A time to live, and a time to die;
   A time to plant,
   And a time to pluck what is planted;

4. A time to weep, and a time to laugh;
   A time to mourn,
   And a time to dance;

8. A time to love, and a time to hate;
   A time of war,
   And a time of peace.

Ecclesiastes 4

A time to live, a time to die

Published by Holy Ground Mission Society
ISBN No. 0 9537405-0 1

Printed by:- P.H.P. Litho, Barnsley, South Yorkshire.

DEDICATION

With deep appreciation to my husband Paul, who has given me the gift of friendship, much more than I deserved.

I trust that in retrospect through reading this book, he and the reader will realise that Paul is my hero. He has totally underpinned the work with his constant friendship. He has my love and respect much more than I am able to show.

I bless him for the freedom he has given me by allowing me to grow within the safe space of his love. May his eyes continue to be veiled from my weeds, and may he through his own beauty continue to search for the flowers within our relationship.

This work is also offered with much love and deep appreciation to all our family and friends, especially to our youngest son Richard, who during the war, willingly opened his heart in unselfish love, by allowing us the space to love an ever-growing family.

To each person who has touched our lives:
Please receive this offering as gift, in the clearest truth I can express from within myself.

Please find yourselves within the pages, as we have tried to honour your loving support, by being your hands and feet for the people in Bosnia. J.R.

INTRODUCTION.

These words were penned in 1980.

"To be moved to put pen to paper, is like not being able to find the paper quickly enough before the thoughts go! Often, I have been willing to share the deep part of myself only to recoil from fear of being judged or ridiculed."

Over the years many have asked. 'When are you going to write the book?' Each time I responded. 'Probably only when I am old and grey and in a wheelchair.' For each of us the very spark of life, the inspiration is in the now. We need to be people of the now. What we are, what we have to give away is for the now. We can so easily miss the opportunity and block the channel, for fear of not being approved.

Each of us is unique, and to allow ourselves to be known at a deep level can become the gift. In five seconds time, something outside ourselves can infiltrate our space, and the pure inner movement within our spirit, which has been given us to give away has already been lost into memory.

What I discovered in 1993 when attempting to write this book was that the 'I' kept getting in the way. I became ashamed of my imperfections as I struggled further to move along the Monopoly board and found myself desiring more of the 'living waters' and less and less of the deep contaminated darkness within.

The more we heard people say 'Aren't you brave' the more Paul and I questioned our motives. We know hearts are deceitful and the enemy of our souls is prowling about like a lion waiting to devour us.

In some ways, this book is not so much about Bosnia but more a commentary on constant choice. A choice that is open to all of us who are prepared roll up our sleeves against self-hypocrisy, self-darkness, self-ugliness and the constant desire for self-gratification. There is a dark oppression, ugliness, so deep within, that can consume us if we let it. Only we who have dived into the depth of our own darkness can begin to penetrate any understanding of our own weakness.

For years I have experienced that weakness reigning in my life. I know the damage I have inflicted. I have watched helplessly as people whom I have loved sunk headlong into the game of justification, happier to blame you than to admit their own weaknesses. I hate that darkness. I hate that deception. I hate the passiveness of any of us that dares to ignore the damage, which is done through our games of pretence. The game which says "I'm the victim, look what they have done to me." I hate that darkness with an energy that is so strong there are times my body can hardly contain the only message, which when reacted upon, will release us from the evil of Satan's bondage.

We need to fight the negative spirit reigning in us. Dare we continue to ignore the inner voice of repentance? Can we make a new start? Are we willing to grow? Are we willing to become a tool in God's hand? As Jenny Hales once said:

'This book is not going to be an entertaining little account but it is an outburst against evil. It is an evil none of us is immune to.' The evil to which I refer is not neatly and safely in the context of other peoples wars, thus making us the goodies, the knights in shining armour running to the rescue. The fact is we 'Christians' can be the very stumbling blocks to the Kingdom of Heaven. We can be very detrimental to the spiritual health of others. Maybe a government health warning should cover us.

For those of us who wear the label Christian, it is good we wake up; time is short. How dare we try to stand in the presence of an omnipotent and awesome God and think we are not guilty? May we all be encouraged in our own relationships to continue to choose to make the changes towards being constantly forgiving, which leads to healing. May we all continue the process of surrender that we may not have to learn from the pain of external war.

I pray that all who read this book will do so with an open heart. So from what started in a moment of time, I pray this offering will, by God's Mercy and Grace, become a tool in the hands of the Living God.

This book belongs to you.

It is dedicated to each one of you who saw the name Bosnia and made a move in your heart.
It is dedicated to each person who walked around a supermarket and bought an extra bag of sugar or flour for people whom they had not met and probably never will.
It is dedicated to every person who sent food through schools and churches in response to the quickening within their hearts.
It is dedicated to the person who sent a sewing machine complete with every colour of cotton; to the many persons who sent shoes, clothes, blankets, doors, radiators, paint etc.
It is dedicated to every person who turned out from a warm home on a cold night to raise funds in support of the people in Bosnia.
It is dedicated to you, the church workers who were concerned first that there would be an audience for your guest speaker on Bosnia and then who were more concerned when the speaker was running late! To all those who washed the cups behind the scenes facilitating yet another gift to be given towards the many hundreds of gallons of diesel necessary to keep our lorry from getting thirsty. To the children who sent pocket money along with the elderly who sent pension money, all sacrificial giving. To every soul who felt the pain of the Balkans, who asked our Heavenly Father to intervene and then went on to pray for our personal protection and

deliverance from danger, without which we would have not survived.
To every heart which felt the pain of Bosnia.
To all of you who have loved from where you were, in the way in which you could.
Please read, knowing you were there. We honour your love for the people in Bosnia.
You have given of yourselves; you did not cross over on the other side of the road.

We are all players in this story. I ask you to read between the lines and see how God has moved the Chess pieces about, and what can be achieved when love is given a chance and faith is put into action.

To you all: -

'THIS IS YOUR STORY'

'THIS IS HIS STORY'

One in which we have been privileged to serve.

CONTENTS

Security Incidents 3 September 1992 - 30 November 1993

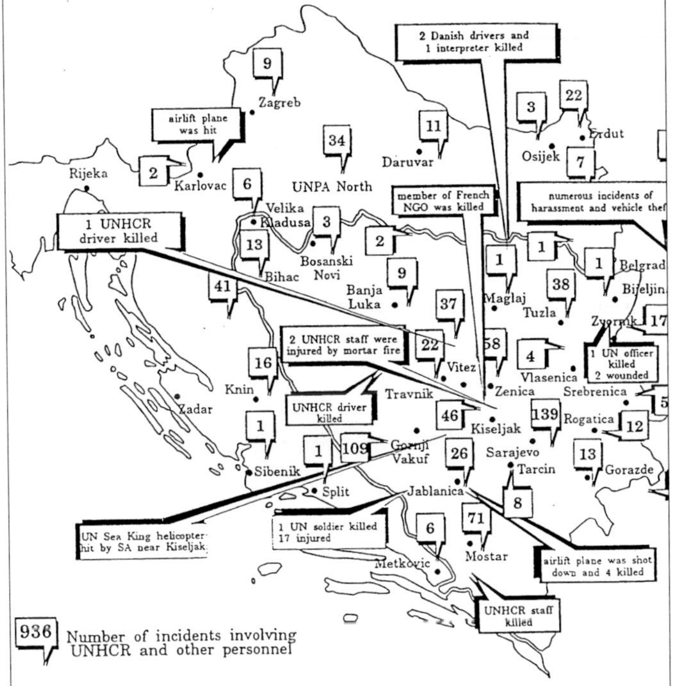

Notes: Not all incidents have been reported to UNHCR thus the above map only shows a partial picture of the security problem.

By 30 November, 64 soldiers had been killed - 29 in war related incidents - since the deployment of UNPROFOR.

Since the start of the war 34 journalists were killed (+2 missing)

Ten UNHCR staff or staff associated with UNHCR's operation have been killed in Bosnia and Herzegovina.

Map 1: Security incidents involving international staff in Bosnia

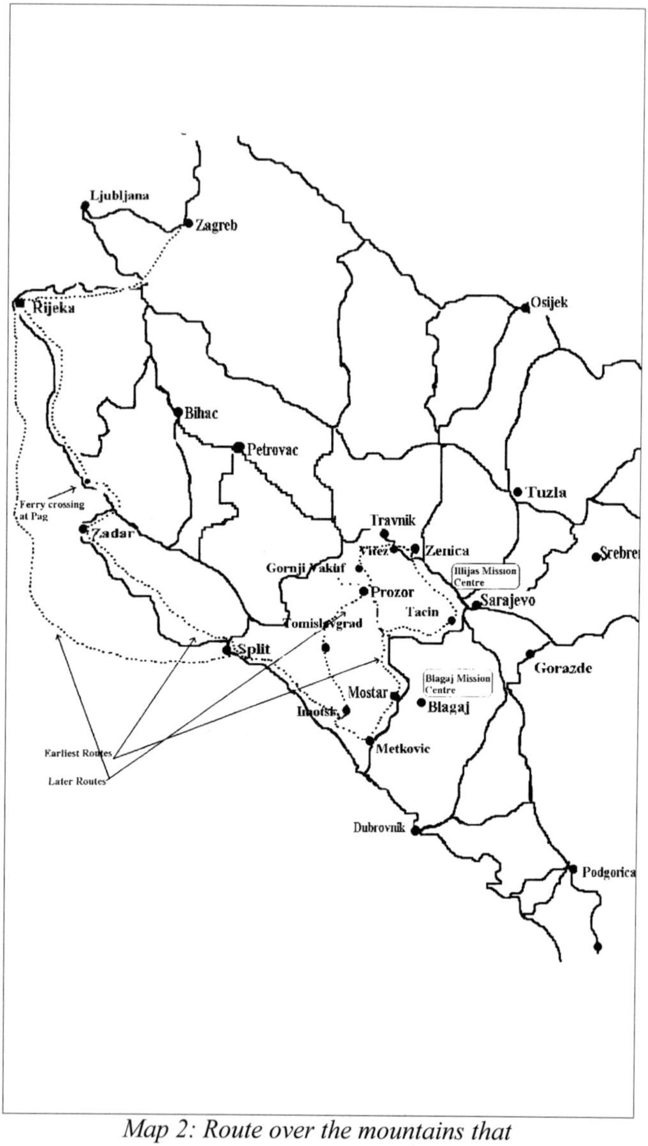

Map 2: Route over the mountains that Paul and Jackie took over the war-years

Chapter 1.

CONVOY OF HOPE

"... and he is looking for one hundred vehicles to take aid to refugees in Croatia," came the words droning over the radio as I listened with only half my antennae directed towards the worldly sound waves.

Trying to ignore the whole report I looked across at Paul who by this time was blissfully enjoying his rest, cocooned in the warm sweet smelling sheets, with his head comfortably resting on the cream satin pillows. He, like most men in time honoured style, was soon asleep with a look of complete contentment on his kindly bearded face.

"...and I heard the audible voice of God," continued the interviewee on the airwaves in Autumn 1992.

Snuggling into the warmth, and trying to settle down by bending my body around the contours of my relatively new 'God given husband', I tried not to listen, but was unknowingly hooked by the inciting message.

The interviewer continued, "and you are looking to raise a convoy of one hundred vehicles to travel across Europe and meet on the outskirts of Slovenia?"

"Yes that's right," he continued, "anyone who can bring any kind of vehicle full of food and clothes for the refugees in the camps out there, contact me. These people have lost their homes and have nothing. The trip should take about two weeks. If there is anybody out there listening, who thinks they could help..."

"Wake up Paul," I urgently insisted, giving him a sharp dig in the ribs for good measure.

"What? What's the matter?" he struggled to focus his mind on returning to planet earth.

"This is just right for you. You've always wanted to go to the Congo or something. Your van's sitting outside and you've always wanted to do something worthwhile. Well, this will suit you down to the ground!"

Having already grasped the vision of a hundred lorries, vans, trailers, in fact all sorts of vehicles rolling across Europe, I tried again, confident that Paul's response would be one of placating me, in the hope of being allowed the opportunity of returning back to the land of nod without more irrational ideas being hurled at him at this late hour.

"Imagine one huge convoy of hope gaining ground under *His* banner, weaving its way through all those countries." I mused actually seeing the scene in my minds' eye.

"What are you talking about Jackie? Go to sleep! Stop being a pain!" Paul bit back. By now beginning to show signs of not really appreciating being 'got at' at this unearthly hour.

"No, seriously. This is just right for you. Listen!"

Much to Paul's irritation, I jumped out of bed and scrambled to find pen and paper to write down the contact number.

He turned his back, grabbing the bedclothes as a form of defence and protest.

"Why do you always come alive when everybody else is trying to get some sleep?"

I was now walking on water.

"Seriously," I insisted, "this really *is* just for you. We will send off in the morning for the details, I've got the number." I was quite triumphant at pulling such an opportunity off the conveyor belt of life as it passed my view, especially when I wasn't even looking.

Little did we realise at the time that everything we had been through in life, had been the preparation which led to this very moment. The first chess piece was now in position, our lives were about to take on a new almighty dimension. Almighty being *His* operative word. After all isn't this what we expect when we pray, 'Lord use me?'

Next morning, in a more conscious state, Paul had no trouble agreeing that it all sounded very feasible, possible and even quite exciting. I assured him, although only just out of hospital after major surgery, I would do everything possible to get behind him and help him join the convoy, if that was what *he* felt he would like to do.

It only needed a few phone calls for us to fill the van with aid. We didn't need to reach out very far as most of the help came from our immediate neighbours, family and friends who were happy to support such a venture.

Our biggest problem was transport, for although our home had all the hallmarks of our more affluent times of the past, we both now lived very modestly, supported by Paul's plumbing work.

Paul and I had both been married before and he was very understanding of my needs for inner healing from the emotional scars which inevitably we bring into our relationships. I was by this time learning to trust him. For me he was a straightforward answer to the prayer of,

"Lord can you make him a divorcee, because I don't want to follow in the wake of a perfect wife." It was Paul's unquestionable love over the years, which gradually allowed me to let him discover the child in me, which few were privileged to see.

Although my early memories of childhood are fragmented, I can recall a few scenes from a period between 1943-1949 when many children were moved from industrial cities and placed with a variety of different families.

During the war years, my Mother needed to work to support the family, which inevitably freed Father to play hard away from home. However it was my father who fetched me back from one family, when he discovered I had been sleeping six in a bed with other children, and that my shoes had been given to the daughter of the household.

I can remember the hem of my dress showing about four inches below my coat and already could sense the shame of such a situation in the eyes of my Mother.

In contrast for another period I lived with a Bank Manager and his wife near London, and can still visualise the bright colours in the beautifully embroidered tablecloths. I can recall the taste of honey from the jar placed strategically by the French Windows, and I remember I was allowed to lick the sweet-tasting nectar off the end of my finger as I passed into the beautiful garden.

Apparently that couple had wanted to adopt me, but on hearing of the proposed plans, again I was hastily brought home, but this time by our mother. I had often wondered who the couple were and were they still alive?

After this near change of fate, I was promptly dispatched to live with an aunt who was eventually to become the Matron of Broadmoor. (Britains Top Security Mental Hospital.) I know I would have trained to become a nurse had my formidable aunt not insisted I should live with her, and follow her into mental nursing. So, in spite of the desires of others, my path was held within the family unit to run its God-given course.

By the end of 1945 our parents declared 'new start' and I remember as a five-year-old child being awe struck by the spectacular colours of the autumn trees as my elder brother and I were driven in a taxi through the beautiful Wye Valley. We went to live in the Anchor Hotel, Tintern, where my mother took the job as head cook to earn our accommodation, whilst my father worked away in Chepstow. I am not sure if it was their intention that father worked away, I think the truth is... he seldom came home.

For my brother and I, at least for two years in the glorious Wye Valley, our lives were idyllic. I can still recall the scent of the sweet smelling meadow grass and the soft, pale coloured primroses. Tiny wild strawberries could be found in the hedgerows, and the giant walnut tree was generous to extreme with her excessive fruit. The juicy nuts could be found nestling in the soft mud at the entrance to the cow shed. I thought my heart would break the day we came to leave this peaceful place and I could only hide my disappointment, and promise myself that one-day I would return.

Back in the city of my birth Coventry in 1947, it was hard to find any beauty in our surroundings. We lived above a cobbler's shop where our Father kept greyhounds which were only accessible down an open iron fire escape. The dread of my life was for him to ask me to feed the hounds, because it first meant I would have to run the gauntlet through packs of giant rats. They would run down the fire escape ahead of me and back track under the fifth step from the bottom, at which point, my feet would curl up beneath my legs as I attempted to jump down the final steps without completely losing all the sloppy food.

The grey upstairs bathroom needed to double as a kitchen and my brother and I would need to sit on the edge of the bath to eat at the old wooden table. We learnt that any attempt to touch the boiling water from the saucepan on the electric cooker nearby, would definitely produce a severe shock.

My place of refuge was a single black iron bed in the same room as my parents, and because I found the ugly metal bars at the head so offensive, I used to decorate them wih bows, which I made from the silver paper found in my mother's cigarette boxes. The little bed however, did afford me the protection to hide under the bedclothes when my father returned home in the early hours. It didn't take him long to find reason to fly into a rage, and tip up the double bed if my mother dared to refuse to turn over… whatever that might have meant.

In the daytime there were times when I would hide behind the green settee clutching my pet greyhound for protection. One Sunday afternoon from my vantage point, I could see my father standing there the worse for drink, with blood running from the corner of his mouth... raging. Although able to hold her own verbally, our mother for once, retaliated by throwing a full pot of boiling tea straight at him.

Looking back now, it is hardly surprising that I was a chronic asthmatic and missed so much schooling, consequently, I left school hardly able to read and with no academic skills. I realise today I inherited much from my mother's strength of character, and thankfully through it all she never lost her sense of well being and she certainly passed that sense onto us children.

For me the need for spiritual development had started at the age of twenty-five, way back in 1965 with one glance across a crowded dance floor. 'Strangers in the night' as the song goes. Little did I realise the life and death pain of every emotion was just a dance away. With just one glance, a chemical reaction had been ignited and in a moment of time, without either of us realising it, the man standing in front of me was to become the very purpose of my life for the next twenty years.

Soon I was to worship the very ground on which he walked. This meant he held the ultimate balance of power in the relationship, which for the survival of the subsequent marriage, proved to be emotionally and spiritually disastrous.

Over the years I had plenty of opportunity to get well aquainted with a negative oppressive spirit which was never far away. There's a state of helplessness; a place of darkness relating to emotional bondage and my addiction to this man was as lethal as any addiction to drugs or alcohol.

Neither of us could understand why the ups were sheer ecstasy and the downs were so dark. We were both in continuous emotional pain and both failed to get in touch with what was going on in the spiritual realm within ourselves.

Again, following my mother's pattern I began to feel used. The more I worked and provided the trappings of prosperity, the more it highlighted the imbalance in the relationship. The resentment grew and so did my outbursts of anger in frequency and verbosity.

The more we tried to fight ourselves out of the painful situation the more we were both consumed by guilt, and again the unresolved conflict was passed through our children onto another generation. In the end for the sake of peace, despair and defeat forced him to make choices, which I did not want to make.

After years of living with the effect of the negative power force all around and within, I was relieved to discover my Heavenly Father loved ugly people like me, and that *He* in *His* infinite wisdom had purposed a way of escape.

At a particular time of conflict within the marriage and in the eternal plan, I met a young lady whilst walking in a park, who told me that two thousand years earlier Jesus Christ, the Son of God, had been crucified on the cross for *my* sins. It turned out that the babe that they told me about at school, who was born in the manger, and who was crucified on the green hill, had something to do with me.

To be truthful, the whole experience of surrendering in my heart and receiving the free gift of forgiveness from God, felt much like being asked to jump off a high mountain and trusting that a parachute would come out and save me. But after much wrestling within, I made the absolute choice by faith to accept that God was real. Jesus Christ was in fact the Son of God and *He* had hung on the cross for my sins.

It was therefore no surprise that my husband asked me to make another choice, which would change my life and that of thousands of others.

"Jackie, choose between me and your friend Jesus."

"Please don't ask me to make that choice," I implored, knowing the final battle lines had been drawn.

So after 16 years of marriage the 'Stranger in the night' had left the matrimonial home, which in turn placed us on opposite sides of the spiritual divide.

So by the age of 40, and for the next four years, I walked constantly through the valley of darkness, mourning everything I had said or done throughout the marriage.

When we had moved into our last home together, complete with swimming pool, there were three children, four horses, two dogs, two goats, and several cats, yet, within an eighteen-month period, I found myself completely alone. "Lord you only have to let Satan send the boils," I challenged out of my place of despair. Then… the doctors told me I had breast cancer.

Thankfully the cancer was soon dealt with through some minor surgery but for nearly 4 years I continued through the refining process. I teetered on the edge, being tempted by the thoughts of Satan to end it all and the sheer gut determination of survival. I hung onto life by my fingernails with faith only the size of a mustard seed as I struggled to come out of the addiction.

Finally in bed-sit-land, staring at my worldly wealth of four ten pound notes, I thought, "Well girl, for an half intelligent person, you are an absolute fool. Eighteen months ago you were driving a Porsche…now you don't even have a home for your son," I braced myself, pulled myself up by my boot strings and agreed.

"OK Lord…I give in… You lead and I'll follow, but Lord, I really don't want to be alone, so please Lord, can I have a husband who loves you… and Lord if you can manage it… can he please be six foot tall?"

Paul said, that after we met several months later in 1985, I practically produced the tape measure to check his height, to make sure he was God's man for me. Today Paul and I can both say; *"All things (really do) work for good, for all those who love God, and are called according to His purpose." Romans 8v28.*

As a God given gift Paul has the most buoyant cheerful disposition, a kind, friendly nature, and is seven years younger. I think it is fair to say one would *not* put us together as the perfect match, but as years have gone on a deep love and affection has matured which has become more precious than gold. I can now look back and know 'The Potter' had decided it was time to seriously mould that rough old clay into some sort of useful vessel, and because of a well-worn body, my professional working days in the rat race, aged 52, were over. God had my full attention at last.

It was a bright, sunny, winter's day late in 1992 as Paul and I enjoyed each other's company, giggling and chatting on the way to take Paul's small van to be serviced, in anticipation of the forthcoming trip. We asked the garage owner to do a good job, as the van was to go out to Croatia. We were a little surprised when, having serviced our only means of transport, he held his sides with his large, black, greasy hands and just fell about laughing.

"This van won't get you to the end of the motorway lady, let alone Croatia!" he exclaimed with what seemed to be some delight.

A little dejected, but now even more determined, I thought, "O yes... well, we'll see about that!" By insulting Paul's little van, he was insulting my husband and that in turn was touching my 'Mother Hen' button.

After thirty-five years in business I was used to getting things done. Now, tuning in at a different level, I added, as if as an after thought, "If this trip is *really* in God's plan for you Paul, I expect *He* will provide a vehicle for you to use."

I was still nursing the internal and external scars from some major surgery, so of course going on such a trip was not in *my* plans either for convalescence or retirement. But, this did not stop me from getting quite frustrated with my own inability to function efficiently with all cylinders blazing. I knew I was still in the no lifting, no driving state of a six month recuperation period but, I thought I could make a few phone calls and get things moving better. I went on alarmingly, verbally whipping myself in preference to whipping Paul.

Thankfully, within days, a neighbour came to our rescue with the offer of a new Transit van, which was a company demonstration model; the only problem was it had a two thousand pound excess on the insurance. Whilst we appreciated the offer, we had no idea how we would ever pay the money if there was to be an accident en route and this of course increased the tension between Paul and I. Nevertheless, we were grateful for the vehicle and accepted it with much appreciation.

A local paper printed the story with Paul's need for a co-driver. We had quite a few phone calls, but began to realise most of the callers were probably not suitable, as it seemed many just wanted to escape from their own circumstances.

I was very uncomfortable with my own discernment in this matter and actually warned Paul. "When the next enquiry comes, ask them what contribution they are prepared to make, apart from their offer of time. Hard work and the need to raise funding have a way of sorting the men from the boys."

A few days later we received a call from a young man in Bristol who said he wanted to help and had already been in contact with the main group of the 'Convoy of Hope.' The organisers had put him on to Paul, yet immediately we both sensed there was something not quite right about him. Maybe it was nothing, but because of my unease we decided to be a little careful if this man came on the phone again. We had yet to learn, especially in this type of expedition, that any weakness of character would soon show up and cause havoc in a team.

In the meantime a middle-aged accountant, pleasant in manner, came offering his services. We instinctively liked Joe, welcomed him as a co-driver, and excitedly made our initial plans.

Within a few days, and much to my disappointment, the first young man, Freddie, phoned again having collected one hundred and sixty pounds and still wanting to join the team, but this time, he was even more earnest. I perceived we had a problem, but Paul still trying to be fair, decided the only thing we could do was to try to take two vehicles, which meant we would need to find another driver. Not wishing to fall into 'a weak little woman act' and as the days were getting short, I agreed to try to drive the thousand miles there but was even more surprised to find a great peace flood my heart.

This decision sent me into petitioning prayer.

"Lord, I'm sorry to come again over this matter of transport and you must know what you are doing sending this young man Freddie to us for a second time." I went on and on, filtering the matter over until, eventually, quietened and silenced, responded to my inner voice.

I had this deep desire to phone the Minister in Coventry who had married Paul and I, and with whom we had a deep spiritual bonding. I discovered his 'first in command', Graham Banks, was now working with a group in Leeds, called 'Alert', an organisation who were deeply committed to helping Bosnian refugees in this country. With Graham's encouragement and with more confidence now, I contacted the local churches and, within a few days, we had enough funds to hire a second van and enough aid to fill them both.

At no time in retirement had I really envisaged the thought of such an adventure. I had plans for long hours in our new little garden catching up on a lifetime of reading the likes of C.T. Studd and Catherine Marshall, to quote extremes. Yet, all of a sudden, having agreed I would go and much to my own alarm, all the old enthusiasm just burst forth, so I argued. "Lord I don't want to get involved with that world out there any more. I have done my bit, I'm tired and I need a rest!" I winged at the gates of heaven making them squeak, yet somehow every time I did so, some dear soul arrived at our door with two pounds of sugar for Bosnia. Somehow, my words just seemed to come back and hit me full in the face...who was I kidding anyway?

At last, with all the logistics settled, and due to catch the 3 a.m. ferry the following morning early November 1992, we agreed a meeting point with the other one hundred and twenty vehicles at a motorway service station. Our two transit vans would help make up a 'Convoy of Hope', all moving across Europe independently, and meeting again (God willing) in Austria three days later.

I was still tender inside, but nevertheless with the excitement of the last minute loading, I decided to put my body on hold for later care. After all what difference would it make? I simply decided none of this would inhibit our quest to experience in full what life had to offer us together as a couple.

I have to admit I was vaguely curious to know what pattern God was planning to weave into His tapestry for our lives. What we didn't yet know was that the main problem of this trip had still to appear.

The difficulties started when we naively picked up my co-driver Freddie. He had hitched a lift to the agreed meeting point. At first we chatted enthusiastically over a cup of tea at a service station.

It didn't take long for us to realise Freddie was interested in Eastern Religion and we anticipated there might be some clashes of opinion, our spiritual experiences of a 'Living Saviour' being very different. I didn't have a reputation for suffering fools gladly and as far as I was concerned, Freddie had little or no spiritual discernment, so I was indeed beginning to pray for a lot more 'Grace'.

When we made our second stop a few hours later, our fears were realised. Freddie and Joe, the two co-drivers, were soon at each other's throats. Paul in true conciliatory style tried to put all the niggles down to the late hour. "Come on you guys, let's learn to work together. We have a long journey to make."

"Let's draw a line, clear the decks of all that stuff, and start again," I interjected in support.

To enable Freddie and Joe to get to know each other a little better, I suggested they travel together over the next stretch to Dover, with Freddie at the wheel. It seemed a good idea at the time, at least until we arrived at Dover.

"That's it! - That's it!" Joe was pacing relentlessly up and down the quayside in the dark. He was refusing to go another mile with Freddie. "He's just a nut case, a bloody nut case!" he snorted.

Freddie, by this time, was standing menacingly at the open window my side of the cab, his finger wagging in my face. His breaths swirled about in the cold night air like that of a fiery dragon. Paul knew from experience, Freddie was making a big, big mistake.

"Do something - do something you bitch!" Freddie snarled, right into my face again. "He says I can't drive. It's all your fault!"

"Really?" I responded very softly, whilst at the same time, slowly and deliberately lifting myself from off the seat. I rose about four inches taller and fixed him firmly, eye ball to eyeball. "Why don't you back off friend, back off... Now!"

Quickly, Paul tried some light banter to diffuse the situation but we both knew we had a big problem, which needed sorting.

"I suppose I'll have to make a move before this gets out of hand." I told myself, deep down resenting the fact that Paul was relinquishing responsibility. I felt quite reluctant to take the initiative so late at night, equally, neither Paul nor I wanted confrontation.

I moved out into the cold night air and with the sea breeze getting under my light clothing, I approached Joe in quite a deliberate manner. I could sense Paul waiting. He knew without any doubt I was making a move on behalf of the whole team. "Are you prepared to do extra shifts with the driving Joe?"

"I'll do whatever you want, but I am not having that maniac in the same wagon as me!" Without compromise, Joe was clear about his agenda. He knew what he was not going to do and still trying to make his point he was pacing back and forth stamping his feet.

"OK, fair enough. This then is what we'll do." Wiping some sea spray away from my face and turning to Freddie. "OK Freddie you have a choice. Either... I will drive you back to the motorway, then you can hitch a lift back, or you can come for the ride as a passenger/navigator. The choice is yours, but... what we are *not* going to do, is have you going over the top every time a difficult situation arises, insisting on blaming everybody else."

Recognising that I had sussed his game, he immediately flipped into a rage, hurling abuse at me for all he was worth.... on and on. "No more words Freddie! Cool it! Make your choices!"

Paul knew I would not move or be manipulated by Freddie's temper tantrums or his threats. I was far too long in the tooth to buckle under that sort of pressure.

"I'll do my fair share of driving. We'll take shifts, two on, one off...all the way." With that I simply turned away. Subject closed. I already knew what Freddie would do.

As usual my husband began to soften his stance. He already felt sorry for Freddie and having experienced me in these situations before, knew I would be unrelenting but, remembering the two thousand pound excess on the van neither of us were planning on taking chances.

We eventually boarded the Ferry with Freddie in tow. The excitement of being with the other 240 drivers saved the day and broke the strained atmosphere.

By morning the only thing on our minds was adjusting to right hand driving through France's rush hour traffic. Joe and I drove the first leg in our respective vehicles, Joe leading the way.

Paul soon realised Joe was setting a much harder and faster pace than I would be prepared to drive, so we had to devise a system of communication signals.... Three flashes on the brake or headlights meant an emergency, two flashes meant slow down.

Within an hour, all the one hundred and twenty wagons had spread out and it soon became heart warming to see another truck with the 'Convoy of Hope' Red Heart sticker on the side. This, after all, reassured us we were still following the correct route.

We had no map, only a written itinerary, stupidly thinking that the whole convoy would be travelling together. It was amazing how we all managed to finish a thousand miles further on, all at the same place, all within a few hours of each other.

The only serious casualty had been one car with a trailer attached, which had jack-knifed en route. We all felt sick and disappointed for the drivers, who were fortunately unhurt, and gladly took on board, as best we could, their load of aid.

Two days passed and I was learning to 'really rough it' for the first time in my fifty-two years of life! I became quite accustomed to sleeping across the vehicle's front seats, trying to nurse a fourteen inch stomach wound, whilst the gear lever seemed to stick into every conceivable tender part of my body. Paul knew this was not too much fun with my condition or for my disposition.

"Staying in anything less than a five star hotel is your idea of sleeping rough!" He teased knowing the one thing that would affect me most was lack of sleep. He knew it was wise to give me a wide berth! This type of experience would certainly bring out the worst in my character.

It would only take Freddie's negative responses, coupled with my tiredness and 'Old Spiky' would have a hey-day, but we both knew my weakness and would be careful not to give Freddie or 'Old Spiky' the opportunity.

By now we were sure Freddie had some deep psychological problem so we were all quite determined to be pleasant and supportive towards him, and were certainly prepared to be as kind as possible. During each change over of drivers, the question was always, who will travel with Freddie?

In my wisdom, I suggested Paul as he had the kindest disposition in the team. He was elected as the safest companion. At least that was my theory until we arrived at the Austrian border when, to my absolute amazement, Paul came running over.

"I have a deep desire just to stop Freddie's continual insinuations and innuendoes. It's like he is determined to cause friction. Do I have your permission to punch this guy right on the end of his nose?" he pleaded.

"Absolutely, categorically NO!" I replied in one of my typically authoritative voices, which says... I'm not joking!

"Jackie he's driving me crazy. I can't stand any more of him. I've done everything, prayed and praised and still he eats away at me."

"Come on Paul, we are supposed to be 'Christians' and would you believe, 'Christians' just don't do things like that!" Paul could see I was trying hard not to laugh, and at the same time trying to deflect his growing frustration.

"OK you're right," he agreed, determinedly planting a quick kiss on the end of my nose and returned quite happily to his vehicle.

I was sitting back, reflecting on Paul's unusual response, when suddenly, Joe approached the wagon quite heated. "Paul's just been arrested! He's had to go with the border guards."

Joe's words were coming in quick succession. Apparently, Freddie had found, and pressed with sheer delight, Paul's red button.

"We were going through passport control when Freddie let out such a mouthful of stuff about you. Paul gave him a warning signal that he just completely ignored. Then, I couldn't believe it! Paul just simply picked him up by the front of his clothes and..."

I gulped, but whilst Joe was telling his story I noticed Freddie peeping round the corner, his facial expression smirking, fully triumphant. He had finally pushed Paul over the edge.

I felt sick. I knew Paul's loss of control would hurt him a lot more than it would Freddie. In Freddie's sick way of thinking he would now glory in being a victim and feeling justified in saying, "Look at what those so called 'Christians' have done to me."

Thankfully, Paul's so-called arrest came to nothing and by this time feeling quite ashamed of himself and not wishing to be beaten by Freddie's cruel sense of injustice, suggested they both try again. Needless to say it wasn't long before the old pattern resumed.

In Slovenia we had missed our way and were hopelessly lost when Freddie started to goad Paul again.

"This is your entire fault. Look what you've done." He was gnawing away like a dog at a bone, pushing Paul to his limit. Freddie seemed to have no awareness that maybe, just maybe, he was contributing to his own difficulties and that of the team in some small way!

Personally I was amazed how Paul just kept turning away, and didn't close Freddie's mouth for him, once and for all. I certainly had to wrestle with that inward desire myself.

However, instead of reacting, as one would expect under such provocation, Paul just decided to pray in tongues. Freddie couldn't understand what was happening and, when we inadvertently managed to get on the right road soon after, he exclaimed he had just seen a miracle. I nodded my head in unbelief. The real miracle was Paul had been given the Grace to respond gently.

Soon after this, one of the other drivers, a Catholic Priest, reversed over a tree trunk whilst parking. Much to his dismay, he had lost his reverse gearing.

On hearing from Freddie about the so called *miracle* of finding the way, the lovely priest approached smiling, half-joking, half-serious, but definitely tongue in cheek and asked. “Do you think you people could have a word upstairs about my gearbox?”

Chapter 2.

THE BOY AT THE FENCE

It's quite a sight seeing one hundred and twenty vehicles of all shapes and sizes, all wearing red hearts emblazoned with the words 'Convoy of Hope' stretching along a dual carriageway. Our team was about number twenty-four in the line and as we looked back from a bend in the road, we could see a two-mile line of 'love on the move.'

"Isn't it a great privilege to be part of such a gigantic love gift to our fellow man in need," I commented excitedly, proud of the love demonstrated by the sacrificial giving of the folk back home. There was a very real sense of 'the cavalry's coming' and our expectation was to deliver the aid directly into refugees' hands.

In Zagreb we were led into a large industrial compound, with many large units surrounded by a six foot high, steel safety fence. All the vehicles were eventually parked neatly in rows and we convoy drivers formed into groups for photographs. The media wished to maximise the arrival of such a large amateur convoy of private individuals.

Everyone was graciously entertained that evening by fresh-faced youngsters singing, although the general feeling was we didn't need entertaining. That wasn't why we had come, but we were appreciative of the kindness shown to us. Freddie, thankfully, had used the social atmosphere to join with another group of unsuspecting travellers and we gratefully breathed sighs of relief.

It was announced that the convoy would, the following day, be split up into smaller groups, going to various districts and different refugee camps. Volunteers were required to travel to the most dangerous areas, and we were disappointed when our team was not chosen.

"Maybe, they think women should not be sent to unsafe areas," Paul commented ruefully. He knew this would not satisfy his 'little woman' for long!

Having been booked into a hotel in the centre of Zagreb for a mere ten pounds, we had our first sight of beds and showers for days. Naturally we all looked forward to a nice hot shower followed by a good night's sleep. With the lifts not working Paul and I trudged to the fifth floor looking forward to a time of reflection and sharing. In customary fashion Paul took a full-length dive onto the single bed, wanting only to stretch his long body. Sinking into the bed and enjoying a few minutes peace, he reluctantly responded to my plaintive cry from the bathroom.

"Oh! No!...Paul...I can't believe it! No hot water!" I was by this time stripped off and freezing in the cold. "Please bring me that phone and a towel." I squealed through my chattering teeth. It only took a few moments on the phone for the shivering wreck to find a use for femininity. "Hi you guys. Have you got any hot water up there on your floor?" I waited with bated breath for their positive response. "Then please keep your eyes closed, we are on our way up!" This was no time for false modesty. At a time like this a girl has to do what a girl has to do.

Eventually Paul and I enjoyed the pleasure of a hot shower together, and it was an even greater pleasure later for me to have a warm husband cocooned around me. I was not blind to the fact we were one of the convoy's few husband and wife teams, a privilege we enjoyed.

The following day, after an early breakfast, we were back on duty in the compound champing at the bit, eager to be off. As each small group left, the stark sounds of blaring horns accompanied them. We noticed the Catholic Priest had no personal food for the journey. With a mischievous glimpse across to Paul first, I wondered if the Priest would like a couple of bars of chocolate as we enjoyed a few words of mutual encouragement. "No packed food? Maybe you thought God would provide! ...Well maybe He has." I smiled, patting him on the shoulder for good measure in my role of tarnished angel.

At last it was our turn to leave and we felt we were finally going to be able to do something positive to help the victims of this crazy war. We were destined for an area about twenty miles outside Zagreb called Petrina and we all set off feeling quite warm inside. Two vans, plus two other cars with trailers, made our small group up to six. We had no difficulty in finding our destination but we eventually found ourselves being shown to a double garage, adjacent to a smallholding, where we were asked to unload.

The family directing operations were most welcoming and assured us these goods would be used to feed refugees in the area. "Hey, wait a moment." I interjected. Whilst we had no reason not to trust the family, we had difficulty in hiding our disappointment at not meeting and feeding refugees directly. After all, it was the only way we would know if the food would be given freely to those for whom it was intended, plus we wanted to know it was not going to be sold on the black market.

At one level, however much we tried, we could not come to terms with the request to just unload into a storehouse with no understanding, or proof, as to what would happen to the food next. Instinctively I knew something else was going on. What did we need to learn? I started to probe further.

"Where exactly are the refugees at present?" We all felt we needed answers and were trying not to insult the family in question. The family was most gracious with their responses. Their sixteen-year-old son made a few phone calls to the local army and it was decided our whole group could be taken further up country.

With Paul and I now driving together followed by Joe. The family in their car led us for about four miles until we reached a steep riverbank where the brown mud somehow supported a pontoon bridge. We were expected to drive across the choppy waters along two eighteen-inch metal tracks. Immediately Paul jumped out to help in the guiding process, clearly confident that I could handle the rest.

A van with a trailer was in front so I told myself, "if the man in front can negotiate this bridge with a trailer on the back, so can I!" I took heart in the fact that at least Paul *thought* I could manage. The van in front skidded from side to side, its back wheels spinning in the soft brown mud. The whole exercise was a near impossibility for him but at the third attempt, the van driver successfully negotiated his way across the bridge and up the steep, muddy bank on the far side.

Now it was my turn! Paul was by this time on the bank guiding my wheels with frantic hand signals, maybe now not quite so confident in my female driving skills. I fixed my gaze on him. A big cheer went up when, much to Paul's delight, his 'little woman' managed to negotiate the crossing the first time. I thought of Dean, an old sparring partner in business back home, “This is just the sort of stuff he would have enjoyed, so why am I here instead of him? After all, this was adventure with little danger; but. “Lord where are the people we have come to serve?”

Eventually we stopped outside a family bungalow, and it was decided this was the end of the line and we could all unload our gifts. Somehow, something was still wrong, I had no peace within. How could we feel or for that matter be satisfied? Would leaving the food here honour all the people who had given back home? Why would our guide think this garage would be any better than the last? We still had no guarantees as to where the food would finish up.

We could see locals gathering, pushing and shoving. The sense of mounting tension and aggression indicated to me that we were moving in the right direction. But maybe we hadn’t yet arrived at the area of greatest need? A heated discussion arose between the self appointed leaders. We stood back and observed like flies on a wall. My questions would not go away. “Who is going to get this food? Where are the really needy people and what is the extent of their needs?”

Amidst all the confusion of the unloading with which the others were occupied, one of the locals in a thirty-five-year-old Austin Somerset pick-up truck beckoned Paul to follow him. Maybe now we could quietly slip away unnoticed.

The guide beckoned again and pointed to some woods about two miles ahead. Mist was hanging in the sultry air and I experienced a scary sensation running up and down my spine. “Serb front lines,” Paul commented, to give me a chance to change my mind. I simply gave him a sweet smile trying to ignore the rapid rise and fall of my chest as my heart pounded frantically.

We continued on in blind faith, following a stranger down narrow lanes, in a strange country and were exposed, for the first time, to the devastation left by war. Burnt-out homes had been raped by men's hatred and greed. Grenades had blown apart families, destroyed them and their homes in seconds. An old thick walled type house had a huge, jagged hole in the gable-end, exposing the remains of children's posters on their bedroom walls. The rest of the house contents had long since been burnt or stolen. Such extra-ordinary sights had an air of normality, which we found absolutely chilling.

The devastation indicated we were now on the right track to serve, and our apprehension increased as we drove closer to the threatening woods. "Paul, do you realise we are now well within the sights of snipers?" I was testing his awareness. He simply smiled, patted me on the knee and kept his foot well down on the accelerator. I felt as secure as I could under the circumstances, given we were in uncharted territory.

After making a right hand turn we came upon a dirt track path leading to a farmyard where many local residents soon gathered. These people, who had been carrying out their everyday tasks collecting wood, feeding a few chickens now gathered silently and stood uneasily around the van. Nearly all but the children were wearing black. Neither they nor we knew what to expect. I could see that in these circumstances my blonde hair must have made me seem like an alien from outer space. Thirty or forty people congregated and it was not long before, much to Paul's delight, the men were inviting us to share some home-made wine. These smiling, yet weather worn-faced people were looking to give.

The women seemed old and most of them were wearing cut down, men's shoes all very worn and mostly held on by string. Thankfully that was something with which we knew we could offer some real help. The women quite understandably were pushing and shoving trying to get as near to the open vehicle as possible. First out of the box was a pair of shoes ideal for a little girl. I looked around. There were quite a few children so we sorted out all the children's shoes we could find and passed them to the rear of the crowd to enable the little ones to be fitted first.

One of the younger women held a very attractive, black velvet slipper and was beckoning for the other. Paul pulled the complete box out of the van and in seconds, in a frenzied air of desperation, the crowd devoured about fifty pairs of shoes. Next Paul produced a big box of sugar and started to hand out individual packets to the heaving mass of battling women.

The men seemed to be holding back, apparently quite amused by the situation as Paul passed food out as quickly as he could. No sooner had an item come into the open air, than there were about six pairs of hands trying to grab it.

The pressure in front of him was growing, and he realised this scene was becoming ugly; someone could get hurt. Paul must have sensed I felt quite vulnerable and we were both relieved to find the next box contained a large box of chocolate bars all wrapped in Christmas paper as little presents. Immediately, as Paul handed out the bars as quickly as possible, the atmosphere changed. The women started to laugh, Paul and I began to laugh and even the men at the back joined in. Soon we were sharing the very joy, which we had come to bring! Paul knew I would not have missed these moments for all the five star hotels in the world!

Pulling out a jar of expensive face cream I laughingly mimed what it was. One younger woman nudged my arm. "Please," she pleaded. I knew that jar of cream would have been like gold dust to me, had I been in the young woman's shoes. It was a pleasure to give. After distributing goods for over two hours we finally surveyed the empty cardboard boxes and paper strewn over the disorderly farmyard.

We were about to depart when, to my dismay, I noticed the young woman, still standing with the one black, velvet slipper in her hand. Frantically Paul and I searched, but did not find its partner. I knew from experience what she would be feeling. It was as if Father Christmas had just come and given her an empty box.

I remembered how as a 7/8-year-old child I had pretended to be asleep under the bedclothes on Christmas Eve. My father and brother came in and out of my room several times, filling a pillowcase and my mind with words of "Oh, she will love this." or "this will taste good." The next morning what my imagination perceived as wonderful presents from Santa soon turned out to be cabbage, dirty old potatoes and a few oranges thrown in for good measure. It was awful to realise that now we could be the instruments of further pain for these people and, not the pleasure we had intended.

By late afternoon we were forced to think of the rest of the convoy, and how the others would feel about our subtle disappearance. Reluctantly we bade our farewells with an extra hug for the young woman with the 'half gift' and resolved to do better next time. As an after thought though, I went to the van, brought out my own shoes and gave them to her, so glad to be able to uphold the name of Jesus.

We all hugged each other again, waving goodbye, realising we had received much more than we could ever have given. We were in fact so filled with the joy of the experience, which we had just shared that we had no fear as we drove past the woods on the way back; in fact a simple lesson in the risk factor.

It was understandable: we found the others including Joe hopping with frustration. Arrangements had been made for an army lorry to take the whole group further into the area, which had been under attack, and Paul and I were delaying their departure. Thankfully there was no time to discuss the situation and the entire group hurriedly piled into the back of the camouflaged lorry as we tried to keep a low profile.

It nearly took a crane to get me on board and, for the first time, I probably showed my age and condition. To ease the pain in my back and stomach I perched on my heels, crouched down and used my knees as a spring board to counteract the effects of the continual bumping as the heavy lorry travelled over the rough ground. "You should be at home taking it easy," Paul encouraged...just a little too late!

"Taking it easy! What's that? Come on Paul, you know me better than that! We all have identical suitcases, it's just that some of us pack a little more in than others."

The lorry continued over rough dirt tracks; through an area where every home had been shelled, sprayed with bullets, and then left to burn out, exposing the devastating effects of evil engulfing a whole community. This awful sight is scored into our memories forever. These souls had their way of living raped, their privacy hacked to pieces. How do victims of man's desire for power and greed live with these scars? Could the people who had laughed over the chocolate bars have suffered similar experiences to these people?

I was just beginning to understand a little and wanted to put my arms around them as a nation, hold them and somehow be the very channel through which they could receive healing.

"Put that camera away, you idiot!" shouted one of the drivers. I was shaken out of my thoughts. The lorry stopped abruptly. Half the group was acting as if this was a guided tour around Central London.

I found the anger well up inside me. "How dare we come and take photographs of these people as if they are exhibits in a zoo? And how dare we come here with left over clothing with buttons missing?"

I wanted to lash out, but at the same time I was also deeply embarrassed. It seemed to me, we were piling insult upon injury. I felt alone, as if the only one seeing. It was isolating, yet I questioned, "How dare I think I am the only one to feel all these emotions?"

Again, I was wrenched sharply away from my internal struggle.

"Be careful where you walk! There could be landmines!" called the driver.

"Come on," I suggested eager to get us amateurs out of here before we insulted these people further. I felt sick within. "Who do we think we are anyway? What do we think we are doing coming here to look at the sights?" I felt a sense of deep shame and embarrassment. I had finally got in touch with the hidden agenda I had sensed earlier. 'The feel good factor.' That's it, we have done our bit, we have got the 'feel good about ourselves' factor. So now it gives us the right to take our photographs and go home to show how brave we have been. Screaming inside I banged the air with my fist. How dare we? How dare we? I looked around wondering what the others were seeing and how they were reacting inside.

One of the men's trailers was still full with aid, so we decided to stop again in the village on the way back. We off-loaded at one of the local homes and, within a short space of time; people were streaming from all over, as if summoned by a Heavenly Call. The aid looked impressive.

There were commercial sized packets of soap powder, boxes of cereal, which looked more like pan scrubbers than food, and many tins of baby milk. When we reached the stage for the clothes being un-packed, I did my best to hide a white, straight skirt that would have looked wonderful on Princess Grace of Monaco but was not really suitable for these ladies. It brought home to me how little I had previously understood the plight of these people and that there were many people who were still unaware of the reality of the situation in Croatia at that time.

Thankfully, before I blew a fuse, my attention was diverted as the host of the house beckoned us all inside for some welcome refreshments. The kitchen/living room was quite large and life revolved round the black, wood burning, cooking stove. The whole team were hungry and quite worn out by this time.

Small children looking tired were whining around their mother's skirt, whilst they looked at the hard, abrasive, brown cereal. It was then I realised the mother didn't know what this cereal was, or what to do with it. Standing up and quietly moving towards the kitchen stove, I found a burnt saucepan, mixed some of the baby milk and put it on the stove to warm. Placing two brown squares in two dishes with spoons full of sugar; I carefully poured on the improvised milk. The two children eagerly took the bowls, and moved onto the settee next to Paul for some comfort.

Somehow I managed to communicate to the mother, "now, tomorrow you show the other mothers what to do."

The mother smiled. What joy! At last I personally had been useful. Now, I was more than ready for bed. "Come on you men. Please can we crawl back into our own little foxholes?"

The next day started exceptionally cold and very damp. A brief meeting this day would change the course of our lives forever. Quite a few of the convoy had already left for England and Paul and I were about to leave, when one of the other drivers came running over.

"There are two men at the compound fence and it looks as if they're trying to attract your attention," he panted.

Tentatively I followed Paul over to the fence to see what the men wanted.

Immediately we came face to face with a young boy about fifteen years of age. He had a lovely facial bone-structure, beautiful teeth with a winning smile. The other man was about thirty-eight-years-old and had a kind and gentle face.

Both were shivering with the cold as they were wearing light summer clothing, which, although of good quality, was little protection against the now falling snow. The young boy spoke in broken English.

"My name Haris. You...please...help us! We need food. Medical Aid! Our town… Breza in Bosnia."

"Bosnia? Where is Bosnia? Isn't there a war going on there or something? How far?" I enquired, wishing I had paid more attention in the Geography class at school.

The tears, either from the cold or emotion, ran down the young man's face.

Paul looked over to the car, which was parked nearby. "Fairly new! How come they need help?" I knew I was following his train of thought. We were both trying to rationalise what we were seeing with what we were being asked.

"Paul, can you call the lady from the UN over, and ask her to get an interpreter."

The young boy was quickly writing phone numbers on a small piece of grubby paper and desperately pushing it at us through the fence. Again, I searched his face. "You must help us. Our people dying! You don't understand. Please, you come?" He tried to explain.

"We are empty and it would take us three weeks to go back to England and return with food. That's assuming we could find out where Breza is, and will it be safe?"

"It's OK, my Father, many soldiers, will protect you."

"But we don't even know where Bosnia is," I kept protesting trying to buy thinking time, by which time the cold was biting hard. The two men seemed desperate. By now I realised this boy was deadly serious.

At last the lady from the UN arrived, bringing an interpreter to help in communication. We watched attentively as the conversation became more and more heated. He really *was* desperate for help for his people.

My senses were by now working over-time. Now turning towards us and looking us firmly in the eyes, the UN lady was ready to give her advice. "Forget it, you two. Go back to England. It's not safe. It's a job for the Army. I'll pass on the need to Brussels. You would just get hi-jacked."

My computer brain did a quick re-take. "Many soldiers will protect you. Hi-jacked? Not safe?" How did we know whom to believe? Who should we trust? Confused and helpless I turned to Paul. "Can we give them your new jumpers from the van?" Paul was quick to respond, fetching over his new, red birthday present, for one of them."Lord, what do you want us to do now? We want to help, but I just can't see how."

I tuned into my inner voice. "Pray with them?" At first I tried to ignore the inner voice thinking maybe I was imagining things because I was not good at this praying for strangers bit. But if I wanted answers then I had better listen and what's more obey.

"Please." I hesitated. "Could we pray with you?" The men agreed somewhat apprehensively but we all held hands through the cold, wire fencing. The wind was biting. The men were blue in the face but looking a little more comfortable in their new English sweaters.

We prayed simply, asking for help and wisdom to know what to do to help these cold souls. They could be genuine. It didn't have to be a trap, but if it was, we certainly could get hi-jacked.

"Lord, we desperately need to know what you want before we make a decision so please direct our path." Suddenly, Paul became aware of the tooting of horns. The others were impatient to set off back to England. Reaching again through the wire fence to shake hands, we bid our new friends farewell, not making any commitment, other than, "We'll see what we can do."

"Was it not Martin Luther King who said, 'I have a dream? Paul is killing ever justified? Where would we stand if an aggressor came to the door of our home or country? Do we have the right to try and stop them?" Now, raising my voice, "What would have happened to us, in the 1939/45 war if others had not been prepared to die for our freedom?" A few days later in England, I bombarded my long-suffering husband with endless questions.

Paul gave no answer, for he knew from experience, I was about to go through one of my soul-searching exercises. He had seen me wrestle many times before and knew I would have to find my own way out of this uncharted territory and find answers in the pit I was digging.

One part of me was asking: "What are we doing in this country? Have we completely stopped refugees coming here for safety? It seems that you cannot enter our country without a visa. But, you cannot get a visa in Bosnia either."

What a contradiction? I knew in my heart that we were blessed to live in a country, which at least tries to protect those fleeing persecution, torture and degrading treatment. After all, isn't our country second to Germany only with such a large number of people asking for protection from persecution in their home-countries?

"So why does our country close the door?" I now reasoned for myself, "I suppose we would sink down to Australia with the weight of millions of immigrants if we didn't. Paul, what would Jesus do?"

A few days later he found me sitting in my study staring at a copy of the UN Universal Declaration of Human Rights. Although Paul knew I was not willing to get involved in politics, he also knew I needed to make up my own mind about certain issues for which I had more questions than answers.

"Paul listen to this, Paragraph thirteen states, 'Everyone has the right to leave any country, including his own and return to his country.' and what's more," I went on getting quite excited, "paragraph fourteen states: 'Everyone has the right to seek and to enjoy in other countries, asylum from persecution.' Surely, this must be as God intended it to be.

Message to the World

Do you out there, well fed, and sleek,

know what it is, when there is no sleep?

Do you REALLY care that I'm unfed?

That I can't find my Dad, and Mother's dead?

They torched my home - how can it be -

'They' were the friends who came to tea?

Each cruel night the cold wind bites,

While you admire your Christmas lights.

What Christmas present waits for me?

- Just a sniper's bullet -

That will set me free

From you, who condone my misery.

Ron Kaye.

Written in 1993 at the height of the Balkan conflict.

Chapter 3.

THE CALLING

"Why is it my greatest adventures in life always start with an argument with you God? No Lord, you don' t really want us to go to Bosnia do you? Not me Lord. I will die there, it'll be so cold!" I knew 'He' always manages to touch my heartstrings whenever 'He' wants, and 'He' always wins! "There are times, Lord, when you just don't play fair," I complained as I had one of my inner battles.

It was about two weeks before Christmas. Paul and I were doing our family gift shopping, having just returned from our one off trip to Croatia. We stood motionless at the checkout as the till rang up ninety-four pounds. I took a deep breath, looked at Paul, knowing we only had about eighty-six pounds to our names in the bank.

As we walked out of the shop with our parcels, I stood on the sidewalk confronting my poor husband with full force. "What are we doing? We wear that label 'Christian' and we are spending money which we haven't got, to give to people who don't need, and those two men are still waiting at that metal fence in Zagreb, still trying to get help for starving people! Paul, what are we doing as Christians?"

Another argument upstairs. "Don't be silly Lord!" I was aware that I was being moved within my spirit in a way that didn't even make sense to me. "We couldn't possibly get everything together before Christmas. You can't be serious!" I sounded more like McEnroe, the tennis player arguing with an umpire. I knew all these thoughts were ridiculous!

Within days and with no inner peace but wishing to make sure I was not just being an emotional female. I decided to share my thoughts with our Church on Sunday and ask if any person had any guidance on the matter.

After the service a young woman approached us very tentatively, "I don't know if this will help, but I will tell you what we were told by a missionary some years ago!" The young woman spoke now with authority. "When Jesus said, 'Go! Out into all the world, and take the Gospel message.' He actually didn't say anything about coming back."

"That's it! That's it!" I nearly jumped out of my skin. I had caught the ball, hardly able to believe my own clarity of understanding. It was just as if the light had come on. "Of course! Of course He said go! So, as long as we are prepared to be obedient, and go, that's all that matters. We actually don't have to worry about coming back. If we profess His name, as disciples all we are called to do is be obedient, and trust Him for the rest."

Now there was such a surge of energy I could hardly contain myself. "OK, Lord, I'm not a doctor. I can't save lives, but we can do whatever you ask of us. You lead, and we will follow." I looked to Paul for confirmation. "We don't know what He will have in store for us in Bosnia, but if we are willing? I searched my dear husband's face for confirmation. "We don't know what He'll have planned for us in life's game of chess, but are you in agreement? If He will provide all we need, food, transport and funds, within the week, then could we go on Christmas Day? That has to be the safest day to travel into Bosnia," I reasoned in some sort of illogical way, and as an after thought, but not waiting for Paul's answer added, "and please Lord, give us the grace and courage to follow."

Within two days, on faith, all the funds and enough food aid to fill a Luton van, which we planned to hire for the journey, had miraculously been gathered in. We approached Smith Van Hire's counter with the agreed hire charge of one hundred and ninety pounds in Paul's pocket. The lady behind the counter smiled.

"With the extra premium that will be two hundred and forty five pounds please!"

We stood like children in embarrassment. An extra insurance premium needed paying, as the vehicle was to go into Central Bosnia. It seemed a blind eye could be turned for Aid lorries going into Croatia a relatively safe area but not for vehicles travelling into the much higher risk area of Central Bosnia.

"Oh! Wait a minute, this must be for you" said the lady behind the counter as an after thought, "some gentleman heard your appeal on the radio and has just phoned us and paid seventy five pounds off your account with his credit card." We quietly smiled towards Heaven wow, is this what it is like walking in the will of God?

Through willing hands and hearts everything necessary had been provided. It was now up to us to keep our side of the agreement. We were already learning we could not plan two steps at a time but had to put away any preconceived ideas and be willing to follow each move as it was revealed to us.

A few days later, in our Yorkshire home sat the wife of Emir, a refugee who was still in Central Bosnia. She was a young, attractive lady with two well-behaved young sons. Not only did she care for her own two children, but also she mothered her four-year-old niece, Elma. This child's life had been saved one dreadful night when the civilians in the whole area were besieged and under attack.

Their home and those of all their immediate neighbours were actually burning when the father, Suad and mother in a moment of immense courage and terror, jumped out of the back bedroom window. They took the only chance they had. The young mother jumped first. An immediate burst of gunfire reverberated around. Suad hurled out the child, quickly following in a desperate leap. Again, blasts of gunfire. Life and death all in one moment.

The young mother lay dead. Suad, shot in the chest, lay bleeding profusely. Mercifully, the child was still breathing and alive. Only nine of their immediate neighbours survived that night. The rest were mown down by gunfire, or burnt to death.

Neighbours later rescued Suad and Elma and we eventually met this child in England. The child would sit happily on my lap allowing me to gently comb her curly dark hair, and in turn she would delight in combing my absolutely straight tresses. Together we were wrapped up in a special place of tenderness where we could share a deep trust.

Now here we were with Emir's wife in our lounge sharing the story of how her husband had been sick in hospital, at the early stages of the war, when she managed to escape to England with her two children and the blessed young Elma.

Since the British Government had ordered a halt to all refugees from Bosnia without visas entering England, they, like many other families, had become separated and naturally were quite desperate in their need for reconciliation. Emir could not come to England without a visa. He could not obtain a visa in Central Bosnia because he had no passport and there was no British Embassy in war-time Bosnia. It seemed our Government had forgotten when such people fled their homes in nights of terror they did not stop to pick up their passports.

Many families were simply separated, through no fault of their own. Emir's wife had come to us and nervously asked if a letter could be delivered to her husband in Zenica. I looked at her compassionately and promised that if, by some miracle we managed to find this one man out of the millions of refugees, then the wife could be sure, not only would we give him the letter, but a big hug from her as well.

We had been warned about the risk of carrying anything exclusively for Muslims in the political climate of that time, so I took the precaution of hiding the letter inside my body. I didn't even share the secret with Paul, as I did not want to compromise him.

Travelling south in winter, through the night in England and trying our best to avoid the black ice on the roads, we caught the 4.30 a.m. ferry. After compiling paperwork, driving through France, Belgium and into Germany, my fatigue was getting the better of me and I was beginning to nag Paul unmercifully. Why was it so difficult for him to hear my need for rest after thirty-six hours of travel?

The pain in my back and neck had increased beyond the level of my tolerance. Up until then I had actually thought my back condition was a blessing because Paul and I would not have been free to go to Bosnia if I had to go out into the commercial world as before. I was well past my sell by date, and the limits of my endurance had by this time well surpassed my patience with Paul's blindness. It had always seemed to me the more I was prepared to endure, the more the men in my life seemed to expect. "When will they hear or see?" was my inner cry.

In my last two years in the Bridal business I knew inside myself I would not be able to carry on punishing my body much longer. There were days when, as I tried to carry heavy gowns, my legs would seize up and I would only be able to move like a beached whale.

It became clear I would have no option but accept a letting go of a way of life that was taking its toll. There were many things Paul and I needed to take in hand if we were going to survive as a couple. So the pain proved to be a useful gift. It gave me the incentive to try to close the business in the least damaging way to all concerned. It had taken several difficult months to orchestrate, only six months previous, and in financial terms had cost everything. But we both gained an inner peace as the complete change in lifestyle was made for my sheer survival personally, and for our marriage. I was officially retired.

First I had time to really be aware of what was going on inside my body, and after a visit to an osteopath I discovered a fall from a horse twenty years earlier had healed, leaving nerves trapped. The discs above and below were having to do extra work as the spine had solidified to protect the injured areas. The problem is there permanently, but at times of self-neglect the pain comes into full focus. At that moment it only takes someone asking the same question three times for my patience to fail, and yes, I blow again like an old steam ship. So was it surprising Paul was about to get a verbal backlash if he didn't stop the vehicle soon.

Paul and I knew very little about the current fighting or the political situation in Bosnia. Our only lead to re-connecting with the young stranger we had met, for a few minutes, at a metal fence previously in Zagreb, was a phone number quickly scribbled on a crumpled piece of paper. However, with child-like trust and in simple faith, now in Germany we made the call.

Chapter 4

THE MISSION FIELD

"Haris? No Haris! Haris... school!" replied the female voice on the other end of the phone. "O.K, I phone tonight." Automatically getting into broken English, as it wasn't difficult to realise the person at the other end of the phone could only understand a little of our difficult language.

That evening Paul phoned again and arranged for us to meet Haris at 8 a.m. on Christmas morning at the same six-foot metal fence in Zagreb where we had previously met him a few weeks before, this being the only place we all knew.

Paul and I had not yet discovered anything about the mountains of paperwork needed to get through customs. We were relying only on our passports to get us through borders, with a lot of expected help from 'upstairs!' Without that extra dimension, contemplating this journey would have been totally unrealistic at the best of times, let alone in wartime.

After a lot of negotiating at customs we managed by some miracle to get through the borders on Christmas morning. The temperature was below zero and a light covering of snow fell, we waited in Zagreb excitedly anticipating the look on the young man's face when he saw all we had brought for his people.

Being Christmas day the whole area had an uncanny feel about it. There were only a few cars on the roads and of course no buses. It had not occurred to us that Haris would have to walk several miles to make the rendezvous. "Look, he's coming!" I said excitedly.

In the distance we could see the frame of the tall, good looking young man, and as he got closer we could see he was red in the face from his long walk in the biting winds. He almost danced up to us. His broad smile and the spontaneous hugs exchanged soon put us all at ease.

Haris was soon on board navigating us out of Zagreb past the majestic old buildings but in a moment of irritation, whilst trying to negotiate the vehicle through what seemed to me a complicated one way traffic system, I let rip with, "Oh! For goodness sake Paul, do shut up!" Immediately there was a roar of laughter. "You like Basil Faulty and Sybil! From the television programme." Well, that was one way of looking at us as a couple.

I was pleased this young man could find some humorous way of handling being in our company. Sadly we have discovered over the years, that some people get hurt when they experience being around us at first. They seem unable to handle the disappointment that comes up in them, as their false inflated image becomes tarnished. Paul and I know we are still being refined. We know as a couple we continue to struggle to communicate well with each other. The truth is we interact openly, unwilling to play the game 'perfect people,' so of course we are at high risk. Usually when there is a problem in retrospect we can identify where and why we came adrift and, are happy to make adjustments and deal with that. But I am clear, we all need people around us who are prepared to love us as we are and not judge us from their own expectations.

Can we 'the church' begin to understand why at times there is so much hostility flying about? People are disillusioned when their pain continues to be ignored. We all need people around us whom we can trust, who will even protect us from ourselves at times. So I was pleased that this young man could be so open in his responses. It wasn't long until I found myself comparing him with my own sixteen-year-old son, Richard. As the journey progressed Haris started to try to explain the war and began to tell us about some of the horrific stories of brutal killings and repeated rapes. What a stark contrast there was between this boy's life and Richard's.

It had been Haris's father, Hasan, who had instigated the two men coming to the fence for help in Zagreb, which initiated our original meeting. Now, after a fourteen-hour drive over snow covered mountain roads, Paul and I had arrived at a flat in Split on the Adriatic coast in Croatia, where we were about to be introduced to the man himself.

Although Paul and I were exhausted, these Europeans seemed to come to life at night! A meal was hastily prepared even though it was 2 a.m. and we had the opportunity to unwind. Only Haris spoke any English, making it difficult for any of us to communicate at all verbally, so now all our other senses had to come into play to help us learn how to build bridges of understanding.

Haris's father was a very charismatic man, with so much presence it seemed to flow out of his very pores. I was not surprised he had such a good looking son and wondered what his mother was like.

It turned out Hasan was a Muslim and Haris's mother was a Croat, now evacuated with him to Zagreb for safety. The family had previously lived in Sarajevo and owned another weekend house by the sea. Hasan had a factory in Sarajevo and each time I asked what he did, the reply came, 'business man.' We are all 'business men' I thought, the question is, "whose and what business are we about?" Quite understandably, it seemed there was only one business for Hasan at this time and that was the survival of his family and his country.

His older son, Rusmir, had been sent to America at the start of the war and was now at university studying to be a doctor. Hasan wasted no time showing us press cuttings about Rusmir. He was clearly a man who inspired his sons and cared deeply about his people. He explained how his people had to try to defend themselves with their hands tied behind their backs, because of the arms embargo set by NATO.

When he heard our story and realised we were just two ordinary people, who had come in faith, trying only to answer a call for help, he immediately went over to a drawer and produced the most beautiful leather document case from which he extracted a certificate.

"My Government has awarded me our country's highest honour, 'The Golden Lily'. After the war is over, we will honour you also."

I smiled inwardly thinking that, if we receive our reward on earth, we have no need to receive it in heaven. Aloud I said, "Thank you, but there is no need," shrugging my shoulders too tired to communicate further.

The following morning there was much discussion about what would happen next, and it was decided Safet (the older man who had been at the fence with Haris) would accompany us for the rest of the trip into Central Bosnia. Safet was a family man with two young children and a wife whom he adored, but I could not get my mind around the situation when I saw this same man pack a revolver into his small bag.

"What are we getting into?" I'm sure we both thought, watching apprehensively. I felt a little easier when I saw Hasan go past the chair and place a loving hand, authoritatively, on Safet's shoulder. If it was any consolation to us we were, I was quite sure, in the presence of a great leader.

As if to confirm my thinking as we were leaving, I saw Hasan take his son by the shoulders and plant a life time's amount of courage within him with just one firm loving hug. It was a precious moment of immense beauty. No wonder this father was the inspiration for his sons.

We drove out of Split, along the coast road, beside the most beautiful of coastlines. The views of the little fishing villages blending into the shimmering deep turquoise waters made us see anew God's gift to mankind.

"Why? Oh! Why do we work so hard to destroy that which He has made?" I cried within.

After many hours of breath taking scenery we turned inland, heading towards Mostar and we were quite unprepared for the abrupt change of mood. Scars of the most brutal cruelty could be seen around every bend. All the roads were pitted with potholes caused by exploding grenades. Every house without exception, as far as the eye could see, was burnt out. Only the broken shells of homes were standing where once on the balconies, amongst the grapevines, families had eaten evening meals in the deep red setting sun.

Amongst the ruins, the odd dog scavenged for food and a few old people walked dejectedly, leading their surviving cow to try to find some grazing. I tried to imagine what it must have been like when tanks fired shells into every home and people tried to flee from the flames, only to be slaughtered by automatic gunfire. The fear! The screams as families saw their loved ones cut down in front of their eyes! The sky alight with the flames dancing silhouetted against the black of night.

"How are these people going to survive? How are they ever going to recover from this?" My mind raced on and on.

"How do we ask them to forgive?" I reasoned to myself.

"Do we have the right to teach about forgiveness. Given we have not lived through this, how can the bridges of forgiveness and reconciliation be built?"

I was relieved to be distracted when we stopped to buy a few fresh oranges at the wayside. Safet and Haris wanted to take this gift of fresh food for their friends. An old man approached our vehicle and I wound down the van window to give him some chocolate. Haris became very agitated.

"Jackie, please don't open your window in Bosnia. You don't realise. They can just throw in a grenade!" I was quickly getting the picture, but still felt very much unprepared for our new role. I was very happy that this young man was giving us a crash course on the art of survival and a new learning curve was taking place.

After pressing on for many hours we passed over the remaining half of a blown up bridge across the Neretva River. The river was a clear, jewel-like turquoise. One could never accurately describe its clarity of colour or the truly magnificent scenery surrounding it. Such beauty only helped to heighten the ugliness of what man was doing to his fellow man.

We proceeded through two tunnels, masonry dangling precariously overhead. I drove carefully being aware of the need to go slowly enough to avoid bringing down any loose concrete, yet fast enough to avoid being too long passing through in the dark.

As we came out the other side we skidded on thick ice, formed by constant drips falling from the long, thin icicles hanging from the craggy, grey rocks. It seemed as if the giant rocks viewing the scenes were themselves crying. I imagined God's heart must have been bleeding. No wonder He had given us a heart for these people.

By early evening we were approaching the mountains and Safet suggested he drive, as the terrain was to become more difficult. I couldn't imagine how, but I let him take control. This was his country and he needed to find a way through back mountain paths so our presence was not seen.

The cold night air began to grip as we slowly approached a checkpoint. The local militia came towards my side of the van smiling.

"Dobar Dan," I said putting out a hand.

"Dobar Dan Lady. English? You cigarettes?"

"Sorry! No!" I searched my mind to see what else I might have to ease our way through. As I was thinking, I saw the guard blow his warm breath into his cold hands. Paul's gloves lay on the dashboard. "Here, try these. You are going to be cold out there all night" I stretched my hand out through the van window. "Please take them as a gift." Haris and Safet looked on absolutely bemused. "Definitely mad," they must have thought. Paul took the giving away of his gloves in good spirit knowing the need justified the end.

"OK, you go. Good Luck!" I smiled but didn't like the, "Good Luck" bit. "Why did we need Good Luck? What's ahead?"

Gunfire was heard coming from Sarajevo over to our right. Our route was to the left, over a mountain pass. Safet was now increasing speed, sensing the impending dark would present new problems. "We need, go along a smaller road," Haris was explaining, "fighting ahead." The dirt track we turned into was frozen solid and ice was covering it, disguising the eighteen-inch holes we hit every couple of feet, which rocked the van from side to side and then bumped it high into the air. Every time I came back down into the seat the pain shot through my spine almost forcing me to shout out, but I was determined not to, the men needed my support, not my weakness.

Safet's eyes darted everywhere. Haris was on Red Alert. I could sense the tension as Paul started to sing clearly determined not to show any apprehension. The others joined in and this calmed us all as we made our way even deeper into more difficult terrain.

"There is no way we can get through here," I thought, as the van continued to teeter on the edge of the cliff, wheels spinning, then surging forward, up and down all at the same time. This was getting rough! My back and neck were taking unwelcome punishment. There was no way my already damaged body could take this constant banging. I looked to Paul for re-assurance, but he, like most men, seemed to be more comfortable with the safari experience. I was in the minority, so had better keep quiet, after all the only way out was forward.

"We will have to cut across the top of this field. The frozen ruts are just too deep here," advised Haris.

Tracer fire burst across the skyline to our right. The track climbed up at an angle of about one in five and it was a struggle to keep traction on the top edge. As we tried to pass between two old trees, the van's nose was reaching towards the stars. The wheels started to spin as they became lodged in the roots of an old tree. The vehicle sank further down between the hard ruts, and came to rest at an acute angle, its exhaust, by this time, well and truly at the risk of being broken off.

"We'll have to push it," Paul suggested.

"Push it! How are you going to get it out without breaking off the exhaust?" I questioned.

"OK let's take the load off then we'll be able to get some branches underneath and lift it, hopefully in one piece." I was pleased Paul was using his experience creatively, it made me feel a lot more secure after all, here we are in a strange land in the middle of a war thirteen hundred miles from home and if anything happens to the van we are lost. We'll have no other way of getting back. My mind was running through the logistics.

Without much enthusiasm for the task in hand the men started to lift the heavy boxes until the whole area of about fifteen square yards was covered with boxes of every shape and size! None were sealed and, as the occasional one was dropped in our haste, it burst open revealing its contents of toilet rolls, toothpaste, sugar and washing powder all mixed together.

"How crazy these things look scattered on the glistening, frosty ground in the dark!" I thought.

The men tried every conceivable way to move our stricken metal friend, but the more they tried the more it skidded in the lightly frozen mud. I wandered a little way away from the activity.

"Lord, we could do with some help. I am going to trust you." I returned to find Paul alone.

"Where are the boys?"

Paul replied looking fairly tired and alone amongst the problem. "Gone to get help."

With a quick change of thought pattern, I suggested we had better get some blankets round us. It was well below freezing, and it was going to get worse. I could feel the odd snowflake falling softly on my face.

Silently, I became aware it was Boxing Night in England. Our friend, Jenny, had given Paul and I ten pounds each to buy a Christmas present. With unusual wisdom, I had purchased warm hats for us both. Mine was a white, woolly ski-type one which covered all my head and neck, exposing only half my face. Paul's came well over his ears. I snuggled down into the treasured gift and thought about all the family at home. What would they all be doing?

By now the cold was beginning to creep deeper into my bones and I could not feel my feet. The night sky was clear with hundreds of bright stars twinkling in the heavens. We could hear bombs thudding as their shock waves reverberated into the heart of the earth. We could see tracer fire darting across the skyline and home seemed a long way away. I surveyed our position. Dark woods in front; solid, frozen mud behind; sheer drop to the right; more solid mud and rocks to the left.

I retreated deeper into my hat to feel again the warmth of Jenny's love. Would there ever be a way back to England?

"Lord I am just going to keep my trust in you but, whatever happens I must just tell the children I love them. I searched for my little tape recorder and as I recorded my message, I heard my own voice trembling with cold and full-blown fear. "This is quite ridiculous," I kept telling myself, as Paul moved towards me and together we walked back along the hedgerow, further away from the white van.

"I want you to know you have been a wonderful wife, and I so love you," my dear husband was saying. Now I knew for sure he thought we were in real trouble, his loving words did nothing to calm my fears, but did everything to make the future, whatever happened, OK. I said nothing in response but gently pressed my cheek against his.

"Paul I can hear voices coming out of the woods! Shush! Be quiet!" The slight rustle from the movement of Paul's anorak sounded like thunder in the still of the cold night air. I mimed to him to drop the white blanket from around his shoulders.

"Let's go to the van," he indicated pointing the way with his hands. I shook my head.

"No. Stay here! Shush!" I beckoned him into the hedgerow. We were about twenty yards from the van when the voices grew louder. "We could get our throats cut for the food we have around that van." At the same time I wondered if Safet and Haris would ever come back.

Our hearts were thumping as we crouched down closer to the ground, desperately trying to become invisible. The night was still and the light snow and frost glistened. The voices grew even closer. Dark figures loomed out of the woods as if in slow motion. Voices became distinguishable as the people appeared like trees moving towards us.

We each held our breath, our hearts thumping, waiting apprehensively! The tree-like figures headed straight towards the white wagon. It must have seemed as strange to them, parked there, as would a spaceship from Mars. The men began to poke amongst the open boxes, getting excited and speaking much faster, in a strange tongue, their breath swirling in the ice-cold air.

On the ground, in the moonlight, I could see a large, round, tin of Roses chocolates. Now was my chance! Leaving Paul, I slowly moved forward, speaking so they could hear immediately that I was a woman. Shocked yet unsure, the men looked up. Hesitantly I moved gingerly closer to the tin of chocolates, taking off my gloves as I tried to pick it up. Still smiling and talking I struggled to get the sellotape off the lid. They waited. What was I trying to do? My fingers were solid with cold and I had to use my teeth to solve the problem. At last, still smiling, I calmly moved in amongst them. "Help yourselves," I invited. Immediately huge hands grabbed the brightly wrapped chocolates. Now everyone was smiling.

Paul appeared as if from nowhere. Thankfully, at that moment, Safet and Haris also emerged from the woods followed by Chug! Chug! Chug! Could we believe our ears? Yes. It was a tractor brought by the locals to try to pull out the stricken wagon.

The next half-hour was a mixture of men doing what men like to do best in such a situation. Chains were being harnessed round the van's chassis; many men gave instructions while others groped in the boxes to see what they could find.

As I opened a box of food an elderly man was asking, in sign language, if he could have the trousers and thick jumper he had found spilling out from a black polythene bag. I was happy for him to have something warm for himself in return for his assistance and most grateful for the help of all the others. Safet suggested we give the farmer with the tractor a few Deutsche Marks. This we were pleased to do as we piled the Aid back on board our happy, white horsepower.

We waved these tree like figures goodbye, cold and hungry we settled back in the wagon but at least we had the comfort of the working heaters. I wondered how much further we had to travel.

"Oh! Only about another fifty miles, about two or three hours!" Haris said it in a way that indicated it was just up the road. My heart sank, as we were all by this time extremely tired so the prospect was not good news. Tracer fire and shells were still falling in the distance.

"What are we doing here anyway? How did we get into this stuff?" I thought with more than a hint of not wanting to play anymore. Fixing my eyes on Haris my heart was again melted by his youthful smile, and I knew why we were here. Although the bumping, rocking and sliding of the van didn't get any easier, we were still much happier to be well on our way, at least until we came to the next checkpoint. Straight away I could see the guards had been drinking, so I decided to keep a low profile.

Safet spoke with the guards but to no avail. They beckoned for the van papers. As Paul reached into the dashboard for the paperwork, his hand slid back and forth, nothing! There was nothing there! We passed over our passports hoping these would do. The men climbed out of the van and, for about twenty minutes they waved their arms about and bounced words back and forth.

"You go Commander!" Overhearing and, thinking a feminine touch was needed, I reluctantly moved my weary bones and forced myself into action by sliding across the front seat towards the unshaven leader.

Outside I ran my hands up and down his two-day facial growth and said, as seductively as my pride and husband's presence would allow. "You naughty man. You've been out with ladies? Tut! Tut! What will your commander say when he sees you, he no pleased!"

He put his arm around my waist; I went stiff but managed a, "come follow me!" as I headed towards the back of the van, searching with my mind and hands to find the bars of chocolate which I knew must be there somewhere.

"For you," I said triumphantly, handing over some chocolate. One of the other soldiers immediately took some bars of goodies uninvited and put them in the inside pocket of his uniform. He seemed satisfied.

To our absolute amazement the guards moved back a couple of paces and allowed us all to move towards the cab.

"Come on! Lads! Let's get out of here before they change their minds!" I lie when I say it was with just a hint of satisfaction, that I was quite pleased with the result of my Marlene Dietrich performance.

There were no more hold ups that night and we arrived safely but very wearily at our destination. Zenica looked how I had imagined Russia to look. The buildings were all grey and uninteresting, in a state of decay, covered in graffiti. The only grass we could see was worn out, and the area was almost tree-less. An air of total neglect hung everywhere just as if the lifeblood had been wrung out of the town's very heart.

With a combination of tiredness and cold we stood at the entrance of a high block of flats, ten floor's high, looking up virtually stunned me into immobility. Staying close together we followed our guides into the darkness. Safet lit a match, which gave a brief glimpse of the depressing concrete jungle.

"Feel for the banister," urged Paul, as his hand reached out for mine in the dark. "Press your toe against every stair as you climb the steps." We clutched our heavy bags. Eight stairs...five paces...eight more stairs. Then long walks along the landing to repeat the whole exercise again and again. Where were we going? I gritted my teeth against the darkness and long climb, gripping Paul's hand in the dark.

"Keep smiling," I told myself, "God knows where we are, even if we don't."

There was plenty of light-hearted banter between Paul and the men as we continued to climb to the sixth floor with twelve lots of stairs. As if by magic a light appeared. Silhouetted in the glow from the half-opened door was the round figure of a lady who was already speaking a welcome in an unfamiliar tongue. She reached out a warm hand, which gently wrapped itself around mine, at the same time smiling a warm welcome. We immediately hugged each other.

Paul and I were home. This was “a Mummy.” Graciously we were given refreshment as Mummy Narjia, sensing my need, led me to a cramped, but spotlessly clean, bathroom. After about three inches of tepid water had been run into the white enamel bath, the water started to run icy cold. Only three inches of water for a bath! Although I did not relish getting undressed in the cold, thereby further exposing my already frozen, tired body, I was grateful for this lady's understanding of my need.

Both Narjia and Emin, the husband, were economists working at the local bank. They had two daughters, both in their early twenties, who had been well educated and were sick that the war had interrupted their studying, one wanting to become a doctor, the other a dentist.

Jeannana, the eldest, could speak good English, and soon she was able to translate our story to the family. Amazed anyone would have come so far to try to help complete strangers, the family suggested the Aid should be taken direct to the hospital the next day but for now, some sleep was in order and we were shown into the girls' bedroom/study. The room was furnished with good quality modern, furniture and also contained a piano standing proudly upright.

"Perhaps tomorrow one of them may play it for us," I thought, but for now the bed looked much more inviting.

Chapter 5

THE GIFT

The next day we awoke to snow, which had improved the scene in the market square tremendously. However, the inhabitants still looked like the grey figures out of a 'Lowry' painting, all with drooping shoulders and bowed heads. Their postures conveyed the pain they had suffered when war invades overnight and catapults family life into a desolate hell.

As arranged, Paul and I accompanied by Jeannana made our way to the local hospital. She introduced us to the hospital director, Muhamed Vejzagic. He spoke no English, but this did not detract from his sincere welcome and the warm accompanying smile. Muhammad was a small-framed man with beautiful silver hair. He had just come off duty having personally delivered many babies the night before. As he proudly introduced us to various members of his staff, their love and respect for this man was evident and straight away I was in awe of him, not in a worldly sense, but because of his gentleness and beauty. I knew from the very first moment we met that we would do anything that would support this man's love towards his patients. Do it willingly and know we were privileged to be called to help.

He said the hospital normally catered for a thousand patients, but now, because of the war, there were about two thousand. They had no X-ray film and little in the way of painkillers. He particularly tried to impress on us the necessity of telling the outside world of their many urgent needs; although they had supplies of dressing for normal times, because of the nature and extent of the wounds of so many of his patients, there was now a desperate shortage.

Here was a deeply compassionate man whom we both loved. He had already found a place deep in our hearts. We were impressed by his care as he showed us around the hospital, personally explaining the patients' various needs. He told how, at the beginning of the war, that they had twenty working incubators for around two hundred babies. Now they were down to three.

The wards were crowded; beds packed in every available space. The midwife in charge of the baby unit told how there was no baby bottom cream and how they were desperate for teats for the bottles. Quietly I left Paul's side and moved cautiously towards the small cots. Although clean, most of them had two or three new-born babies packed into them. Each tiny mite was bundled tightly in an individual, closely wrapped blanket. I was grateful; knowing each baby would feel secure being held firmly. One baby was in full vocal flight whilst being changed exercising his lungs to full capacity.

I moved towards him, his tiny arms and legs were blue and so very thin. Observing this child being consoled by a dummy, I was thankful realising this was a simple thing we could bring which would give so much comfort to the babies, and therefore to the mothers and staff. Suddenly I was drawn to a baby with an enlarged head. This child, though apparently peaceful, seemed near to death and I dared to ask.

"How long?" A doctor walking past overheard my question.

"This baby will die because we do not have the valves

to drain the water off the brain." I could sense his frustration. This was yet another situation, which illustrated the stupidity and inhumanity of war, and although I could do nothing at the time, the need for valves to drain the water off the brain was stored in my memory for use at a later date.

Some other babies quickly caught my attention. These little souls, so desperately ill were given individual cots. Some just screamed in fear as I bent down gently to comfort them. "Lord, be with these little mites. Heal their pain and cover their fear. Come in and dwell in them that they may know your peace, in Jesus' name."

Immediately a new peace seemed to fill the room, we all seemed to sense the God of the universe had responded to humble prayer so both Paul and I continued to quietly move about, trusting to bring a touch of warmth and comfort to each little soul. We must have prayed with over fifty babies, and all the time Muhamed smiled patiently, for he knew any help from above for his little souls was welcome.

Soon we moved towards the adult wards, where the smell of death and oppression seemed to hang like an invisible haze in the air. To see the grey faces and amputated bodies pained us deeply. Again my heart wanted to touch and pray with all of these broken bodies but I felt drawn to one lady in particular, who lay weeping. She could speak no English but with arms out stretched, "Help me! Help me!" she seemed to cry. She had a bullet wound in her arm, her leg and in the side of her stomach. She was also seven months pregnant.

"My baby, my baby, please help my baby!" She seemed to say. I reached out and clasped her out stretched hands.

"Oh my God, what can we do? Please help!" was my simple prayer. How can we help these people? They need real help. Inside I was angry at our inadequacy, and at the same time feeling drained and empty. We have so little to give.

My lady urgently pleaded with her eyes again, her arms reached out.

"Help me," she continued, drawing me closer, showing her wounds. Bending over her and trying to reassure her the best I could, I again beseeched the gates of heaven.

"Oh my God! What can we do to help? Show us! Please show us," still pounding the gates of heaven in desperate prayer. Bending down further, I took the lady's face between my shaking hands, and gently kissed her, inwardly promising to return with help thinking this must be a job for the big agencies.

Eventually I tried to release myself from the desperate grasp but was drawn back into the morass of pain and despair. Soldiers lay with open wounds. The smell from stale blood in the sodden mattresses made my heart sink even further. Paul was touching my arm trying to draw me away. In a state of shock I must have pulled away and wandered from him along the dull, damp corridors, mentally carrying all that I'd seen, taking deep breaths to try to restore my equilibrium.

Within a span of time for which I have no account, I looked into another ward where Paul was praying with an elderly man. My heart reached out in compassion with him, pleased at the beautiful scene in front of me. There was Paul at his most beautiful! This is the man I love!

Thankfully I was free to continue round the ward praying with the men injured in circumstances which I could not comprehend. I tried humming a tune, trying to lift myself trying to be cheerful, joking where I could, but all the time my heart was being wrenched out and cut up. "Lord, why do we do this to one another? Why? Why?" As usual I had more questions than answers and still

Muhamed the Director stood near - love and compassion pouring out of him like some never ending stream.

Next entering a ward of women, most of who appeared to be about sixty years of age, although they were probably only in their late forties, I approached a lady in a middle bed. She grabbed me with both hands; her urgency bordered on desperation and I was pleased Muhamed kept close to interpret. Already this lady was trying to tell her story. Apparently the Chetniks (the Serbian extremists) most of whom in Bosnia are described as renegades, had come to her village on a night of killings and destruction. Very much like Hitler with the Jews in 1940, they were programmed to cleanse the earth of all Muslims. Do they see the slaughter of men, women and children as some sort of honourable act?

This lady had been attacked and beaten unmercifully because she had tried to protect her granddaughter. Although I understood little of the detail of the story, I was drawn closer by the out stretched arms and the lady's insistence for prayer. Praying with her brought new feelings of total inadequacy. Apparently, this lady needed to go to the Sarajevo hospital for urgent surgery, but there was no way she could enter the town under siege. Her situation was desperate. The pain of her nightmare could be seen in her every gesture. "Lord!" I exclaimed once again. " Where are you? Come and meet with this lady. Put your arms around her. You know the way for her," I was pleading as I held her as tightly as I dared. "Lord! These people need your healing touch. Please don't respond to my lack of faith, but respond in Jesus' name. Respond through your Holy Spirit. Let your Spirit come down and touch this lady in a miraculous way, Lord I ask a healing for this body and for the memories of this lady and her family, again, I ask in

Jesus' name."

Exhausted and drained I tried to pull gently away, but this lady had a tight grip on my arm. Unable to hold the bent position any longer because of the awkward twisting position over the bed, which was pulling my back, I moved a little nearer and hugged her gently again. I wanted only to love her better, we were one in body, and her pain was my pain. Floods of words continued to pour from her and I wished I could understand more of what was being said. My concern was that the lady was putting her trust in me and not in God. Nevertheless, I kept silently praying in tongues until eventually she calmed again. Through Jeannana I managed to communicate the message, "We will return to England and try to get all the help we can for your people." She seemed satisfied, so I was free to move on.

Next my attention was drawn to a little, round lady, sitting on the edge of the next bed. Her head was bowed, and she seemed to be trying to avoid eye contact. "Lord, what is this?" I was already inwardly asking as I moved quietly towards her. It was then I realised most of her face was blown away. Taking a big breath I just stood over her, placed my hands behind her head and gently pulled her into my breast, just like any mother would to an injured child. "Oh Lord, Lord, please come now and love her better in Jesus' name." I felt helpless and defeated and berated myself. "Why am I not better equipped to help more? Why couldn't I have been a doctor? Lord, what are you doing? What are we doing here?"

"Come on Jackie!" words I could now only vaguely distinguish, shook me out of my thoughts.

"The local T.V. cameras are here, we want to photograph all the gifts which you have brought."

"No! No! It's nothing! It's like we've brought nothing!"

Emin was standing by the van as they all started to unload boxes and boxes of toothpaste, soaps, shampoo, cotton wool mixed with bandages, boxes of beans, soup, meat and the occasional bar of chocolate which was viewed as something really special.

"So much, yet so very little." I felt sick, and I must have looked sick.

"Stop it Jackie! You have done fine," pleaded Emin. "These gifts are incredible. You don't realise what they mean to us. Nobody had done this before like you people." Both Paul and I smiled, grateful for what he was trying to do, but we were not convinced.

"We must get some real help for these people, they need more food and bandages, everything!" I wrestled with the flesh seeing only our limitations, yet deep down I knew God would move and He would honour our commitment.

More relaxed now we bade our farewells and made our way back through the darkness. Again we climbed the twelve flights of concrete stairs, again we reached the warmth of Narjia's sanctuary, glad to be back, to be able to get a sense of proportion and reflect on all we had seen.

"So this is Bosnia, Lord. These are the people you want to touch with your love. I can't see what little people like us can do in such a mammoth situation, but if you will continue to lead, we will continue to follow."

A little more at peace, we began to relax in the comfort of this home as, much to Paul's delight, Narjia presented her home made dishes of traditional goodies. Sleep was not going to be a problem this night and it seemed no time at all before we woke to be greeted with a refreshing cup of tea. Our hosts were beginning to get the message about my weakness and addiction to the English habit.

My mother always seemed to find the answer to life's problem by saying, “Let's have a cup of tea and a cigarette” and whilst I had no desire for a cigarette, tea had quickly become a necessity for me in this place. Maybe there is a way of getting it intravenously? Now, fully awake, I stood and looked out of the window.

"What's that big building just over there?" I enquired of Jeannana.

"It is a school housing three hundred and fifty refugees. These people have arrived, some walking; some in cattle wagons fleeing the Serbs who over-ran their villages. Many have been killed and these are the ‘lucky’ ones."

"Can we go and meet them?" Paul enquired, eagerly.

"It is not good for you two, especially you Jackie.” Jeannana took one look at the expression on my face.

"Well if you must, you crazy woman!" she was by now treating me like her sister, and I liked that.

After breakfast we made our way down the dark stairs, across the road and into the school. As soon as we walked in the main doors, the smell of sewerage hit hard. Undeterred, and pretending not to notice I followed on, I so wanted to get to know these people, share their pain and bring a little hope.

Having received permission from the ‘committee’ we made our way into the first of seventeen classrooms, all housing between twenty-five and thirty-five people. At each door there was a collection of old shoes, most of which were only soles with bits of string to hold the old leather to the feet. We respectfully removed our shoes as we approached the individual families. They were living most of their days and nights on blankets. Each blanket marked out an individual territory. But could this be the school spoken about by the lady in England for whom I now carried the letter in my pocket? "Does anyone know of this man?" I held up the letter.

With the Muslim grapevine working to the full, it didn't take long to locate Emir, the husband. He was hustled before us by a small group of bustling women.

"You Emir? Your wife in England, at this address?" I showed him the brown envelope, creased from being rolled up tightly. The man, who already looked ill, went a further shade of pale grey as I opened my arms to him.

Receiving the letter in total disbelief, he dropped straight into my arms in floods of tears of relief. It seemed everybody was now crying. Man or woman it made no difference, this was a dream many of them had held on to as a means of keeping alive. We were all seeing someone's dream come true.

With joy, I kissed him on the side of his cheek, hugging him at the same time. "This is from your wife." The tears flowed faster. "Your wife in our home last week, very beautiful lady, very pretty." He tried to smile through his tears. Everyone was caught up in this emotional situation. Even the men cried, unashamed of showing their emotions. These people had lost so much, been through so much that they weren't interested in false pride. The more they cried the more we loved them, these were our kind of people, they were prepared to be open with their vulnerability, honest with their emotions.

It wasn't long before most of the women seemed a little brighter but the men were much more sullen, dull in spirit and countenance. One boy, who looked about twelve, was pulling at my coat trying to get us to go upstairs to meet his family. Paul nicknamed him Jimmy, as he had a look of Jimmy White the snooker player back home. As we followed Jimmy, with about another twenty to thirty women and children trailing behind, we were beginning to feel like the Pied Piper, but what could we do for these people? We were impressed by Jimmy's unselfishness, asking for nothing except that his mother meet the English people. I searched my pockets.

"We must have some gift to give. If only we could tell them about our Saviour," I murmured quietly to Paul. But, for the moment, a piece of chocolate would have to be used to help build a bridge. Looking around the room there appeared to be only a few children, so I pulled out one bar of chocolate and cut it into as many small pieces as possible. Each piece was devoured in seconds and placed as the first plank on our bridge.

The grey faces were now smiling. They sensed warmth as the children beckoned for us to sit down amongst them. Jeannana introduced us as "These people from England," their smiles broadened.

"But Lord, I only have one more bar of chocolate. How can we turn this into 'the loaves and fishes' for you?" I was concerned we had no more to give. One man in a corner was gesturing for a razor. Now, feeling a little more confident, I gave him the thumbs up sign to let him know I understood.

"Paul, we have about 15 dinars in Bosnian money. Do you think we could go to the market and see what we could get? We must be able to buy some disinfectant for the toilets at least." He put his hands to his head as if to gesture, 'here we go again.' Having assured the people we would return and accompanied by Jeannana, we made our way through the crowd and back down the stone steps into the fresh air.

The local market was only a few yards away, but most of the stalls were empty. Some had just a few second-hand items. I spotted a pair of old shoes, which looked first class compared to what we had just seen in the school.

"How much are they?" I enquired.

"The equivalent of four hundred pounds," Paul worked

out!

"Surely you have made a mistake! What sort of economy is this?" I asked Paul who was quick to grasp the situation.

"The cheapest thing we can buy for these people Jackie is money!"

He was right. Our money only bought a few rotten oranges, two pots of jam and a tube of toothpaste. But how was I going to get a razor?

At last I spied a yellow razor, one of the plastic varieties on a little old table which was substituting as a market stall. I approached the middle-aged man with the usual Mediterranean craggy features "How much?"

"Don't be silly Jackie." Paul was saying, "you would need a fortune for that."

"Well in that case I will have a word upstairs! That man has asked for a razor, and he is going to get one!"

"Please sir, you give me for my friend, refugee?" He laughed,

"You woman, you crazy! Much money lady! You much money?"

"No, but I have a great God. If you will give me that razor He will send his very angels to protect you and look after you," I went on with great conviction.

"Lady, how I eat if I give you this?" With a broad smile, I replied.

"You can't afford not to! All I can tell you, God will bless you beyond measure if you give it to me." I smiled again. He looked and surrendered. With gratitude I thanked him, sure God would honour as I silently claimed his soul for all eternity.

Like an excited schoolgirl I looked forward to delivering one razor so we hurried back, singing and laughing, eager to deliver the special gift. Jeannana was speechless at what she had just witnessed. I imagined she was beginning to see with new eyes.

We all returned to the flat but Paul had needed to go back downstairs to our van to change into some clean trousers ready for the evening. I was contentedly half way through my first cuppa when there was an almighty explosion. The whole family instinctively ran to the hallway, this being the centre of the building and furthest from the windows. I ran straight to the back window to see if I could see Paul, and at the same time to discover what had happened. Swirls of thick black smoke were rising up into the sky from about fifty yards away.

"Come away Jackie!" Narjia was vigorously shouting. Jeannana joined me on the balcony urging for me to leave the window area. For a moment all was quiet. Just as we were taking a breath of relief, there was another Boom! from high over the mountain, a high pitched squeal, then… silence. For a couple of seconds, we all waited.

"Jackie! Down!" Jeannana shouted. In an instant I grabbed her shoulders by instinct and threw my own body on top of hers before we both hit the floor... An immediate explosion.

"That's done it!" was my first thought. Two more shells fell in quick succession and Narjia was going crazy, shouting for us to join her away from the window. To reassure her we surfaced quickly, but not before taking another quick check to see if the van and the school were still standing.

"Come away! Come away both of you!" Narjia pleaded.

"I must go and find Paul. I want to be with him," I found myself protesting. "It's OK Narjia, we will all be all right." I said firmly. Then I prayed a quick prayer, asking for a hedge to be put around them and the whole building.

As I reached the front steps, Paul was on his way back in and out of breath he was saying.

"That was close, I was just putting my trousers on when the first shell fell. I thought, Lord, Jackie will go ballistic if I get killed without my trousers on!" He planted a quick peck on my flushed cheeks.

We were taking a moment to reassure each other when we were joined by a lady, also out of breath and shaking from head to toe.

"Man dead! On bike. Boom!" She was clearly in shock. We sat her down on the steps and huddled close to her in order to help keep her warm and secure. The lady put my hand on her heart area as I tried to re-assure her. "You O.K? No problem!" At least that's what my voice was saying, but in my heart I wasn't sure that it was the truth. The lady indicated she wanted to go across to the school.

"That's fine. No problem! We'll take you!" Within a few minutes we were entering the school as most of the refugees were just emerging from the cellar. Apparently, in the cellar they use tables to form a catwalk to enable them to avoid walking in the sewage, which had escaped from the broken pipes.

The lady seemed to know which classroom she was heading for, so Paul and I just followed. When we entered the room we were shocked to find ourselves right in the middle of loud moaning and wailing. Over on the far bed a lady was prostrate, arms out stretched, her head rolling about. She had just heard her husband had been killed and was beside herself with grief. Many other distraught women were gathering round the bed, trying to console her the best they could.

"Jackie, Please! Please!" One of the refugees was asking me to go over to the bereaved lady. At first I was reluctant to intrude in her private grief, but now several women were urging me. Straight away I held her hand, then held her close to my whole body as my heart began to bleed alongside the widow's.

"Lord, please come and bring your healing balm for this dear sister. Comfort her and love her in Jesus' Name." I looked deeply into the eyes of this woman. I could see and I knew her pain.

"In everything under the sun there is a purpose" kept going through my mind. What was the Holy Spirit trying to teach me? Hadn't I just prayed? 'Come Lord bring your healing balm, comfort her, love her in Jesus' name.' Suddenly there was a realisation, He had, He did and we were it!

My mind flashed back to a day twenty years ago. Oh how I remember old Jack's words to me the day I collapsed into his arms all those years ago. He simply put his strong arms around me and said, "He knows, He cares." and he was right. The man Jesus knew all about suffering and so did Jack Howells.

Jack had been a Welsh Rugby International in his younger days who had been caught up in drink and, I imagine from listening to him, had his fair share of lady friends. He had been saved during the time of the Welsh Revival and he frequently shared how one night he had run down the centre aisle of the local chapel, threw himself prostrate on the floor and begged God's forgiveness. From that time on he was a new person.

By the time I met him he was in his seventies, tall, lean and with a smile which reflected an intimate love with His Saviour. He had the longest arms I ever saw. He always said he only wanted to stretch out those long arms and put them round the hurting people and love them better. I was beginning to wish we could have Jack's arm's here with us now.

Oh yes, Jack knew pain. One day his twenty-two year old daughter was upstairs singing, "I surrender all.... I surrender all" arms stretched heavenwards in complete abandonment. Within seconds she had fallen down the stairs and lay dead. Then as if from a broken heart, his wife also died and within a three-week period he had buried his wife and daughter.

Yes, Jack Howells knew pain. Yes, Jack Howells knew how to get alongside pain. At the very worst time in my life, Jack Howells had been love, in action, there for me. It had been Jack Howells who had handed over the baton in the relay race of life to me. It had been Jack Howells who had commissioned me to; 'Go into all the world and take the gospel message.' I was now without doubt that God again would honour His own word.

As soon as this lady calmed a little more, the other ladies seemed more willing to take over, so discreetly and quietly Paul and I moved away making our way back to complete, what we hoped would be the final scenes of this very emotional day.

Chapter 6

NO WAY BACK

As we approached the school the following morning to say goodbye to our new friends, a light covering of snow once again improved the appearance of our surroundings. To our surprise a shivering Emir was waiting, clutching one very small bag. The bag he was carrying should have given us some sort of clue as to his hopes, but the women who were gathered around, a sort of supporting committee, distracted us. They began asking, pleading and then begging us to take him to another small town, in the hopes of maybe getting a passport. It didn't seem such a big deal but neither of us felt quite right about the request and hadn't yet learnt to say the hardest word: No.

"What do you think?" Paul asked, stroking his beard.

"Search me, well I suppose so, it won't do any harm and who knows it may just help him get back to his wife one day." I realised for me, I had responded with unusual vagueness, so added, "but there's no point in us both having to suffer the red tape of form filling, if you would rather rest," as if to cover my own lack of clarity.

Paul would have none of it and with plenty of room in the vehicle and no problem getting through the check points we thought we were well on schedule to obtain Emir's passport and deliver him back to the school by lunch time. How naive we were.

The first office we found ourselves in was drab with dark brown peeling paint work. Having waited about three quarters of an hour we were told by a grubby looking man in an even grubbier uniform. "It is impossible to get a Bosnian passport in less than six weeks, and then only for V.I.P 's."

"What does that mean?" Paul enquired. "Very Inflated Price?" We had heard the going price for a passport on the black market was about fifteen hundred Marks. The thought of a thriving black market at the cost of war got well up our noses.

"We can't give up at the first hurdle and we're definitely not going to play their games. However, this man may not get another chance to ever see his wife and children again if we can't find a way through this maze of red tape for him. We'll just wait for someone with more authority to come." I was beginning to dig in.

A second man behind a desk shuffled piles of papers with small photographs attached to them, into some semblance of order. "Maybe he would help?" but before I could formulate my thoughts another soldier came in through the door. Immediately Emir shot to his feet to greet him.

"Dobar dan," the newcomer turned and addressed me courteously.

"Dobar dan," I displayed my only knowledge of the language proudly, hopeful of some brownie points. Emir and the young soldier, who beckoned us to follow him outside, were clearly discussing the situation.

The pavements were full of soldiers, each one carrying a gun and almost immediately I was having a job to keep up with these burly men whilst Paul strode on in front seeming to enjoy the male company. Trying to pick my way along the broken pavements whilst at the same time weaving in and out of the heavily armed military, I was soon left yards behind. I wondered why God had not given me roller skates instead of feet.

It took about twenty minutes to arrive at the new building and, showing my age, I was out of breath after my unexpected hike. Again we ascended some stairs and now waited on the top landing, sitting on the old wooden chairs provided. The ceilings were extremely high and were all a dirty shade of sludgy cream. Once more a soldier shuffled papers back and forth as we all anxiously watched the time. It took another half an hour's wait before we were shown into the room behind the outer office.

The smell of damp filled the air. An old painting of Tito did nothing to enhance the room. I had the feeling it was only the paint, which was keeping the wall in place. The soldier behind the desk was unshaven, and where his hand used to be, an ugly stump protruded from his jacket sleeve. He barely glanced up as Emir stated his case and asked for a pass to be free to move out of Bosnia. As we watched their interaction, hopes of Paul and I getting out of Central Bosnia that day were fading fast. After more wrangling and more waiting, we were eventually shown into an inner office.

"This is certainly the inner sanctuary, and that picture of Tito hanging on the wall, is a definite improvement on the last." Paul was trying to break the tension.

To my absolute amazement a smart,good-looking young man came and sat at the large desk in front of us. On hearing we were English, he immediately sent for refreshments before going over to a large glass cabinet. He removed a cassette and brought it over to the desk. In broken English, "Please, we wish you have this. We would have you know we still great people."

Graciously we thanked him. "On behalf of the English people, we would like to assure you, there are a lot of people in England who care deeply about the plight of your people. Many people in England are frustrated that our Government seems unwilling to get involved further to help your people more."

"Yes we don't understand that, but thank you and your friends for what you are trying to do for my country-men, and Emir. He is most fortunate. I will be delighted to sign these papers, please do all you can to help our friend." Smiling and wishing us well, he signed the papers.

We could hardly believe our luck as we made our way back through the town, now quite comfortable walking amongst camouflaged, uniformed males until I spotted the sight of dozens of hand-made wooden headstones on the freshly dug graves. There was a profusion of photographs of dead loved ones displayed on every lamp post only a few yards away which made me feel quite sick and vulnerable.

I could feel the mothers' agonising pain in the loss of their young sons, and had to fight to break out of my own depressing thought patterns. "As it is so late, it probably will be best if we take Emir back to the school now." I was already projecting my mind forward to the task of how we could possibly help him further. "If he has a passport and a visa to enter England by the time we come on our next trip, then maybe we'll be able to help him further." I didn't know what else to suggest and, thinking that was the end of the matter. "Let's go back and make an early start home tomorrow."

"Fine with me," agreed Paul, cold, tired and bored with the whole procedure.

We started on what we thought was to be a short trip back to Zenica. The journey went well even though by the time we were stopped at the first check point the snow had thickened considerably.

"Zenica?" I chirped to the guards, expecting no problem.

"No. Sorry Lady! Much fighting! You no go through."

"What do you mean no go through." I questioned if my powers of comprehension had seized up. "We have got to get through to take this man back?" Thinking aloud and having a full conversation with myself. "Paul, that's fun! Fighting! No snow chains! A Muslim man on board with enemy mountain roads ahead."

At last coming to some positive conclusion. "With Haris and Safet wanting to stay in Zenica, we needn't go back for them." Taking a breath and reasoning further. "Our own bags are on board the van, so we'll have to try and make our way forward, but, there is no way we can make it to Split before dawn. So it looks as if we are taking Emir whether we like it or not. We'll have to try and follow in the tracks made by the other lorries which are ahead of us."

"Actually we don't have any real choice," agreed Paul in a calm, matter of fact way, which made me want to hit him.

Over the next couple of hours the men frequently had to get out and push in the ever deepening snow, whilst behind the steering wheel I did my best to keep the van facing forward.

"I wish we could have gone back and started fresh tomorrow," I murmured as the cold began to bite into my bones. One didn't have to be an Einstein to see this journey out of Central Bosnia was not going to be fun. "Let's stop at the first UN base and see if we can get the loan of some snow chains and maybe a hot meal."

Paul was relieved and pleased when we eventually arrived at Vitez a small town where the Cheshire regiment from England did their best to help us.

The burly sergeant after offering us a meal scratched his red hair whilst considering the possibility of snow chains. "Sorry, we don't have any chains which would fit this van, but by coincidence we do just happen to have one set which are in stock by sheer mistake. It just so happens they don't fit any of our vehicles so we will cut them down and try to make them fit but," he continued, just as all three of us were drooling over the thought of hot food and were about to head for the temporary canvas eating-house. "Before you go, young lady, " looking down at my light footwear in total disbelief.

At this point I wanted to crawl under a stone.

"Lady." Putting on his Sergeant Major's voice and looking me straight in the eye.

"We in the army survive... to fight! You...however...before this night is through, will have to fight... to survive!"

It was a blow below the belt, but he was right. If we were going to come into a war zone, then we had better get equipped to do so. As we pondered in thought over a welcome cuppa, we both learnt a lot from the remark. We knew, we needed to become more professional in our approach if we were to survive the terrain and climate, let alone the fighting. We were grateful for his honesty.

"These chains should at least help you, maybe even stop you, from being frozen to death tonight." We thanked the sergeant warmly, knowing he had given us more than snow chains, tea and sympathy.

At that time the only road open ran through a Muslim/Serb front line. It was now dark and we tried to keep our spirits up by singing. Over the airwaves came a familiar sound "Oh when the Saints...come marching in..." Emir's face lit up, as he recognised the tune. Singing as quietly as we could we began to enter a pitch-black tunnel. Surprisingly Paul accelerated. Puzzled at first by what appeared to be his reckless driving we realised he was trying to get through before the tune finished. Bonded together just a little more by Paul's kind gesture we travelled on deeper into the darkness.

Suddenly a flash of blue fire darted abruptly in a straight line across the nose of the van, jolting our senses. My instincts would have been to accelerate but Paul slowed down, waited, slowed down more, listened, then slowly came to a halt turning off the engine and all the lights. The snow glistened on the ground in the bright moonlight. We sat there motionless, like mice listening and waiting silently for the cat's next move.

Time seemed to pass in slow motion until Paul started up the engine, which catapulted us into instant vulnerability. Slowly he dared to drive on. The compacted snow crunched under the tyres. We had this overwhelming desire to be out of there but could only drive as fast as conditions would allow. I did not complain as he swerved in and out of fallen trees, presumably blown down by the wind. At least that was my explanation to myself. I didn't want to acknowledge any other possibility.

Haris's remark 'What they do is, leave an injured person in the road with explosives in their mouth,' flashed into my mind. We were soon past the shadowy areas and the road conditions improved immensely as we approached lower ground without further incident. It was quite amazing when looking back over the landscape, how the trees actually sheltered the area once we moved further south. The fir trees protected the narrow tracks, the snow actually giving way to slush, then slush giving way to thick brown mud.

Paul stopped to check the route. "We need to take a narrow left turn over a ten mile mountain stretch," pointing at the map, but I hardly registered what he had said as my attention was caught by a group of soldiers standing by the road.

"Lift, you give lift?" One of the soldiers growled as he rolled about unsteadily, hardly able to stand. My concentration sharpened.

"Yes, but only one in the cab, the rest of you must go in the back." This suggestion offended them. They declined the offer, with the exception of one soldier who scrambled over me into the middle position in the cab, almost sitting on my lap. As he did so, I found myself withdrawing from the stench of alcohol. Emir used this opportunity to take the sleeping bag and curl up in the back of the van ignoring the whole situation as quite normal.

To be truthful, I found very little joy in having a smelly Gorilla sitting next to me and inwardly thought "Yes, I should have had more sense than agreeing to have a drunken primate in the cab in the first place. It's not a good idea."

Knowing we had been naive to accept the passenger, I tried to console myself.

"If we get stuck in all this mud, then at least he will be another pair of hands to help push. " Of course I should have known better than to tempt fate. We had only travelled a further five hundred yards over the first part of the track when the van became embedded up to the axles in mud.

"Blato...Blato," our travelling companion was shouting. 'Blato' means mud.

"Mud! Mud! Glorious Mud!" except it was anything but glorious. It was thick, brown, slimy and, worst of all, it hid the real danger.

Paul could not see the huge hidden potholes and for our little van it was disastrous. The under carriage was so low to the ground that if we weren't careful, we would completely seize up and be held captive by this dreadful 'Blato' stuff. Slowly and carefully we edged our way forward as our crude companion took another swig from his bottle, burping fumes of fire into my face.

Turning away I tried to cut off from him and concentrate on the job at hand."Pull right Paul! Watch it! Be careful! Slow!" It was too late. The vehicle had hit a rock. A raw crunching, grating sound came from beneath the seats. We had grounded!

Paul threw the gears into reverse. The wheels spun, churning up a shower of brown mud upon everything in its wake. Now into second gear. The van moved just a few inches but the back end was spinning. "This won't work Paul! We are getting further in."

I turned to our new companion, now was the time to find out what he was made of.

"Come on, let's get out and push." He shook his head and shrugged his shoulders.

"Yes! You friend. If I can do it, so can you. Come on! Move your big butt over here!" His day as a passive passenger had ended.

He crawled out of the comfort of the warm van, and stood with an indignant expression on his wrinkled leather face. "Who you tell me?" he exclaimed raising his fist.

"It's simple pal," I went on, "if we don't move, neither do you!" Again I moved my eyes from his resentful glare to the job in hand. I knew only too well, we couldn't even begin to push that van, never mind have any real impact on it, and it was clear this particular passenger wasn't even going to attempt to help.

He just started picking his way slowly through the mud to the lorry behind, greeted the occupants, climbed into their cab and folded his arms in total defiance.

Paul was furious. "Look at that so and so!" He moved to get him by the scruff of the neck.

"Slow down, Paul. Slow down. It makes no difference. We don't need him. He's the last person we need."

"You're right," he begrudgingly admitted, composing himself.

"Now, lover let me get in the driver's seat. Get Emir out of the back then he can help you push." I knew it was essential not to accelerate too much or too fiercely. Gently, Oh! So gently! We slowly inched our way along until at last the van gave a huge surge forward rather like a child being delivered from out of the womb. The 'Blato' gave up its hold.

Paul, triumphantly gave a thumbs up sign to the lorry behind.

At least…I think that's what he gave?

By now the moon had completely gone behind gathering clouds. "How much further?"

"I think this stretch is about ten miles. It should take us, at ten miles an hour, about an hour. Then we should be back on tarmac." I said nothing but thought Paul was being a little optimistic. At that moment I couldn't even see us getting to the other end of this monster mountain without a few mighty miracles.

In the distance I could see the rear lights of a small, single-decker bus. It was higher off the ground than the van, travelling much faster, moving easily along, rocking merrily from side to side as it bounced along the rough road. Suddenly, it came to an abrupt halt!

"If they are stuck, we stand no chance. Please can we

stick close Lord, I've a feeling it's going to be a long, cold night!" I was happy to have my inner friend with which to chat.

By this time Paul was accelerating uphill, back end spinning. “Do you have to go quite so fast?”

"Hold on tight! I can't stop now!" Paul was right.

We bounced from side to side. I held on to the door handles trying to take the weight off my spine. Each time we hit back down to ground a fierce shock wave went through my whole body. It was as if my legs were being severed. The whole of the bottom half of my body was enveloped in a cocoon of pins and needles. "Paul, please take it easy. I can't take any more of this!"

"I, I can't do anything else. Just hang on." Hang on I did, until suddenly, with an almighty crunch, we came to an abrupt stop. We had completely grounded at the exact place where the bus had come to grief.

"That's done it!" Now Paul was concerned, and he had needed to be. Not one of the four wheels was on the ground. We were completely incarcerated by the brown slime, held up only by the under carriage pivoting like one of those circus plates impaled on the end of a stick. Glad to be stationary for a while to enable the jet lag to wear off, I tried to move out of the van but my legs were like lead.

"Come on, you stupid things, get moving! This is no time to pack up." With what little energy that was left, I willed my legs to move. "Lord, now what?" I was crawling out of the van door and into the thick, brown sludge. To my amazement I straightaway sank down about two feet. The mud was well up and over the top of my thighs. "If it wasn't so dark, and we weren't in the middle of Bosnia, I might just laugh at this!"

"Laugh anyway!" came the inner response.

From a distance we heard sounds of merriment and looked across to see some soldiers sitting on a mattress in front of a log bonfire rolling about, roaring with laughter at our predicament. "Come on, you guys come over here and Push! Push!" I mimed the gestures. This made them fall about laughing even more. Whilst I was willing to concede the whole situation must have been quite entertaining, I could not understand how they could just sit there, without moving a muscle to help. "Come and help! You lazy...!" My blood boiled as I beckoned them.

By now the thick brown mud was over the vehicles door ledge. "There is no way this van is ever going to move without more help. Of one thing I am quite sure we can't call out the AA here!"

I realised on such a narrow path, if any vehicle got stuck and blocked the way for others, eventually the other drivers would just have to push the offending obstacle over the edge. There was nothing for it. I would have to put my pride in my pocket and try again with the soldiers and, maybe this time, just a little bit more sweetly. At least that is what a tactful woman would have done but somehow I didn't feel sweetly disposed towards them.

Moving forward I was conscious of lowering the tone of my voice and could see they were still enjoying our predicament. "You guys! Just what do you think you're doing? Do you think we've come all this way for the benefit of our health?" I was now almost on top of them gaining momentum. "Come on! Get off your backsides, you idle good for nothing so-and-so's!" Not the best way to get a positive response from the opposite sex. "Get this wagon out of here!" I sounded more like a sergeant major than a female from England who would stand no chance of becoming a diplomat.

They were so amazed any woman would dare speak to them in this tone, they just stood up and followed, half-bemused, maybe thinking I had some authority, which they should know about. "Come on lads! You can do better than this!" I kept up the pressure, but softened my voice just a little.

It was obvious to everybody; all the pushing in the world was not going to move this van. It looked stuck for the duration. Under all the bravado my heart was beginning to sink, but I was determined not to let them see any feminine weakness.

In any group there is usually one person who will shine. On this occasion one of the younger soldiers, realising the need and taking full responsibility, started to take command. He gestured to everybody to wait whilst he waded towards an oncoming lorry. To our amazement, the lorry driver, at the request of this young soldier, produced a solid tow-bar. It took only minutes to get things organised and, very slowly, to the sound of metal crunching beneath our under carriage, all four wheels plopped back on to solid ground. Much to our relief we were being pulled towards the safety of the inside edge of the mountain pass, right on a bend.

After thanking them and feeling half embarrassed, not wishing to cause any more trouble, Paul and I decided to stay put in the curve of the bend and take a breather. A long line of wagons had gathered, some in front, some behind. Paul counted every one of them. There had been twenty-six held up on our behalf.

Conscious of the narrowness of the track I tried quite unconsciously to contract my body, as if by getting smaller the van would also shrink. "Maybe, Paul, this would be a good time for us to become invisible."

"Maybe it would be a good time for 'The Rapture!" he responded back with his unmistakable dry wit.

Very slowly the train of vehicles began to move past. First one, then another, carefully and slowly inching their way along. I was still unconsciously trying to use my mind and body to edge us over to the inside of the track, but it didn't make any difference, the traffic was still getting by us with only inches to spare. "Oh! No! This one will never get through!" I gasped as a massive articulated lorry approached.

We just sat, waiting for the crunch. The huge vehicle came at us like a giant caterpillar. Paul, starting the van's engine, tried desperately to move nearer the edge. It was a futile effort. Cccccc……rrr. The screech of cutting metal shrilled in our ears. "That's done it!" was my immediate response.

"Maybe it just sounds worse than it is" said Paul who was trying to comfort himself and at the same time wondering what Smith's Van Hire in England would say? He jumped out. "Oh! No! You should see this!" The damage was even worse than it sounded. Down the whole length of the hired van was one clean cut; the metal had been neatly sliced through like butter. "How are we going to explain this to Smith's Van Hire?"

It wasn't long before the wind whipped up the glutinous mud, ready to ensnare its next victim. Clearly we will have to move on but this time we were going downhill and, of course, that made quite a lot of difference. I looked forward to a much easier descent until, sure enough, another white truck was embedded in the thick, brown slime, held captive by the treacherous, gooey stuff.

"This mountain track must claim more exhausts per yard than any other stretch of track in the world!" There was only one thing for it, sit, wait and enjoy the star-lit sky until the white truck was towed free. I reached for my lipstick and as I applied it, took time to enjoy the constellations in the clear bright sky.

Paul moved forward, time for take-off! He revved the engine determined to plough his way through, leaving a good distance in order to give him the best chance of driving through the mud unhindered.

In the challenge of this anticipated mud bath we had completely forgotten about our passenger. Emir was riveted to the seat, his huge, frightened eyes staring out of his drawn, ashen face. Then, to our amazement we heard another engine roar into life. A huge JCB crawled from a siding and started to clear a way through all the gunge ahead.

Mounties to the rescue! Our way was now clear. I flashed a smile of appreciation at the driver. "Thanks pal! Perfect timing!" Then looking heavenward. "Thank you, Lord! You never fail!" As the speed increased I found the fact I could hold on to the side of the door handle quite useful, at least I could rise up out of my seat as I felt each bump hit the wheels. It almost became fun! It certainly wasn't what I would choose in my 53rd year of life, but since we were in it. "Hi Ho! Silver!"

Chapter 7

THROUGH THE DARKNESS

We had only travelled about two miles of the ten and already it had taken about four hours. I anticipated we still had major obstacles to overcome, and it was nearly ten o'clock at night.

In these regions nobody is out after dark. These areas have to be defended daily and night-time is when the fighting starts again. Even the locals don't travel the mountains at night. "Jackie, maybe we should just decide to stay here the night. After all those soldiers back there were bedding down near their bonfire."

"Paul, I'm already bursting to go to the loo. No! Come on! We must press on. Why do you think all these drivers are so anxious to get off this road?"

Without words he continued to cautiously edge forward inch by inch. We managed about another four miles in the pitch-black night. The clouds kept covering the moonlight and the intermittent darkness only added to the tension. Deep shadows danced all around us and the ferry in Split seemed a million miles away. With the onset of the bleakness in front, I was beginning to think Paul might have been right to suggest we stay where we were. "Want a few dolly mixtures?" Passing them to the two men.

"Thanks lover!" Paul responded taking a few seconds to look over at me. "We'll make it tonight somehow. Don't worry," trying to make me feel better.

I could have believed him, had it not been for the sudden loud crunch again beneath us. That 'look' and words of comfort had cost us dearly.

"Not again Paul! I really can't take another mud exercise. What do you think I am ... a hippopotamus?"

Paul tried to reverse his way out of the mud but we were only sinking in deeper.

"Paul, take it easy. What do you think you are doing?"

"Look Jackie, if you can do any better, come on. If not, shut up!"

His words went in like a knife. I knew I had blown it and also knew neither of us needed confrontation. "I had better remove myself or this could get nasty between us."

I knew there was nothing left in me and I didn't want to make it worse as we were both tired. "Paul, I'm getting out. You'll do better on your own."

Reversing the truth and letting self-pity and pride come into play I told myself, "if he doesn't need me, then I'll simply keep out of the way."

Jumping out of the cab, I found myself standing in the darkness alone ... up to my thighs in thick, squelchy mud, not quite sure what I had done to be standing in this goo?

Convincing myself I would be more of a hindrance than a help, I determined to keep out of the way until the four wheels were back on terra firma.

With unstable ground moving beneath and deep blackness surrounding me I stumbled towards a monster lorry in front. It was so high I couldn't even reach the first step up to the cab. "O.K if I join you for this next section?" I shouted. "You give me lift?"

The two middle-aged men smiled down at me. 'Locals?' Too hurt and tired to care; I was now well away from the protection of my husband.

"You.... Come up here!" one of the men said putting out a grubby hand to help me. "You very beautiful lady. Where you go?"

"Split," I replied, wrestling with my internal confusion and adding, as if to re-assure myself, "My husband behind … in lorry behind."

The men laughed. Soon there was no lorry behind. We were travelling further into the darkness, bumping and bouncing. I began to panic inside, as the shadows flickered through the window on my side. The branches from the overhanging trees were swiping the side of the cab as the vehicle gathered speed. The terrain was becoming easier but my heart was beating harder and harder. "Where is Paul? Why isn't he here?"

I felt like a child who had lost her father in the crowd. "What am I doing here? Keep calm!" I was saying to myself, not daring to look across at the faces of the men in the cab in case they thought I wished to be friendlier.

Taking advantage of the darkness, I allowed my right hand to feel for the door handle. Slowly I moved my fingers over the cold metal and along on to the Rexene panel. Still nothing! "It must be somewhere, keep going Jackie! There has to be a door handle!"

Still there was nothing and my heart raced even faster. I looked in the wing mirror, still nothing behind! "Of course, Paul is not there... He's way back still stuck in that damned mud I expect."

The fear in me was growing by the second and I was beginning to give myself a whipping for my own stupidity. "Well," I reasoned, "I put myself here - I must get myself out of this mess." My thoughts turned again to baling out. I felt again, this time more desperately, for the door handle.

The man nearest to me put his arm across my chest to indicate the door. "Nema Problema! Nema Problema!"

"No problem for you," I thought with little charity.

I decided to bide my time. The path ahead was still dark and, by this time, there were trees on both sides. We were travelling through a cutting in some woods. My heart raced. No other vehicle in front! No Paul behind! "Oh! Lord! Forgive my disobedience," I called out in my heart like a child.

"Who's to say anything dreadful is going to happen? These men may be perfectly OK. After all, they are just giving me a lift aren't they?" The more I tried to reason with myself, the more I was not convinced. "No, this is stupid," I decided, "I am going to get myself out of this mess now!"

Again, I felt for the door handle and this time found the place where it should be. The end of my fingers moved over a small, exposed screw thread. Nothing there! My heart was pounding like a base drum. Moving my hand further down the door I reached for the window winder ... Yes! There was one! "That will do," At last my brain was back in gear but I would have to wait for my chance.

"Thank God!" Ahead I could see some lighted cigarette ends moving in the dark, glowing like miniature torches. The lorry was slowing down! They were actually going to stop! Yes! It was a checkpoint. The barrier was down! "S'truth! ...I've no papers. No passport. No money ... Nothing!"

The driver leapt out, waving his arms, talking to the armed guard. The man in the cab turned to me. "You very pretty lady." I moved away as far as I could, putting up my hand to clutch the top of the zip on my ski suit. At that moment the driver at the barrier was calling my admirer to join him.

I breathed a sigh of relief. "NOW's my chance." Again looking in the wing mirror. "Pitch black behind ... only this small group in front of me! I must get out now!" Searching for and finding the window handle I carefully wound it round and round until slowly and stealthily, I could reach out of the open space. I felt for the cold, projecting metal in the dark. "That's it! I've found the door handle on the outside."

The handle squeaked as I pushed it down ...metal on metal. I waited tentatively ... no they hadn't noticed the sound! Opening the door I jumped straight into the brown slime, jarring my spine. Not daring to look around I tried to move my legs towards the cover of the darkness. I couldn't believe the black density of the night. I could see nothing, absolutely nothing!

Frightened, like a child in the dark, I was consumed with aloneness and fear in the ebony night. Thankfully my legs were transporting me forward automatically, but I could hear the voices of the men behind me demanding I stop. "Hey you! Stop! Polako (slow down)".

I blocked the sound of their voices still needing to drag each leg about two feet out of the mud for each step. "No turning back now! Just keep going! Paul is there somewhere in this blackness." The thought of him pulled me along like a magnet, further into the darkness.

I reasoned. "They'll not come after me in this... mud. No! They're not following! I am free!... Free to go where?" Nothing in front, except darker shadows in the pitch-black night as the mud squelched with each step I took.

This slimy enemy was well up over my knees as I battled forward. "I must have come about two miles in that lorry which means Paul must be two miles away ... not even a torch! Why haven't I a torch? Everyone else in the world would have a simple torch!" I berated myself, punishing myself again and again for my own stupidity.

"Stop!" I could hear something... "Yes, it's an engine. Must get out of the way." I tried to move over to the left but sank down another few inches. The mud clutched at my boots determined to hold me in bondage.

Bright lights were now coming at me. I froze in the beam of headlights like a mesmerised rabbit. A soft 'peep' in the distance told me Paul had picked up my silhouette in the headlights. With a sense of relief and shame, my knees began to buckle.

"Want a lift, Lady? Been having fun dear?" Rightfully Paul was having his moment of triumph and I would have plenty of time to reflect on my stupidity

It had taken eight hours to do a ten-mile stretch. Blato! Blato! I didn't want to see any more mud as long as I lived. There was as much mud on the inside of the new van as there was on the outside, it was a wonder the wheels could still turn at all.

For one brief moment away in our thoughts from the mountain road, we seemed to be the only people alive. No cars, no lorries, no people, not even lights coming from the small shuttered houses. “We're not going to make Split tonight are we? Can we stop at the first house where we see a light and ask if we can park the van?" The ‘little woman’ in me pleaded.

"Yes, you're right, it feels awfully eerie around here. I wonder what our friend's feeling?" Paul was very graciously not maximising his esteemed position.

"There, Paul! Over there! It seems like a café type place." We pulled over on to the forecourt. Some soldiers could be seen inside the café, their guns propped up on the wall beside them.

"Paul, this will have to do. Let me go in first with the maps and see how the land lies." As soon as my feet touched the road, my legs turned to jelly. I stumbled into the café trailing mud behind me, ashamed to be soiling the clean floor with dirty boots.

"Sorry! Sorry!" I was saying to the smiling face of the lady sitting at the second table. I pointed to my muddy boots.

"Nema Problema! Nema Problema!" responded the hostess. Relieved and putting the large map on the table I asked. "Can you show me where we are?" Realising the café owner could not understand my English; I pointed to the last place I could identify.

The lady understood and indicated a place on the map. Moving her finger a little further along she pointed again. "Where you go?" She seemed to say. I pointed towards the coast road on the map. The lady shook her head slowly.

"No tonight! You no get through ... road closed" and she was right. There was nothing else for it, I went straight to my pocket and triumphantly ... produced a teabag!

Whilst all this was going on I took a sideways glance towards the soldiers to check their reactions. They were Croats and seemed to be quite happy with my presence.

Paul was making his way into the café; having stayed outside with Emir to inspect the damage which ran the full length of the van.

"Jackie! You should come and see the van! What a mess!"

"No thanks dear, I think I can do without that pleasure tonight!" Tea was brought to the table and, delighted at the thought of hot food, we ordered some egg and chips. Again, the service was good and we felt quite at home and cared for by this lady.

She seemed to understand our predicament and, to our surprise and delight, offered further help. "Would you like to stay here tonight?" she communicated with hand gestures and a few words. She pointed upstairs. It was not difficult to get the message and we were all more than pleased to gratefully accept her gift of hospitality.

"How wonderful Lord!" I was thinking as we followed her out of the café, up the stone steps outside and into her kitchen/ dining room.

It took only minutes for the lady to pull out a bed-settee from the back wall and make up the bed, taking great care with clean white sheets, whilst at the same time gesturing her third guest to another room.

This loving care was a real treat after what we had been through and we took every precaution to avoid dropping any mud in her home. “In as much as you have done it unto one of the least of these my brethren, you have done it unto me." This lady had just brought this scripture to life for us, and we received the blessing. She would probably never realise what a precious gift she had given.

As soon as we snuggled under the warm bedclothes, I set about a concentrated time of prayer for her. Even though I was tired and had been on the road fifteen hours, the more I prayed the more excited I became. "Lord, please protect this home! You have said I can ask anything in Jesus' Name, so I am asking you, by the power of your Holy Spirit, to protect this home and family. Put a hedge around them Lord. I ask it in the Name and on the authority of Jesus Christ my Saviour." I knew the Holy Spirit was releasing His power.

All tiredness had left me and I was filled with so much energy I could hardly stay in bed. Thankfully, Paul had immediately fallen into one of his deep sleeps. I was free to praise and worship without disturbing him. I could hardly contain my enthusiasm. We had been on a physical mountaintop that night, but, Praise God, I was now on the spiritual mountaintop.

As the dawn broke I peacefully put my head down for a quick nap before the household woke. It seemed only a short time before a blond, curly haired little girl, peeped around the side of the door, and came to examine the strange lumps under the bedclothes. As soon as she saw Paul's bearded face looking at her, she hid again.

Getting dressed he fetched a five pound bag of dolly mixtures from the van on which the child nearly made herself sick. "Come on Paul! We need to be getting on our way, perhaps we have done enough damage with that huge jar of sweets!"

I pondered on how we could possibly repay this lady for her kindness without offending her. Paul brought a couple of food boxes out of the van. The gift seemed insufficient and we were embarrassed, however, I knew we had already given her the greatest blessing possible, the covering of prayer. We trusted God would honour and keep this family safe throughout the war.

Chapter 8

THE MILK FLOAT

The following day it was only the fact we were heading for home which encouraged us to keep up the pressure for another ten hours of driving, before Paul finally totally exhausted, stopped the vehicle. By this time it was 2.30 a.m. We were at the top having completed the last uphill climb before our final descent down on an ice covered tarmac road which had not been treated with grit or salt.

The temperature outside the van must have been minus 20/30 degrees. Absolutely exhausted we tried to curl up in the sleeping bags in the back of the van but as soon as the engine stopped the temperature dropped and we all became so cold, I just knew something radical had to be done. Paul was finished. There was no way he could drive another inch. Anyway, he was sleeping soundly and not wanting anything but sleep.

Reluctantly, gritting my teeth, I forced my tired body into the driver's seat and turned the key. "Lord I can only sit here. Will you guide this wagon back down to safety?" My eyes were hardly able to focus on the road, my spine and arms felt like one solid piece of bone but we had come this far, I simply had to help Paul, as he was unable to help himself. I just could not give up.

We had planned to take the twelve-minute ferry from a deserted peninsular, which would serve as a short cut in the long journey. The vehicle was skidding rather than being driven down the glistening narrow mountain roads and it's at these times one becomes aware there must be unseen angels in support of our frail bodies.

Finally, as we hit the coast road, the excessive cold gave way to torrential rain and gale force winds. As we approached Zadar, I knew the Serbs were still pushing down from the North and wanted to make sure I didn't make any wrong turns and end up in the middle of fighting.

Stopping on a dark, deserted, coastal road I crawled out into the heavy rain. "Are we still on the right road? I think maybe we should be getting near to the turn off for the ferry," I shouted trying to wake the men.

Immediately loud, ferocious barks came from a nearby front garden. Paul and Emir leapt out of the back. "OK Boy! OK Boy!" They were trying to pacify the Alsatian when, out of the darkness and in the pouring rain, a small figure of a lady appeared. "Dobar dan. Dobar dan," she was saying.

"Dobar dan" we respectfully shouted over the barking dog.

"Rex!" his owner commanded and pointed to the house. To our relief Rex obeyed and disappeared inside. I approached the lady, holding a wet map disintegrating by the second.

"Ferry?" I pointed to the map, then to the way ahead. The lady raised her hand, palm upward to the sky indicating the wetness, then pointing to the house she beckoned us inside. We took no persuading to follow. The dog started up his loud barking again.

"OK Rex! It's O.K!" Paul was saying. "I wonder if the dog understands English?" I quipped in a small attempt at humour.

The home was large and well furnished. It had been a guesthouse before the war. One could imagine this lounge bustling with people, full of the bright lights, activity and the warmth of entertaining. Now one family was huddled together by candlelight in the cold.

Sitting with the father of the household was his tall, young son. This twenty two year old man could speak good English, and it was not long before, over a meal, he was telling us how they were surviving. Although having problems feeding Rex, the family was determined to keep their pet guard-dog. They told how armed soldiers in a flat they owned in the town had confronted the father. The soldiers just burst in, pointing machine guns, and took everything of value away with them.

Just as the war began the family had been helped by one of their previous guests (a German) who had come to them with food supplies. He would have been trapped in the area had it not been for the son using his army pass card to get him through on the last ferry out of the area. The family said they would be forever grateful for the courage and unselfishness of their German friend.

When they heard about our very amateur efforts they were emotionally moved and thanked us on behalf of all the people in Croatia and Central Bosnia, Muslim or Croat. The son and I stayed locked in deep conversation. "You are my number four son." Two grown up sons of my own, Haris number three now my seal of approval was on him. I had inwardly made a personal commitment to him and his family.

Before retiring to a spacious, bitterly cold, but welcome bedroom for the night, Paul and I exchanged many ideas as to how we could best help the family and their neighbours. One thing we were sure about, there would be tins of dog food on the next mission.

The next two days we drove for another thirty-six gruelling hours to reach the Austrian border. Paul and Emir were asleep in the back of the van and I was quite nervous about what the officials would do if his paperwork were not acceptable. With very little energy or resistance left, I decided to play it by ear.

"Cigarettes, Lady? You have any cigarettes to declare?"

"No. I don't smoke," I responded completely forgetting Hasan had given me a packet of six hundred cigarettes for Ljubica. "Oh sorry, I have these," I hastily admitted, pulling out a packet of two hundred.

"O.K...You go." With a sigh of relief I drove slowly through automatically checking in our wing mirrors. By that time I had no idea what I was supposed to be checking for but merely acted out of instinct.

Finally when Paul emerged I asked at a service station, " Will you please go and see if there is anywhere, anywhere I can have a few hours sleep?"

"No problem Jackie! You can sleep in those empty cardboard boxes in the back of the van."

"BOXES! CARDBOARD BOXES! You are offering me CARDBOARD BOXES to sleep in after three days horrendous driving!" I was hurting. My pride was on fire like a beacon and Paul had to take the full force of my hurt feelings.

"You two go and sleep in those cardboard boxes, if you think they are so comfortable!"

I tried to fight with nothing in the tank. Paul simply picked up his things out of the cab, took me at my word and got out of the firing line. Emir, not wishing to get caught in the crossfire joined him.

Fuming I now withdrew to be alone with my own anger. Every time I thought of Paul sleeping soundly in the back of the van, my frustration became stronger and stronger.

"How can he sleep when I can't even close my eyes!"

Throwing the gear lever into first, wheels spinning and with no thought for the poor souls still trying to sleep in the back, in fact especially designed for the poor souls sleeping in the back, I pulled straight out on to the motorway.

"Now, where? Which way?" I was asking myself through the tears of hurt and anger. Seas of headlights hurtled towards me; long concrete tunnels, stretches of endless tarmac. It was only the energy from the anger, which kept me going.

After long dark miles, dawn broke bringing some sense of newness. The sun began to penetrate my darkness. A beautiful new morning was about to be born.

Travelling became easier and I started to feel a little brighter by feeding off the rays of the sun. "A nice cup of tea is what's needed now." I was beginning to love myself again but I wasn’t so sure about loving my husband.

A log cabin type place which Paul and I knew well was coming up soon. "Great! We can have a cup of tea at last." I beamed inwardly, "maybe the sugar in the tea will sweeten me up!" Full of optimism and high expectation of the medicinal effects of the brew ... I couldn't believe it ... the cafe was closed!

Emir took the opportunity of stretching his cramped legs and having a smoke. I eventually took the opportunity to curl my body around the gear stick trying to rest and soak up more of the warmth of the sun's rays.

Paul stood back apprehensively, not sure if it was safe to approach me, the gap between us had become a chasm. The drive back through Germany, Belgium and into France did nothing to endear me to my husband, but thankfully we were nearly in sight of the end of our journey.

It was 12.30 at night, Paul was driving and Emir, as usual, was asleep in the back of the van snuggled up in a sleeping bag. We were only about half a mile away from the ferry at Dunkirk.

"Oh! No! I think we have missed the turn. No problem," I said, with an unusual amount of cheerfulness for the situation and the time of night.

"Just go down this slip road under the motorway, and up the other side." With that Paul turned into the slip road stopping to check the route before driving under the Motorway Bridge only in second gear.

"That's it! Go under this bridge. We're right. Go on! We can get up the other side," I urged.

As Paul moved the van steadily forward there was an almighty ... crunch

"What's that?" He shouted. After dodging Paul's verbal exclamation I looked into the wing mirror. The road was littered with stepladders dirty washing and the tall purple rooted Lupins, which we had dug up in Germany. Paul's muddy boots lay amongst my lace smalls. All our personal belongings were strewn over the road.

In a sickening moment I said quite pathetically. "We must have killed him Paul! Emir must be dead!"

Paul shocked by my words naturally couldn't understand my comment. "What are you talking about you crazy woman?" He shook his head and tentatively climbed out of the cab. Looking in the wing mirror again I saw him scratching his beard and looking up at the back of the van in disbelief. "Oh! My God! What will Smith's

Van Hire think about this one?"

I joined him standing on the dimly lit road to see exactly the full extent of the damage. The whole of the container part of the vehicle was suspended high in the air from, what we could now read, a seven foot high concrete bridge. It was a sharp, clean amputation. Instead of a Luton Van, we were now pulling a milk float! The only part that was still connected, was the padlock to the roller shutter door, which lay as a carpet in the road.

To our amazement, there still lying comfortably in his sleeping bag, with glazed eyes, looking dazedly up at the stars, was our Bosnian friend.

"I think you would have been safer in Bosnia than with us!" I burst into uncontrollable laughter with relief that the tension of the last few days had at last been broken, even if in an unusual way. As I helped him to his feet to survey the chaos. I just could not stop laughing almost hysterically which was infectious to the other two. "Paul, I don't believe this is happening. It looks like one of those Key -Stone Cops films, where a lorry goes through a haystack and comes out the other side with just an engine and wheels."

Although we could see the seriousness of our situation Paul and I just could not stop laughing. "Paul, I really thought we had killed him when I saw all the washing in the road." I was trying to be serious through the tears of laughter, which just would not stop flowing. “What are we going to do? Here we are with all this metal hanging from a bridge in a foreign country, next to a port, in France, with Smith's Van Hire written on the side in English."

Holding my sides with uncontrollable laughter "Paul! It won't take much working out for the 'Gendarmes' to figure this one out and,” nearly curled up in two, “we don't need a tussle with French bureaucracy.

Where's the number plate? Which half is it on?" Again I roared at the sight of what I was seeing.

"It's on the chassis half!" Paul responded not quite knowing where my questions were leading us this time.

"In that case, unhitch that door and let's get out of here fast!"

With no more delay we quickly gathered up the dirty washing, step ladders and Paul's boots and roped them all on to our new milk float! It looked like Steptoe's rag and bone dray. I climbed into the driver's seat, still giggling in shock but trying to take control.

I could see the real implications of the situation and was certainly questioning my own morality. "Come on, Paul, we need to get a move on! The consequences of this accident could be very expensive for us, and the sooner we are on home territory the better. If we are going to have an argument with authority I would rather it be on British soil, than from a French cell!"

We gathered my precious German Lupins that were lying in the road. "You know you can't take those Lupins into England" Paul struggled in confrontation.

"Why not?"

"Because it's against the law to take plants into England cotton head."

"Then let's dig them into the ground to pay for the damage." I am sure Paul could see he was not going to get any sense out of me at this time.

"Paul, I keep listening expecting to hear the sirens of a police vehicle. Someone, somewhere must surely investigate how half a British vehicle became suspended from a bridge in France!"

Waiting in the embarkation compound at three o' clock in the morning and tucked in amongst the big 'artics' the little 'milk float' was anything but inconspicuous.

"Where have you people been in that thing?" was the pointed question from our nearest driver.

"Oh...didn't we say." I struggled to keep my face straight "...well...would you believe? ...BOSNIA!"

Note:

It was many months before we had the joy of seeing Emir reunited with his wife and two children, and united he surely was. Needless to say we did not even attempt to get Emir into England. Thankfully, our Heavenly Father was faithful and guided us over at the last hurdle... even if He had to use a solid concrete bridge to prevent us breaking the British law. As it now stands, it will take Paul and I between thirty and thirty-five years to pay for the damage.

Chapter 9

BLUEBELL OF BOSNIA

Paul and I hadn't long returned from the last trip when Helen phoned to ask about our well being. Helen is an Aussie. A big beautiful blonde, one of those people who radiate life and has a heart, which can reach through the skin of a rhinoceros. I met her when I was in business and we enjoyed a lot of fun together when we had worked on some very creative advertising campaigns. We had a deep, mutual, unspoken love and respect for each other.

It was not long before I was graphically describing the plight of the people of Bosnia and the heart-rending sights we had seen in the hospital. "Do you know, Helen, there was a lady who was seven months pregnant, with bullets in her leg, arm and stomach." It wasn't long before Helen's heart was moved into action. "Jackie! Oh Jackie!" she was crying down the phone, "The poor soul! Just imagine!"

Helen had heard little, but had instantly put herself completely in this woman's place, and was experiencing the pain. "Oh Jackie! We must do something to help her. Jackie! I can't handle this." Helen put the phone down unable to continue the conversation. I was not altogether surprised and somehow I knew this particular lady in the hospital seemed to be the one whom God would use as a catalyst to focus our minds.

It wasn't long before the phone rang again. A much calmer Helen spoke with warmth in her voice. "Jackie, Frank and I have decided we want to help this lady in particular. As you know, things are and have always been tight for us financially, but we have these two beautiful boys and in some way we want to say thank you to God." She went on, hardly taking a breath! "I have already made up a bag with everything for a mother and baby and we have put in a letter and a photograph of our family as we want to really show her there are ordinary people out here who do care and want to help."

Now, taking a deep breath, as if needing to stand stronger because she knew the cost of what she was about to say. "... and we have decided, if she will let us know a bank account or something, then, we want to help her each month. We want to send her money to help support her in some way. She is now part of our family."

Tears welled in my eyes, and I had goose bumps running all through my body. "It looks as if Our Heavenly Father is at work again." I mused in silence. So it was to be. On the next trip in February we would trust to be back in Central Bosnia just before the birth of the baby.

"Barnsley people, they're NOT just generous! They're just absolutely F-A-N-T-A-S-T-I-C!" Paul exclaimed having returned home after doing a food collection in a local supermarket. "I never cease to be amazed at the beautiful giving from the heart of ordinary people. Do you know it is real sacrificial giving?" He went on ... "One lady came and gave a whole carrier bag of food, yet only had one or two items in her basket for herself. Another man came with twelve bags of flour." Paul was shaking his bowed head, in humble tribute to the caring generosity.

It wasn't long before the phone rang. "Would you come and share in the Worship and say a few words about your trips to Bosnia in our churches at Ecclesfield and Grenoside?"

When Paul and I had the opportunity to share, I trust we did so in a simple and sensitive way, so much so that the whole congregation took us and the people of Bosnia into their hearts.

The love and warmth we experienced then and still today, is part of the very foundation of an exciting ministry. We hardly ever seemed to need to make any decisions for ourselves beyond surrender. The only thing, apart from our faith and prayer life, that seemed important was to be available and willing to follow like children.

It was only a few days later when the phone rang again. "Hello, my name is Mary-Anne, my husband and I are trusting God to sell our house to enable us to move out of the area but, if you would like, I will do my best to support your calling before we move. I know most of the local churches and members."

Within days wheels were spinning! Paul and I just stood back in amazement. I was no slouch myself, but when God motivates his people, watch out for the dust of the wheel spin! Invitations to speak came rolling in and the more we just simply shared how God was raising up his love for the war victims in Bosnia the more the love gifts came in support.

We could hardly believe it when, in a matter of three weeks, we had enough to buy a suitable lorry to carry all the food and wonderful gifts to His people in Bosnia. We spent days driving to see all kinds of lorries and I was fast learning which types were suitable.

What we needed was an ex-army four wheel drive, but the more I looked at them the more ugly they appeared to me. “I just can’t see myself sitting in one of those things ... let alone driving one! Lord, I guess I’m not ready to be a lorry driver yet! Just give me a little more time to adjust.”

The jump from working in a beautiful environment to navigating a lorry over rough mountain roads was a big one. I had no problem in being willing, but still needed to make the necessary mental adjustment before becoming a lorry driver’s mate.

The very next lorry we saw was sitting comfortably in the corner of a big building, all warm and under cover. She was a lovely blue colour and had many extras. “Would you like a test drive in this one?” The salesman invited.

“No. How much is it first?” I enquired with my usual direct no nonsense approach.

“Three thousand seven hundred and fifty pounds, plus VAT”

“Big problem: we only have three thousand. Tell your boss we will give him three thousand pounds”

“No chance! My boss won’t accept that!” the salesman interjected.

I smiled again ignoring the whole discussion about money and cost. I turned to Paul, “I didn’t even realise we needed a hydraulic ramp for getting the incubators on board. I didn’t even know things like that existed, but God knew, I think He’s brilliant! She must be ours!”

This time Paul made the offer. Quite sheepishly, three thousand pounds. The salesman laughed.

“No chance!”

“Tell me,” I persisted, “where is the owner of the garage? Can we speak with him?”

"Well if you will come back to the office we can phone him, but would you like to go on a test run first?"

"No thank you." I already knew I loved this Blue Lady and also knew it would weaken our position to show any need of her.

On returning to the office I spoke with natural confidence to the owner on the phone "It's like this, we have three thousand pounds cash and there's another lorry we saw this morning which we can buy. Frankly, we don't mind which one we have so would you like to consider if you would sell this lorry, for this price? We're going to have some lunch and come back for your decision." With that I firmly handed the phone back to the amazed salesman.

"Jackie, have you gone potty?" Paul said in disbelief as we walked outside into the rain. "What are you doing? It's the best lorry we have seen in three days!"

"Yes I know and it's ours. But the owner just needs time to get used to the idea he's going to sell it for that price! Wait and see! Let's go and get some fish and chips, you must be starving?"

By 3 o'clock Paul and I were happily driving out of the yard in our new friend Bluebell! She was an eleven-year-old seven and a half-ton, Ford Cargo, complete with power steering and full service history and what's more, as lorries go, according to a females view of things, she was very pretty! We loved her immediately!

Imagine the scene. A suburban housing estate on Saturday afternoon, but instead of families watching television or cleaning cars, it seems as if the whole estate is out in the street helping to load a seven and a half-ton blue lorry, bound the following day for war-torn Bosnia. The families involved are just ordinary people, but they are achieving extraordinary things.

Hospital incubators are lined up, each in turn being packed to capacity, by eager women with packs of nappies, plastic pants and large quantities of drugs, medicines and surgical equipment.

The wind is blowing a metal stretcher trolley down the road, much to the amusement of the gathered children. Hospital mattresses are everywhere and prove to be excellent packing for the valuable hospital equipment being loaded.

There are boxes and boxes of supplies containing everything from razor blades to tinned food; heavy packs of hospital sheets and pillowcases all wrapped in heavy-duty sacking. Dolls and chocolates being stuffed into any convenient space; it is as if they were saying ... “We’re going and we’re equally important, so please make room for us!”

Large mugs of tea miraculously appear to warm the enthusiastic loaders. The high winds and driving rain work hard to dampen spirits, but to no avail, until several hours later as darkness falls, exhausted but joyful, neighbours hug and kiss, wishing well the ordinary drivers of a very extraordinary load.

There are many heartfelt prayers for our safe return. The lorry, the cargo and the high cost of sending such a gift into the war zone of Bosnia had all been collected and provided by hundreds of Sheffield and Barnsley people over the previous three weeks. Countless numbers of just ordinary folk had been moved in their hearts to help to fulfil our call to the mission field.

There, at the end of the day, stood a precious but seemingly ordinary wagon, full to capacity with thousands of love tokens. This gift was to travel 3,500 miles across Europe, through rough terrain and treacherous weather conditions, be exposed to grave dangers, and all to achieve its aim of witnessing, to the love of God in action, and to fulfil His commandment to: "Love one another as I have loved you."

Jenny was a new acquaintance. Although she would describe herself as elderly, like Bluebell she has an energy, which would put a much younger person to shame. I would lovingly describe her as intellectual, mildly eccentric and Socialist in some of her outlook. She has a deep commitment to peace and conservation, saving everything from the whale to the Amazon Rain Forest. Our shared desire was to do something for the plight of the people of Bosnia, but we had yet to work through our emerging differences. We were each sure of our personal salvation, but had yet to work through to a resurrection within the relationship. Personality wise, we made an interesting mixture. It is at these times when I think our Heavenly Father has a sense of humour and must have been sitting upstairs smiling when we all chose to come together on such an expedition.

The fighting in Central Bosnia was intense. There were daily reports of aid workers coming to grief. In fact the morning we were due to leave, the news reported four Italians had been ambushed on the "Diamond Pass." Two aid workers had been shot in the back and killed, two had escaped. I knew this would mean we would have to alter our route, because the bridge at Jablanica had long since been blown up. The UN named 'Triangle' and 'Diamond' as routes for passes they had cleared over the dreaded mountains.

Because of the increased tension Paul and I had learned to come before the Lord, and to completely empty ourselves, willing to lay down our lives, for we knew that any holding on would make it impossible for us to go in the first place. Hours of emptying. Hours of checking motive. Repentance, and still more surrender. It was at times like these that the prayers from our Brothers and Sisters in the Church would form the only basis on which we were able to travel. We were quite sure; it had only been their prayer support so far which had lifted us above the enemy's grasp.

It wasn't long into the trip across Europe, when I became conscious of different value systems between Jenny and I. We each came from very different backgrounds so it wasn't surprising despite my awareness; the small divisions soon started to appear in our relationship. Sadly for both of us, these cracks quickly became crevices.

Travelling through Belgium we had just experienced a very uncomfortable time trying to restore our sleep patterns. Jenny had tried to sleep across Bluebell's front seat whilst Paul and I tried sleeping on a single mattress on top of the aid in Bluebell's bowels.

Jenny had brought her personal belongings in a high-framed backpack and it was proving difficult to know where to fit something quite so large and rigid in amongst all the other items. As usual the aid was packed tightly and we could only just squeeze in our own personal clothes packed in black plastic bin liners. The simple task of retrieving articles from Jenny's backpack ten foot up in the back of the lorry was an immense challenge. Paul showed great patience each time Jenny needed something from her backpack. After some time, I realised this exercise over a 3,500 mile journey would become too onerous. It was essential for Jenny to keep her overnight personal belongings tidily in the cab. We needed to make some changes, but I could see this wouldn't be easy for a woman who had a routine established over sixty-nine years.

I had a strict rule in the cab. "The floor must be kept clear at all times for quick and easy exit." This meant books; flasks and shoes needed to be kept in order. The only deviation was the drying of our undie's or towels on the dashboard. More often than not my 'smalls' could be seen hanging from the indicator lever projecting from the steering wheel, usually much to Paul's pleasure and amusement. However I had not managed to get Jenny to agree to these methods of operation.

Without the growing niggles fully surfacing we continued on through Germany and stopped at a service station for some breakfast. Jenny and I stood at the beautifully prepared display of fresh fruits, freshly baked croissants and trays of sizzling bacon. "I'll have bread roll and water. It's not necessary for us Brits to eat as much as we do!" murmured Jenny. Only in half agreement, and wondering if Jenny thought funds might be abused, I decided to modify my own intake.

Paul bounced into the service station, full of his usual joy and sheer excitement at the thought of food. "Darling, take it easy," I urged quietly, out of Jenny's earshot. The words of warning fell on deaf ears as usual, so I tried again, approaching my warning from a different angle. "Paul, when your eyes see food, nothing else exists! You are like a nuclear warhead homing in on its target with a heat-seeking device which would put NASA's space programme to shame!"

Jenny continued stating her beliefs about the way so many people over-eat whilst others are starving. Sheepishly I looked at Paul's plate piled high with food, and projected my own guilt feelings on to him.

"Paul, do you have to be so greedy?"

Hurt, he looked me straight in the eyes and gave me one of those 'little boy lost looks,' which says, "Who me?"

Now for the third time a clear open warning. "Yes, you! Can't you hear what Jenny is saying?"

Paul was furious and came in for the kill. He hit back with full accuracy...with me as the target area. "I don't give a damn what Jenny is saying," venting his full annoyance and unwillingness to pick up false guilt. "Look, Jackie, if you want me to drive that wagon, then I am going to eat what I like. I need my strength and I am going to make sure I've got it and I'll do and eat what I like!"

Reeling from this unexpected and uncharacteristic response from Paul, I allowed the light of the sunrays to feed me in a way nothing else could. Jenny was by this time in full flight, lecturing us about the starving of the world and how she was proud to be still wearing the same shoes she bought from Oxfam five years earlier for fifty pence.

Now, disliking my own thoughts more and more, and desperately trying to escape from my own guilt feelings, I listened whilst the two of them played their all too familiar games by placating one another. "I can't stand this any longer! You pair of hypocrites you are acting as if everything is fine."

Poor Jenny now reeling from 'the scorpion's sting' just huffed and puffed, shrugging her shoulders, as if it had nothing to do with her, whilst I went into a sea of darkness.

I tried to figure out. "How did I get here?" Both Paul and Jenny seem fine. They were behaving as if everything was all right. The more they did this, the more I felt left out and the more my resentment built up against them both. "After all," I reasoned. "Aren't husbands supposed to be in loving protection of their wives? Where has all this, 'I love you' gone?"

The more I tried to understand, the deeper I was sinking into a pit of despair until finally I cracked open. “Jenny can huff and puff all she likes, we are going to sort this out and Paul Ryalls had better start hearing or there’s going to be trouble!” Now it was fighting talk within my imagination!

The more I battled against the rejection, the more exhausted I became. “Lord! Show me, what do I need to learn here?” was the cry from my heart. I sat in a sea of emptiness, detached from everything and everyone... completely alone.

Paul could have been a million miles away. He was in his own world, struggling with his thoughts. He was, in fact, mentally and emotionally a million miles away from me. My adult self was asking. “How come Paul can’t see my need for his protection?” Then I remembered something I had read, which had been written by Ruth Graham (the wife of Billy Graham, the evangelist). ‘Don’t expect your husband to be God. He cannot read your mind. How often we women expect this from our partners.’

I moved my being back into the cab. The atmosphere felt as hostile as before. Paul’s eyes were firmly fixed on the road ahead. The perfect cover for staying in his own space. Jenny shrugged her shoulders up then down, wordlessly showing her disapproval, as if fed up with the difficult child beside her.

I did not know how to get from the isolation where I found myself, into the companionship Paul and Jenny shared. I couldn’t see a bridge, and didn’t know how to build one. The truth was I didn’t really know if I even wanted to try! “Why should I venture into that bleak territory?” I retreated into the safety inside myself. Maybe later I would lift up the bedclothes of my mind and peep out again into that inhospitable world inside the tin box.

Eventually we stopped at the Austrian border. The sun was still shining and we decided to buy in some bread and cheese for the long expected wait at customs. There is one thing about the Austrians: They never disappoint with their bureaucracy. Paul would need sustenance before having to wrestle with the miles of paperwork and ploughing through a maze of unknown foreign words.

If he came through this border unscathed and still smiling...you could take it his Guardian Angel must be standing on the very pages of the green, blue and yellow forms with which he would need to wrestle. "Maybe there is a special form factory somewhere in this country where men sit locked in rooms, just thinking up new difficulties for the tired H.G.V. drivers?" I quipped.

Big Brother must be off sick! Paul was triumphant. The whole exercise only took three hours! His triumph was short lived, as we were only fifty yards from the next border where the whole process would need to be repeated. We would again be in another endless line of giant, crawling, and snail-like lorries.

The sun was beginning to beat down. No sharing of food or drink could, by this time, bridge the gap that had developed between the other two and myself. I just had to sit with my discomfort and work it through. I concentrated on navigating as efficiently as I could, trying to justify my existence.

We were four hours out of Austria and into Slovenia and I had hardly noticed the beauty of the scenery, only occasionally emerging from under my thick dark cloud, for a quick glimpse at the outside world. "Why does Paul do this? Why does he leave me in this? Why doesn't he help?"

As the miles were eaten up, we made our last stop before the Croatian border. Now something would have to break. There was no way we could even attempt to get through that blockage without being right with each other and in full positive power, I decided confronting them both. "We need to sort things out. We need to talk things over." The other two were not interested in discussion. They were more interested in refreshments so as to compound the punishment, we went to eat.

By this time Paul could do no right in my eyes. The service was terrible and I gave up the whole stop as a complete waste of time, but now I became determined. I definitely would not go forward into Croatia with this negative atmosphere between us. Neither Paul nor Jenny wanted to hang about talking and I was now convinced I had given Jenny every right to justify her opinion, namely that I was the worst example of a spoilt child she had ever met.

My mind continued to look for a breakthrough yet I had to continue to stand my ground with what I believed in my heart. "I suppose we are just three rough diamonds rubbing together, but we had better learn to live together as Brothers and Sisters in the Lord or perish together like fools." I blurted out in desperation.

Looking back, I asked the question. "How did I get here?" The starting point was when I tried to get along side Jenny in her bread and water exercise. I guess my response was not honest, I sold out in my own need to eat more. Then I tried to warn Paul from making what I thought was a mistake. Was Paul making a mistake? No, ... not for him, of course, he should eat properly, I reasoned.

I saw very clearly, that my first need was to find the truth within myself, own it and then share it with the other two as honestly as possible. I could have said to

Jenny "Bread and water may be OK for you, but we are used to living in God's abundance, so please understand it's His will for all people and this is our choice in life for ourselves, providing there is no harm to others."

I was refusing to ignore the pain and push the rubbish into the subconscious. I was not willing to play the game of perfect people, knowing this would mean accepting a false peace. Instead I decided to confront the suffering and continued to invite the other two to confront.

Thankfully after much painful discussion the door of understanding opened, enabling us all to build a bridge and share responsibility for keeping the channels of communication free, honest and positive. This helped us all to reach a deeper level of respect for one another and to this day we both love Jenny beyond measure.

During the next few days we were to see why God had allowed us to fight so hard to come into harmony with each other and obedience to Him. Coming through that painful situation was only going to be a forerunner of what was to come. "Just look at that! Talk about Bosnia burns."

We could see, in the distance, a pale green haze in the sky. "I suppose it's a fall out of sulphur created by consistent bombing." The heart of ex-Yugoslavia was truly burning. Fearfully we approached into the unknown, against all the odds and advice, to reach our goal, Zenica Hospital.

We were expecting three days drive through bandit country where daily stories of ambushes of aid lorries were shared amongst army personnel, but for us all at 10.30 at night, we were now to experience our first battle against Croatian bureaucracy, at it's best.

We had already been on the road twelve emotionally painful hours. Slowly, we pulled into the parking space along side the customs offices, showing our passports at the barrier. "Spedition!" The guard ordered us over to the offices. Fortunately we knew the routine. This was the time for patience and endurance, and if possible big smiles.

The Croats were at all-out war with the Muslims in Central Bosnia, so there was no reason on earth why they should allow us through to feed people whom they saw as "the enemy." We were totally relying on God to open this particular door for us. The officials took one look at our 'T' form saying destination Zenica Hospital. "No Zenica. You go Zagreb!"

Yes, they would let us go and deliver our aid into Croatia's capital city but not to the perceived enemy. "No Zagreb, Yes Zenica Hospital," I contradicted.

This performance went on for over an hour. I even produced a letter bearing a Croatian stamp, which stated we were to deliver incubators to the hospital for Croatian babies. No joy. They simply were not interested. "You stay! No go. You pay eighty percent your load value, to go through."

"Eighty percent! You really are joking!"

I thought for a moment. "Can you tell me how much is eighty percent of our load?" I was indignant at the mere thought of it. "We are going to Zenica Hospital" was my repeated affirmation! "You'll have to decide what you have to do to make it OK for you to let us through."

The official in charge became more and more frustrated and agitated with the English woman. He marched up and down outside the office, to recover his composure.

A busload of seemingly well-inebriated tourists were returning from some sort of pleasure trip. We looked on in amusement, as the holidaymakers behaved just like children who had been let out of school to play. Watching them 'perform' on their ridiculously rubber legs provided us with light relief from our own situation. Eventually, the bus was let through, and the guards returned to the English problem, which simply would not go away!

After hours of negotiating the officials finally gave in but only after I bent over to their computer screen and saw they were playing a childish game. The truth was, by then they wanted to finish their game and the English looking over their shoulders were spoiling their concentration.

The time spent with Jenny in the cab travelling across Europe and Croatia was not the easiest of time for me. Somehow, a third person seemed to upset the balance of teamwork which Paul and I had learnt to establish. Nevertheless, we were all acutely aware, the very friction was of value. We were being finely honed, more finely tuned, and can always look back on our experience and say it was not easy. For all of us 'Grace' would need to become the cornerstone in our relationships. We knew we had a deep love for one another, not because it just happened, like falling in love, but because we all made a conscious decision to accept our differences, and love one another as the 'Big Book' says. We all found victory in forgiveness, something none of us could live without.

Chapter 10

TESTING OF FAITH

We were trying to find the address in Zagreb, Croatia, where Haris lived with his mother since they had been evacuated from Sarajevo a few months earlier. We had seen the rather tasty sandwiches his mother had prepared for Haris on our second trip and I had a mental picture of an elderly, homely, mother-type person, so was quite taken aback when introduced to Ljubica. She looked about the same age as me, well spoken but seemed quite wary. Still underneath her reticence I discerned she was my type of 'woman's woman,' if there is such a person.

We all knew we would soon come to love her but there was little reason for her to trust us. After all she spent most of her days and nights with a radio clasped to her ear, listening to front line reports of killings and atrocities. She lived with almost permanent anguish in her mind. Was it surprising she was smoking about sixty cigarettes a day?

Not long after our arrival Ljubica had calmly gone into the kitchen and prepared a meal, having first brought a tray of Caj (Bosnian for tea) made from one of our English tea bags, which I always carried with me. Paul tells me I am a Philistine where tea is concerned, but for me a cuppa always restores my sense of home comfort. I mimed my joy of tea to Ljubica in an attempt at small talk, without any understanding of each other's language.

Soon Haris and his mother began to tell of their fears about the war, how at any time, they could expect the military to burst in and maybe try to kill them. Haris said he would have no hesitation in killing his mother to prevent her being taken by the enemy. Naturally we were all shocked by this. I was not sure whom 'the enemy' was and didn't want to get involved in the politics. Still I was taking in the situation. I thought, "There's Ljubica with one son in America; this other son Haris, trying to get his mother to allow him to join the Bosnian army. Her husband Hasan, who we had met in Split, was by now back in Central Bosnia, and Ljubica had not seen him for over a year. Gosh! It's not surprising she looks drawn and without much joy."

I was beginning to appreciate the depth of the intense pain within Ljubica and the darkness, which had all but overwhelmed her. I instinctively wanted to reach out, put my arms around her and somehow make her better, but sensed without doubt I didn't yet have permission.

With the help of Haris interpreting I asked very tentatively. "Tell me Ljubica have you ever thought about prayer?"

"What point Jackie? God no listen!"

"Ljubica, how can you say that? Did you pray for help before you met us?" She had to admit sheepishly that she had.

"Then tell me," I went on, directing my next question to set up a final move. "What do you think we are doing in your lounge now? Please don't tell me 'God no listen.'" Ljubica smiled a smile that simply said, Checkmate.

Silently I prayed, "Lord, will you please, please allow us to be a channel of your healing love to this very beautiful lady, tenderly heal the hurts. Keep her and her family safe and, most of all, let her know you love her." Without thinking, and as if on automatic pilot, I reached for my lipstick, unconsciously offering it to Ljubica just as a man would offer a swig of whisky to a mate. This gracious lady appreciated the sentiment and just as unconsciously, smiled and accepted the gesture without a second thought. We were friends. Unexpectedly and irrevocably bonded together forever.

Ljubica and I sat many hours, following every news report on television about the local fighting situation. Village after village was falling, first to the Croats then to the Muslims.

Paul and I were to learn checkpoints along the way into Central Bosnia could change within hours, so selecting the right documents and routes would become a work of art. I was beginning to get the message; creative paperwork was the order of the day! I knew I needed to collect rubber stamps on paper like children collect train numbers. The more official looking stamps I could compile on the original paperwork the better, and the more chance there would be of getting through.

As we continued to listen to the news reports, we heard there was heavy fighting around Zadar. The Serbs were shelling the whole area. The news broke that a vital reservoir had been blown up and the Croats were desperate. British engineers were being sent to the area immediately, to give technical advice. We felt quite proud to be British and had never before realised the advantages of a British passport.

To learn as much as possible I sat night and day, in a dense blue smoke-filled room, listening to every news report (most of which I could not understand) trying to piece together the political situation. It transpired Ljubica was a Croat and Hasan a Muslim, each of course with different passports. Haris had two passports, one of each, and used which ever was necessary for movement between his mother and father.

Ljubica told us how, in the earlier part of the war, she helped Hasan out of Sarajevo and up country, using her Croat passport through checkpoints. Now things were much worse. There was hardly any civilian movement, and thousands and thousands of families were split apart, anxious for news of loved ones. I cried within. "How responsible am I for Paul and Jenny? I need to hear your voice. Which route should we take? And most of all when?"

When we were ready to leave, Ljubica asked us to call on her brother who lives just on the border between Croatia and Central Bosnia. When we eventually met him we discovered he was a Professor, teaching sixteen to eighteen year olds. This beautiful man, reflecting gentleness and kindness became for the first time in my life a channel for a face to face encounter of Communist thinking.

He clearly found conflict between the way the Communist system worked and his own inner sense of right and wrong. He found himself quite unpopular at college by refusing to take bribes to give good marks to unworthy students. His fellow professors no doubt felt he was not one of them.

Paul and I could really understand the strain on such a man who was walking such a narrow tightrope between loyalty to his entire party upbringing, and the need to live by his own conscience.

We were to learn this beautiful man was willing to endanger not only his own life, but the lives of the rest of his family, by supporting his two nephews who were in hiding under his own roof. They had escaped the brutalities of the Serb invasion of Mostar, in Southern Bosnia. The oldest nephew was twenty-nine and could speak excellent English. His brother, twenty-six, did not or was not willing to communicate so openly and kept himself in the other room with the two teenage children of the household.

Six of them lived in a one-bedroom basement flat, which was a model of neatness and cleanliness. The family's resources seemed to bear up well under the constant extra strain of feeding these two extra hefty young men.

The young men's father was a Serb and had been a top official before the war. He was like the captain of a ship, determined to remain on deck until the last part of his ship sank into oblivion. Their mother is Ljubica's sister and a Croat.

Somehow this lovely family had survived intact despite the difficult political situation, constant bombing and internal exterminations. However, one only had to look into the eldest young man's eyes to see the deep, ingrained fear etched there. One day he was like any other young man training as an engineer, courting a young lady, when overnight he like the rest of the community was plunged into a nightmare of sinister violence and hatred, which drew ordinary families into a life of terror and fear. The strain of the present situation was certainly taking its toll.

Paul, Jenny and I with the residents of the house sat around the small white kitchen table as the eldest nephew tried to share his experience of life in the situation. "You people must turn back," he was saying. "This is no place for you. These people are crazy. You don't understand. They are sick in their minds!"

The more I listened the more I saw his deeply entrenched sense of hopelessness and fear. He saw no future for his country or his family. They were trapped. Not wanting to fight or kill yet, in holding this viewpoint they were held as traitors by their own school friends and neighbours.

The more I tried to explain why we were trying to help his country, the more insistent he became that we should walk away, go back to England while we could. "Jackie, you don't stand a chance of getting through. They will just cut you down!" Lowering his eyes he added, "Or even worse. Why? Why?" He queried. "This is not your war. You don't have to be here?"

Gently I looked deeply into his eyes and smiled, "Please, can you just accept God has planted a seed of love deep into our hearts for you. We come simply in obedience as a direct result of how *He* has saved us from ourselves. Your people are *not* forgotten!" He gestured with his hands in the air unable to compete with this crazy woman! There was little understanding between us but we knew we were one family.

Paul continued to ask various questions about the fighting factions. He needed a greater understanding of the political situation. I went deeply into my own thoughts wondering how we could help. "Tell me young man, have you ever thought of leaving this country completely?"

Roars of laughter at my naivety. "Have we ever thought of leaving? It's the only thing we people ever think about!"

"Then maybe we can encourage you in some small way?"

He stretched his hand out to my arm. "Please, maybe one day, but how can we leave? Our parents are still in Mostar."

Even more gently now, I dared to reply, "You know, if I were in your mother's shoes, the deepest desire of my heart would be for my boys to be safe. That above all, would give me the greatest comfort."

He fixed his gaze on me again, "I tell you, at this moment, we are still one step up from the bottom. When we get to the bottom line, then well, maybe." I knew he was right, and I understood what he was saying.

"OK friend. But please don't leave it too late." Again he looked away with a deep sadness within. "Maybe one day?"

I was beginning to feel the weight of our own situation. Should we go forward and try to get to the hospital and the refugees at Zenica against all the odds, or should we return home? I knew I would make the final decision, taking into consideration Paul and Jenny's lives were at stake as well as my own.

The family was quick to respond and like every single home we had ever visited in Croatia or Bosnia-Herzegovina, the families gave their guests their best accommodation and continued to plead with us to turn back. "Tomorrow, we will have a day of listening to what God is saying to our hearts," I announced, "Then we will make the final decision; but for now folks, anyone mind if we try to just sleep?"

Paul had no problem eating and sleeping under the most difficult of circumstances, but for me, that night, peace within seemed as unattainable as peace for that country.

The following day I decided to test the temperature of the water so to speak, and see what guidance God would give us. Would it be safe for us to go forward? Would we get through? We decided it would make sense first to travel to the pilgrimage town of Medjugorje in the hope of receiving some direction.

So within no time at all Paul was driving Bluebell up the main street and we were soon greeted by the sound of sweet singing accompanied by a solitary guitarist playing under the shade of a big tree. The nearer we homed in on the familiar sounds, the more we recognised our own church choruses. The musical group was made up of half a dozen Germans and, although they were singing in their native tongue, it was easy for Paul, Jenny and I to join in, at least by humming the well-known tunes. Within about twenty minutes we were all having a turn at choosing our favourite choruses and singing at the top of our voices.

In the midst of this sharing I spotted an elderly lady sitting weeping nearby. As quietly and unobtrusively as possible I approached, sat down silently beside her taking a frail hand gently in mine. We could speak no words in each other's language but that was no barrier to the moving of the Holy Spirit.

Although I sometimes questioned the value of my own feeble prayers, I trusted and started to pray silently in tongues knowing my Heavenly Father understood and would listen to the needs of the old dear lady. Face heavenwards, I looked forward to the day when all would be revealed.

As I moved back into the group the lead instrumentalist approached us. "God has just laid it on my heart to pray for you and your friends, constantly for the next week."

I took a deep breath and smiled. "Thank you! Please do just that. It is necessary, in fact, absolutely vital! We all thank you most sincerely."

Having received the encouragement for which we came, we decided to go next to the Croatian/Bosnia border and test the paperwork. In theory there was no way we should be allowed to go through, so the outcome would be a good guideline as to God's further will in the matter.

We approached the border with much trepidation, partly wanting to be turned away. A bit like, 'Take this cup from me.' on one side, but the other half being willing to follow in faith.

With a slight frown the main guard examined our quite flimsy papers. Then looking me directly in the eye, he gave a broad smile, "Good luck lady," and beckoned Bluebell to go forward! Our hearts and bodies moved up a gear as we proceeded forward into the unknown.

We were now in Muslim territory heading towards East Mostar and I suggested we take the next left turn over a main river bridge. Bluebell went happily forward and we were all feeling a little more relaxed as we climbed the incline onto the bridge. "Paul, wait! This bridge isn't going anywhere!" True enough we were just heading into actual deep water. The bridge had already been blown up. It was in three sections. From our angle an optical illusion made it appear normal, but in fact it was broken in two places.

Paul reversed Bluebell, swinging her round as we headed forward again. Sensing many eyes watching, Paul took no persuading to jam his foot down hard on the accelerator!

"OK Let's try just one more thing before we go forward. Let's back track to the UN base," I suggested. "If anyone is going to tell us to go home it will be them. They hate 'amateurs' and will be only too willing to discourage us."

Struggling with an ordinary road map, I hoped it could guide us over the difficult network of narrow mountain roads. It took some hard driving to find the UN base but eventually we pulled into a large compound with a factory type warehouse. We were still testing and searching for confirmation that we were following God's route in His time.

The place was deserted and there was a strange atmosphere. Food was piled to the ceiling; all boxed and marked with the familiar blue starred label. "Anyone home?" I called out, but the only answer was the echo of my own voice.

Eventually a middle aged man appeared. "Can you help me? We are trying to get some incubators through to the hospital in Zenica."

"Umm!" He bowed his head. "Things are bad. The men have all gone to a funeral. One of our wagons was blown up yesterday. The Croatian Guide was killed and the driver badly injured. The trouble is," he went on, "there happened to be an Italian T.V. crew following and they sent the pictures back via satellite and the victim's pregnant wife saw them in Denmark on her television screen. So as you can see, things are not good. They are all at the funeral. What is it you need?"

"Well I think one of your UN rubber stamps on our customs papers would help."

"Sorry, I can't help with that," he replied, "Go and see if the officers will help."

I thanked him and returned to the cab. "Paul, park right outside the offices at the far end please, wait there if you will, and let me see what the situation is."

"Lord, please show me clearly, I don't want to make any mistakes. Paul and Jenny's lives are at stake, so please make the way and your will for us clear."

A self-assured young lady approached me.

"Can I see one of the officers please? We are English and are trying to get to Zenica," I explained. "No chance," was the confident reply? "Our lorries haven't got through for seven weeks."

Totally unmoved by this comment I stood my ground as the young lady picked up the telephone and spoke into it. Within minutes a tall, blonde good-looking

Swedish officer appeared around the door.

Even my faithful eyes could not help but notice his immediate charm! I responded naturally, trying not to allow my femininity to open the door to the way forward. "We are getting quite used to the route into Central Bosnia, we have done it before. We are heading to Zenica hospital with incubators on board. What is the present situation?"

"Well," he stroked his chin thoughtfully, "if you have survived at this stage of the war, then I count you professional enough to know what you are about. Where's your lorry?" he asked, looking out of the window and stroking his chin again. I indicated Bluebell.

"That blue one down there!" he exclaimed in utter disbelief. "No chance! You will never get that over this terrain. The only way forward is over the 'Diamond' route and there's heavy fighting through Gornji Vakuf. Lots of sniper fire."

"Yes, I know. We've been that way before and, you may think this a bit strange, but this is God s work, so *He* will open the doors."

"You have done this trip before? In that? Well I guess if you are still alive and still willing to go, you might just pull it off, but not in that lorry. It would be a bit like the wooden horse going through …then"…he seemed to think again. "If you are determined and you are quite sure, would you like to take some wheelchairs for us?"

To my amazement he continued planning. "I suggest you call at all the UN camps en route, then they will know of your whereabouts and will be able to tell T.S.G. your position. Please ask for a Major Bowers at Tomislavgrad. Tell him I sent you and I am sure you will get all the help you need."

"Thank you, thank you very much indeed." I felt totally released inside, if he thought we could do it then we could do it.

With confirmation, and my confidence back on line, I dared to ask. "Incidentally, have you one of those UN maps? I could do with a decent map!" He gave me a broad smile and left the room, returning shortly with an official UN route map, which even showed the up-to-the-minute front line positions. We shook hands warmly.

The young lady stood up amused by the outcome. "Come on I'll get the necessary paperwork done for the wheelchairs and we'll get them loaded. You do have room don't you?"

"Of course!" I chirruped, secretly hoping we had and realising we had been given a great deal more than wheelchairs. Not only did we have official UN paperwork, but also we had at last been acknowledged as professionals! "Thank you Lord! You don't miss a thing do you!"

Before long we were loaded and on our way. The pieces were in position on the chessboard. There were no more questions to be asked 'upstairs.' I turned to Paul and Jenny, "We will go back to the uncle's house and make an early start in the morning if that's OK with you both?"

The next morning was bright and sunny when we set off at 8 a.m., enjoying the drive to the first UN base about two hours away. We thought we could find it without too much trouble by using our new map. This was fresh territory for us and Paul was quite impressed with my navigation skills. I had to admit I was like the cat with the cream!

We reached the base, showed passports and papers and were eventually led upstairs into the operations room of the UN camp. It was situated in a school where murals on the walls remained from happier days when these rooms resounded with laughter from children.

The Major was polite and business-like, offering tea first, he explained the area we were entering had been under heavy fire, and directed us to the beginning of the 'Triangle' route, adding us as new players to their theatre, we were on our way.

This route started on a flat plain where brightly coloured, wild flowers waved in the light breeze. A few cows were grazing peacefully and I wondered what they thought of the actions of their masters!

Both Jenny and Paul were in good spirits after a first class early lunch at the base. They were happy to be making some real headway. It wasn't long before the plains gave way to hills and the hills gave way to steep mountain tracks. Although the army was constantly maintaining these routes, Bluebell still had to wrestle with deep ruts and potholes.

She had a very low undercarriage, so there was very little room for mistakes. It would only take a moment's lack of concentration on Paul's part and Bluebell could lose an exhaust, or worse still, a hole could be smashed in her sump.

We turned a hairpin bend. Bluebell's nose was facing up to the sky at an acute angle. "Surely she won't be able to pull this heavy load up there!" Immediately Paul double-declutched, accelerating so as not to lose any revs. Old Bluebell spluttered but the dear lady pulled her heart out for us as she slowly and laboriously crawled up and up the steep rugged track. Paul patted her dashboard in appreciation. Our love and admiration for this old girl was growing by the minute.

Maybe the surge of adrenaline the struggle had generated was just what we needed to keep us going for what should have been a twelve-hour drive over some of the roughest mountain tracks in Bosnia. The UN had done an excellent job keeping the paths clear. Anything less than tarmac for dear old Bluebell put her in danger of seizure! Her springs creaked with every bump and pothole.

The elderly lady graciously made her way forward where the big sixteen tonners had pioneered the route. After about five hours in the warm sunshine we were beginning to feel we were the only people left travelling in the area. The only other living creatures in sight were the occasional goat and an odd cow or two.

I repeatedly checked the map as a wrong turn in this terrain could have dire consequences. Through the wing mirror we delighted girls noticed a UN vehicle coming up on Bluebell's rear. To help relieve the monotony we threw a few boiled sweets across from Bluebell's open window into the young men's cab. Delighted to see females still in existence, the soldiers immediately interpreted the gifts as an invitation to stop and chat

"How are you off for diesel?"

"Oh! We're OK thank you. We've half a tank," replied Paul.

"Well, if you like, we'll fill you up from our tank and we have a Jerry-can we'll also fill for you to take." Little did we realise at the time the significance of this gift of fuel.

Continuing to pick our way carefully around the boulders, most of the time in second gear, and occasionally down to first, old Bluebell did her best to climb the extreme upward gradients.

After eight hours of solid, concentrated driving through the second mountain range, we turned a bend to find ourselves on the tail of a convoy we had followed earlier. This line of about twenty trucks had been held up as one of the lorries had managed to slide over the edge and a great deal of effort was going into retrieving it.

"I imagine the military will not be too pleased to lose one of their wagons over the edge of a mountain but, in the warm afternoon breeze, at least it will give the 'tail enders' a chance to take a breather."

The long hours of intensive journeying over the bumpy road became quite tiring and tedious. The only thing which kept me going, was the anticipation of the expression on the Hospital Director's face when God willing we would arrive with the five incubators, now held for safety deep in the heart of Bluebell. I remembered well the needs of the pregnant lady we had met on a previous trip, who had received three bullets in her tormented body. She was the reason why we were making this trip. For her sake we would put up with all the discomfort, for in a matter of hours we hoped to be at her side. This wonderful thought warmed me through and through.

After several hours in the dusk of evening the convoy in front stopped and to Paul's surprise, the officer in charge came up to the cab window. "Would you mind going to the back of the convoy?" he said. "There's a lot of sniper fire in this area. You'll need to go to the back of the line. We're going to put on our bullet-proof vests and drive through as fast as we can. If you can keep up, all the better. But, you must understand, we will be going through check points and if you get stopped, then you are on your own!"

"That's straight enough. Thank you for that at least!" I said politely, if not a little sarcastically.

"It looks like we will be on our own again! He clearly knows nothing about Angels."

With all their headlights on full beam, the convoy pulled away at top speed. Thankfully we were now on tarmac, and Bluebell found it well within her range to keep up. We were feeling very proud of her when a single-decker bus pulled out from a side turning and slipped neatly into the position previously held by Bluebell. Many burnt out houses lined the route and people were trying to flee the area and this bus had probably slipped into the convoy to secure protection. "Look at that lucky so and so!" I thought. Then, just as quickly, "Sorry Lord! I'm sure that bus is just where you want it to be!"

The words were no sooner out of my mouth when lights flashed ahead. "Checkpoint coming up Paul! Don't look right! Don't look left! Just look straight ahead!" Out of the corner of my eye I could see the single-decker bus being ordered over. The guards complete with their AK47's had boarded it. "Come on Paul! Don't stop now. Go through!" The road ahead, opened before us just like the Red Sea parted for the Israelites. In that instant the bus had become a shield to enable Bluebell and her crew to pass through the checkpoint safely.

I looked down at the dashboard. The fuel tank was half full. "Lord if you had not given us the gift of fuel earlier, we would have been out of diesel right in the middle of all this!" Sinking back into my seat with a broad smile plastered all over my face, a sense of peace came over me. "Lord, I would rather have you than all the bullet-proof vests in the world. Thank you."

The convoy, having gone its own way was by now tucked up in camp for the night. Bluebell was on her own but still grinding forward after eighteen hours motoring. In the darkness ahead we could see a lorry parked broadside across the road. It just looked so odd. An evil, sinister atmosphere prevailed and I immediately responded to my primitive survival instincts. "Paul, turn the lady around, the UN base is only about two miles back. Enough is enough for one night!" Paul needed no prompting, as he also sensed something was very wrong.

Although the actual area we were in was very dark and quiet, the skyline behind, was vivid red with the fierce glow from burning buildings.

It took all of my feminine whiles and much gentle persuasion for the UN Commander to agree to let Bluebell and her weary passengers into the camp. We were grateful for the camp beds and showers but most precious of all, Bluebell had received a welcome drink of diesel by lining up with her big brothers.

It was one of the guards on duty who suggested that the road where the lorry was positioned broadside was in fact mined. Many of the Muslim houses had been burnt down that night, the occupants taken away by their enemy, in full view and only twenty yards from the UN entrance. Under their mandate, all the soldiers could do, was to stand by and watch helplessly these appalling ongoing scenes.

Despite the closeness of the horror of the war going on around us, I felt quite uplifted the following morning because maybe today we would be arriving at our hospital, our people.

The only thing, which was causing me a problem, was my concern for the brakes that, because of their constant use were burning and starting to smell during the descent of any slight incline. The smell from them was making me feel uneasy. "Paul, use the air brakes. She won't last the journey at this rate," was my constant cry.

Paul seemed quite rattled at my suggestion, but I chose to ignore his hostile vibrations. Reaching for the flask I tried to give him a drink to soften his staring gaze.

Bluebell rolled from side to side as she got caught in some deep ruts made by the heavy armoured vehicles. "Careful, Paul! Watch that boulder!" He braked hard then stopped. Bluebell's springs gave a screech of exasperation.

"That was close," grimaced Paul, "It looks like we are going to have to move that one," referring to a giant boulder in our path.

The words had no sooner left his mouth than Jenny sprang into action. This sixty-nine year young lady was bending down and heaving for all she was worth in the full heat of the day. Triumph! The rock succumbed to her determined efforts and rolled to one side. This was Samson stuff, and soon I was patting Jenny's arm in appreciation. I felt a little ashamed of my own reluctance to let my back take any sort of strain, but knew if I did, the price would have to be paid later.

The hours passed slowly, and we were beginning to feel the strain of the hot sun as our minds and bodies became more and more tired. We had almost completed the 'Triangle' route, which, at Bluebell's sedate pace, had taken five gruelling hours. When suddenly, CRUNCH! A heavy scraping sound brought us all into sudden alertness. Bluebell had hit a boulder but we thought she seemed to have survived the impact.

Approaching a small town, and not really wishing to stop and check Bluebell, we wound our way around the narrow bends, Paul doing his best to avoid the lunatic, local militia drivers who seemed to hold life on the roads as a very cheap commodity.

The whole atmosphere was uncomfortable and tense. The presence of evil in the air was so strong it was almost tangible. You could have cut it with a knife. "Which way?" Paul was asking as we approached a 'T' junction.

"I'm not sure Paul but turn left and we'll ask these men." I should have known better.

The groups were local army personnel, sitting waving guns in the air, laughing excitedly and clearly high on drink. "Which way Zenica?"

With roars of laughter, they pointed left, the way Bluebell was facing. "Hmmm!" I thought, trying not to be judgmental. Suspiciously, but following instructions, we turned left, took a right hand fork, which became incessantly more narrow the further we travelled.

The further we went the more obvious it became we had been deceived. "Stop, Paul. There is no use continuing. We are obviously going in the wrong direction!"

"But I can't turn here!" He said quite flushed in the face, looking over the edge at the hundred-foot drop, inches away from Bluebell's wheels.

"Paul, you're going to have to. I'll get out and watch the wheels so you don't go over the edge." As soon as I was on the ground, I saw we were in big trouble. Bluebell had been leaving a trail of thick, black oil. The worst possible thing had happened.

"She'll run out of oil before we can get to the next base." Paul stated quite categorically. "This is no place for an aid lorry to break down," he reasoned. "This food on board will well outweigh the value of our lives. Wouldn't those men back there like to have the contents of old Bluebell?"

Paul was careful in his manoeuvres and, as he was negotiating the tight space, I noticed the local militia watching us. A man with a walkie-talkie was clearly describing the scene. "Let's get out of here!" I urged as Paul skilfully swung Bluebell round for the last time on the narrow path, we were at least now able to go in the right direction.

We found our way out of the town without too much trouble and loss of time, and were soon on our way to the base. "I'm glad it's not too far. How much oil is left? Will it last out?" Paul didn't answer. He was not hanging about, but pushing the old lady for all she was worth.

"There's a Warrior, Paul! We can't be too far away now!" True enough, there, up ahead could be seen the compound. The big white iron gates were closed protecting the columns of huge, heavy, armoured personnel carriers.

Approaching, Bluebell limped quietly to a halt as we waited for permission to enter. Her outpourings became embarrassing. I blushed and was not amused by Bluebell's ungracious display. It was a bit like the breaking of the waters of a pregnant woman!

After being instructed in the rules and regulations I signed the register. Only then were we allowed to enter the compound. Bluebell could hold out no longer, and proceeded to disgorge all the thick black oil from her entire sump, leaving a trail all the way from the main gate into the large, factory workshop.

Soldiers came rushing over with trays of sand to try to minimise the damage, but they were too late! Bluebell had truly left her mark on the British Army forever! This old girl would need a full hysterectomy. It seemed her weight bearing days were over.

For two days Paul and an army sergeant called Les, worked relentlessly operating on Bluebell. The hole in her sump was thankfully repairable. It turned out she'd had a miscarriage, however there were still problems with her postoperative condition. The two men toiled side-by-side in a deep pit, first in extreme heat, and then, deep into the night.

Finally the moment of truth! Bluebell soared into life, her heart was again beating, but oil was still pouring out of her womb. The gasket had not been stitched correctly, which meant the whole operation needed to be repeated again. The two surgeons were exhausted and disappointed.

"Sorry, Jackie, I'll keep on working but I don't think we'll make it in time to leave with the convoy in the morning."

There was nothing for it but to make the best of a bad job. Jenny and I would just have to amuse ourselves for another day. Whilst Paul continued working we had little trouble listening to the experiences of the war with the men in the lower ranks.

On hearing our intention to continue to travel over the 'Diamond' route the following day, a young sergeant bowed his head. Slowly, shaking it from side to side, he whispered, "Lady, we went to retrieve the bodies of the two Italians who were killed. There were four drivers, two escaped and were wandering in the mountains for two days, finally finding their way here, exhausted and in a terrible state. The other two" his voice trailed off. He shook his head again as he recalled the dreadful sight. Now looking me straight in the eyes, "Lady, if you saw what they did to those men, what those bodies looked like, then I am sorry," raising his voice, "then you would just not go any further."

I opened my body to the sun's rays, using their warmth to prevent his words penetrating my inner being. I shrugged my shoulders and turned away asking to be excused.

"Lord, it's no use listening to the seed of doubt. I can only listen to you. We have come this far, we need you to guide us." I rested back against the seat, soaking up the warmth, allowing God's creation to feed me in a deep way.

As time passed Paul was delighted and relieved to report Bluebell was fully recovered from her emergency operation.

"Bless you come, have a hot shower, then we'll have a good meal together. Whatever is said about our British Army, there is one thing, which is indisputable. They make the most wonderful custard, and if possible we will both leave room to have seconds of their lump free creation."

"OK you girls, what have you been up to today while I've been slaving under a hot lorry?" Jenny and I looked sheepish. "Well it's like this. We've had a wonderful day with the boys, playing on a tank having our photos taken. At least that was the good bit. The bad bit was they told us about the Italians being shot but, it's no subject for the dinner table."

Not far into the meal we were joined by a large group of Overseas Development Agency drivers. They had nine 'heavy duty monsters' out in the compound, full of bulk food destined for Zenica.

"What time will you be leaving in the morning?" I enquired.

"We're under orders not to go any further if the fighting's too bad. We'll take this load back now."

"So many warnings! Have I misheard you God, or is the enemy of my soul trying to distract us by sowing the seed of doubt? No Satan you are not going to win."

"Go back, it's not worth it." Their leader was saying.

"Gosh! If they think that, and they're being paid about seven hundred pounds a week to do the job, and they know the difference they could make with nine lorries of food, then what right have I to risk three lives to deliver our little offering?" I wrestled silently on this question as Paul and Jenny talked, laughed and shared some of Paul's light-hearted jokes.

I disappeared into my little corner upstairs where I had made my home amongst the filing cabinets in the interpreter's office. We had two-army issue, camp beds between three, one chair and a small table, which substituted as my dressing table in the mornings. This night, it was to be my altar. "Lord, show me the way. We are available. We are available for you. We just want to be in your will." I sank back into the quiet of my own heart. It was still and peaceful. "Yes, Lord, it is OK. We will go forward as planned in the morning and just trust you for everything, whatever may happen."

The one thing of which I was sure: something big must be going to happen!

...Our faith was certainly being tested!

*Destruction in
Central Bosnia*

Chapter 11

THE LOAVES AND THE FISHES

Next morning a news reporter approached us in the UN camp. "Are you going out today? Which way are you heading?" He addressed his questions to Paul who was checking Bluebell's water. Hardly giving Paul time to answer, he continued, "I'm going to Sarajevo but will be calling into Vitez for an escort from there on."

"We are passing Vitez en route for Zenica. Maybe we could travel together?" Paul was saying.

"Yes, it looks as if they will give us a Warrior escort from the 'Picnic Area'" (The army's name for the rendezvous area, before the most dangerous section.) The reporter was driving an armour-plated Range Rover and, once on the road, wasted no time in spite of the fact I had suggested Bluebell might be able to keep up with his pace.

It was only minutes before we were out of the relative safety of the army compound and onto the dusty Diamond route before Bluebell bumped and groaned over the pitted track as her springs were stretched to their limits once more. Listening to her one would think she would break in half at any moment, but this was God's tool, so I tried to quieten my thoughts.

The Warriors were already in position waiting for us at the 'Picnic Area' as the Land Rover sped straight past them. The huge army vehicles remained stationary.

"Paul, weren't they supposed to escort us through this bit? Because if they were… then they aren't. We are on our own and this is no place to be alone!" I found the whole process of travelling, in constant fear, compared quite well with my most miserable nightmare. I wondered if others experience such a degree of fear whilst driving.

We approached a particularly difficult stretch of road. I couldn't help thinking of the poor Italians and their awful fate. This must have been the place where it happened. I thought, "rocks on one side, woods the other, a perfect hi-jack position." The reporter's vehicle was wasting no time as if he too sensed the increased danger at last. Bluebell continued to bounce from side to side.

Jenny was awake for once and fully aware of the danger. She sat silently not murmuring one word of protest. I held her hand for our mutual comfort as her eyes darted into every shadow amongst the trees. "Jenny, I may find you a pain in the backside at times, but there is no doubting your courage," remarked Paul lovingly.

I started to sing. "Jesus, Name above all names." The other two joined in willingly, as the Holy Spirit moved in upon our frail minds and calmed our fears.

From out of my heart, words were now forming in my mind. My inner voice was speaking. I reached for my pen to scribble on the back of an envelope. 'Do not fear man who would seek to take your flesh life, but fear God who would one day judge your time on earth.' "Yes, Lord, thank you for the reminder."

We were now all relieved we had come through the mountains and reached Vitez where we flashed Bluebell's eyes as our reporter companion pulled into the barracks and gave a cheery thumbs up sign. I imagined he was as relieved as we were to be through that section. It was true, the actual physical going forward into the unknown was being done half in naivety and half in faith, but for us faith was something we needed to exercise on a daily basis in order to grow.

At no time during the following hours drive on to Zenica did we feel able to relax our vigilance. In every shadow there seemed to lurk the manifestation of evil. Most of the buildings were destroyed, one house exposing an empty fridge and the shop safe which had all been rifled.

Every few yards the roads were a mass of crumpled tarmac where grenades and shells had destroyed all the day to day normality of living. There was a single decker bus where every inhabitant had been killed, which we had seen on the news in England. I wondered where the inhabitants of these villages were now. Had they fled? Were they able to flee?

The odd group of children played with hand made wooden rifles, re-enacting the horrific scenes they had lived through and which had now become part of their normal lives. Many had huddled, hiding in cellars, their supposed places of safety becoming their very tombs.

It was with relief we turned on to the final stretch leading to Zenica, a town now surrounded by enemy forces, a place sinking with the sheer weight of many thousands of homeless refugees. Excitement was mounting in me, and I could hardly wait to see my director friend's face.

The hospital was bursting at the seams. Patients were everywhere, many lying on blood-covered, broken down trolleys in the main reception area. Doctors and nurses dragged themselves slowly along, showing all the signs of just hanging on, having worked night and day, each with their personal tragic story to hold in a breaking heart.

The Hospital Director welcomed us with open arms, hardly able to believe his eyes. He was feasting on our clear complexions and smiling faces. "Welcome! Welcome, brothers!" he seemed to say with every gesture, his hand frequently touching our arms as if needing re-assurance we were really there!

He showed us into his office for refreshments. Immediately an interpreter was called for, as we wasted no time catching up on all the news.

"How is 'my lady'?" I enquired. The Director's eyes dropped.

"The lady you speak of, Jasmina, her baby was born two days ago." I waited, holding my breath, "...but it died early this morning."

"Oh Lord!" my heart sank. "Where is she? Can I go to her?"

"Yes, Jackie. We will take you right away, but she doesn't know yet the baby is dead."

We had on board the bag Helen had packed in England for this lady. "I must take out the baby things, but Jasmina must still know Helen and the family are there for her, especially at this time." The big black sports bag was brought up out of Bluebell and I searched for the letter and photograph Helen had carefully prepared for Jasmina.

Beckoning to the interpreter we were led through the endless corridors of human suffering. Victims were sitting on long benches or hobbling about on crutches.

As we reached her bed 'my lady' recognised us instantly. Tensely I bent over, desperately trying to control my own emotions.

"My baby, my baby. You see my baby?" Holding back my tears and choosing my words carefully, I managed to whisper, "Your baby is in a good place. We come to love you, to show you that you are so special."

I knew this lady had been used of God, to be a focus for all to see. I wanted so much to love her better that I just reached out my arms and enveloped Jasmina with all my being. Tears ran down both our faces as we embraced and held each other tightly.

Reaching for the letter, I tried to find some composure and see through my own tear filled eyes to enable me to share Helen's love. The letter was full of best wishes for the Mother and the new baby, so I less than skilfully edited the text as I read it out aloud, trusting it would be some time before Jasmina would be able to get someone to translate it in full for her. My voice continued to break as Helen's love reached out to Jasmina's pain. We were all one in the suffering. Silently I prayed in tongues for Jasmina's emotional and physical healing asking God to come into her in spirit and do a work of grace.

"Lord don't let this baby's short life and this mother's pain be wasted," I prayed silently.

Exhausted, I tried to pull myself together having taken into my heart the pain of these dear souls in the hospital. Feeling at collapsing point under the emotional and spiritual weight. "Jesus, I am bringing these pains for your healing, cover them in the blood of Calvary. Heal in a mighty way for your name's sake, Amen." Being with Jasmina had not been a painless experience but leaving her was even worse.

We wandered past an open door to one of the male wards; a nurse called us inside. There, lying on a bed was an elderly man, totally paralysed from the neck down. His eyes reached over to me as the nurse explained Paul had prayed with that same patient on the Christmas trip. The nurse was now asking if we would both have a word of comfort with him. Paul joined me and we drew strength from each other. Far from us serving him, the man was serving us as a couple. The love between we three at that moment was electric and I savoured our brief contact as we all shared a special time in our Heavenly Fathers arms.

After receiving much needed refreshment, the Hospital Director's thoughts turned to the grave message he was holding in his heart. "Jackie, Paul..." he pleaded through an interpreter, "I would not ask you this if it were not necessary." He went on, his voice trailing almost to a whisper. "You know I would not ask you this if it were not necessary but could you go back to Zagreb and get us some more drugs? We have no anaesthetic, no X-ray film, and no morphine." His voice became more urgent. "We have not had any supplies for seven weeks. No one has been able to get through to us. You are our only hope. I will give you the necessary introductions to people who will help."

Our hearts sank with tiredness and despair. For us Zagreb was a week's drive away and, at that moment, Jenny and I felt we couldn't face those mountains again. Our nerves were at breaking point. "Oh Lord! What are you asking? What are you saying?" We prayed, bracing ourselves.

Standing firmly now I looked our friend directly in his eyes. "We need at least a day to unload and feed the refugees in the school. There is nobody else, in Central Bosnia, who could ask this of us but for you, and I know I speak for the others, we will do our best. For you, my friend anything."

After we unloaded the few medical supplies which we had brought the local T.V. crew, on hearing we were at the hospital, came to give us a video filmed on our last trip. It was only later that we were to learn of the significance of this gift.

As we all walked slowly through the large hospital foyer led by men in white coats, I was uncomfortable, being reminded of occasions during my school days when the school governors processed in full entourage amongst the 'little people'.

Feeling quite uncomfortable at the elitist role now, I was very relieved when a man who had been waiting for our appearance pulled me away and asked if we would take a letter back to England. It was amazing that, after so little time, it seemed as if the whole of Zenica knew we had arrived! Receiving it I smiled at his initiative in coming to the hospital to find us. He tried to hang on to my arm but not wishing to be impolite I tried to reassure him " I'm sorry but please excuse us because we must go and find our refugee family in the school but we will deliver your letter in England, I promise."

We bade the Hospital Director good bye with the promise we would do our best to make it back to Zagreb and return with his urgent supplies. How much this man had become a part of our lives.

The school was only ten minutes drive away and as soon as Bluebell arrived, so did the crowds! It seemed the children were everywhere - even hanging from dear old Bluebell's wing mirror ears! A tall Muslim boy called Ricki who was a refugee from the school was there to interpret for us.

Everyone had a good laugh at our dusty state. We had learnt why the professional aid drivers wore bandages over their mouths and noses as the dust gets everywhere! Some of the more caring women shook their heads, sorry we had arrived in such a dirty condition.

"Come on! The sun is shining and we have wonderful surprises for you!" I called from my perch standing high on Bluebell's running board. I produced about two hundred letters. One by one we called out all the names.

Hands stretched out to receive loving messages. There were kisses of appreciation and tears of joy.

Paul and I recognised a woman who by this time, was on her knees on the hard pavement, kissing and hugging her letter, tears of joy streaming down her face. We knew her to be a strong woman of great character. She was tragically cut off from her daughter who was now safe in England. Pushing through the crowds we went over, fell to our knees and bled with her, tears streaming down our faces in complete empathy. The world stopped. A calm spread across the waiting crowd. The frame froze. Everyone's eyes were drawn to this cameo of compassion.

Jolted back to the task in hand by the sound of a car horn, I whispered. "Come on Paul, we've all the other letters to distribute!" With growing excitement we gave out the rest of the letters to the eager families.

There were the inevitable disappointed faces. The joys we brought to some seemed to highlight the disappointment and hurt of others. "Come on, Paul, let's get some of the food boxes off for them."

"Jackie, do you know what you are asking? We've not stopped since we arrived. Can't we have a rest?" but he knew better, nothing would stop us from giving our best. Paul immediately arranged to have the food boxes carried into the largest of the downstairs classrooms. We knew if we tried to pass the boxes through the main entrance, some of the boxes would go astray via the unscrupulous ones amongst the refugees. So Paul decided to make a chain and pass everything through the open windows into the hands of some of the appointed leaders.

There were seventeen classrooms in the school, most with twenty five to thirty five people in each. Many families were living together day and night in one classroom.

Once all the boxes were inside, a team of us assembled seventeen tables side by side to form a counter effect. We then emptied each box and sorted the food into some order. A jar of jam, a tube of toothpaste, plenty of beans, sugar, flour and oil all to be shared equally. There was not sufficient oil, flour or sugar to go around but eventually there were seventeen tables completely full of every kind of gift one could imagine.

Now, the big problem! How to get the sorted aid safely into each classroom through the dense wall of human flesh, pushing and shoving against the door.

"Ask for two representatives from each room to come in, one pair at a time," I suggested to the tall young interpreter. Ricki threw his hands in the air, exasperated at my naïve suggestion.

"Jackie you don't understand! The minute we open that door there's going to be a stampede. The children are just going to get crushed. Some of them will wait patiently, but others will grab what they can."

"OK the strongest men will have to guard the door from the inside, then we will have to take on the whole crowd." Paul positioned our men with their shoulders against the door. Ricki and I braced ourselves as they released the lock taking the full weight of the surging crowd. We pushed our way through the small opening into the heaving mass.

The women were all prepared with blankets ready to carry the first loads away into their rooms but I realised they would struggle to lift their heavy burdens from the ground.

"You!" I indicated, pointing at one strong man. "You! Help these ladies." He shrugged his shoulders.

"Help? Who me? No way!" His response was easy to interpret. I waved my arms at him, now determined. "No help! No food! No problem for me!" my frustration was growing.

"Please tell these men," I now addressed Ricki.

"Please tell them I mean business. They no co-operate. We go home. No food! No more letters! No next time!" They calmed a little.

"Now tell them, if we can get this food distributed, we have some shoes to share out." This seemed to please them, and they gave way to the women to load their blankets and get their much-needed supplies of food back to their rooms.

Having solved the food problem we now laid out the shoes on the tables, which we hoped would also serve as some protection from the crowd.

"Maybe we can let them come in on mass and sort them out for themselves...maybe not."

As I was turning this idea over in my mind, the door burst open and in stormed a throng of sweaty aggressive men, each determined to get their hands on the shoes ahead of their neighbour.

To prevent myself from being crushed, I managed to scramble onto a desk in front of me. The pressure of the heaving crowd pushed the arrangement of tables into the only standing space available. Desperately I grabbed a terrified child within my reach just managing to retrieve him from being trampled beneath the weight of the powerful, hostile mob. Men pushed the rest of the women and children aside, caring only about their own needs. Some men were grabbing hands full of children's shoes shoving them into their pockets. Anger welled up inside me but I was helpless, marooned on top of a table and for a time I was ashamed to be part of the human race.

Within minutes the room looked like an old junkyard, nothing left but empty boxes and paper everywhere. Ricki stood in shock and ashamed. After all this was not representative of all the refugees, but it was still true to say many were coming from greed and not need. The battle inside me raged. "Lord, I have no right to judge these souls. What would I do if it were I?" I could see yet again there could be no lasting change for the good of mankind unless there is a change in hearts first. "Lord, help us. How much we need you to refine us!"

There had been little sense of satisfaction in the day's work, and with very heavy hearts we decided to take a pram and some baby food to the orphanage. There were sixty-five babies there. Some of the women were not married, but were the victims of rape by the enemy. They had been attacked in their own villages.

Paul, Jenny and I didn't stay long, but we were absolutely delighted the following day when we saw 'the pram' being pushed towards the local market with four young children on board. "If helping that to happen was the only reason for us being here, then I suppose we should all feel quite satisfied," I observed. "Come on you guys, a good cup of tea's waiting."

Immediately we were shaken from our moment of satisfaction. Thankfully, Jeannana and Emin were there to gather up the team's aching bodies and ease our shattered spirits by taking us over to their flat to help restore the ravages of the day.

The lounge was filled with the smoke from Hasan's cigarettes, and it wasn't long before Safet arrived. It was good to see the men again, and as they sat round the large coffee table, Jeannana acted as interpreter for us. They all seemed anxious to tell of the desperate situation of the Muslims. Hasan was extremely patriotic and eventually asked if Paul and I could bring food for the hungry soldiers.

Confused by his request I felt I needed more information. Not wanting to take political sides or be guilty of neglecting to help the poor, I asked if we could be taken to meet the officers in charge. I knew this would help me to discern in my spirit what was right.

The following morning we were taken on a conducted tour of the local barracks. It was a complete picture of defeat, grimy and totally run down.

"This is where the eighteen-year-olds are brought to be trained to fight," the mature man in charge told us. I imagined my eighteen-year old son, Richard, maybe leaving home for the first time and finding himself in such a place. Even worse was the thought he would then be expected to go out and kill, all within a matter of three weeks and that's at best.

I wanted to do what we could for these boys, but still I wasn't sure if it was the right thing to do. We progressed over to the medical centre where a young man was being given attention for a severe wound in the calf of his leg. My stomach turned as my eyes veered involuntarily away.

Realising my mistake, I forced myself to look again to try to give the young man some support. I could hardly believe, bless him. He had seen my reaction and had covered himself to save me. A small, sensitive gesture but typical of many we had met.

The armaments consisted of a few broken down tanks which looked as dilapidated as the place itself. Instinctively I wanted to do my sergeant major act and put extra discipline in, to tighten up the place, but I saw in the neglect the reflection of the rock bottom morale of a nearly defeated army.

"Let's go Hasan! I have seen enough!" I said shaking my head despairingly, as we all made our way over to his car. Paul and Jenny were by this time both bending my ear with their differing opinions, but I needed space to make my own decision.

When we arrived back at the flat I wanted to separate myself away from the conversations and thankfully, having done this, it wasn't long before the answer became clear to me. After checking with Paul, I addressed Hasan directly.

"Hasan, I am now clear for myself and on behalf of all the people who support us in England. Firstly, I want you to know we will do anything within the bounds of our moral code and within our power to help you or your family personally. We have looked deeply into your request, but we have decided the answer is… no. I am quite clear now. We are here to help war victims, not to aid the continuation of the war. If your men need feeding, then that is the responsibility of your Government."

Hasan was clearly disappointed but also seemed to respect my direct and concise answer. "Now, if there is anything we can help you with personally, please ask." I could see there was a lot more he wanted to discuss with us. Jeannana was very patient, working hard to interpret conversations between Hasan, Paul and I.

"Jackie, maybe you sell me Bluebell?" Hasan enquired.

"Bluebell! Our lady! Why do you need her?"

"I need to go Italy to buy food and shoes for army."

The thought of leaving Bluebell in Bosnia would feel like leaving my legs behind. The mere suggestion had thrown me completely off balance. "Hasan, if you need a lorry, send the money to England and we will buy you your own vehicle and bring it over for you quite legally."

I could see the right hand drive and the British plates would give Hasan a moment's credibility at the checkpoints and those could just be the vital moments.

"OK I think about it!" Hasan was saying, but I could see there was still more.

"Jackie you help me get to Split. I get papers from policc to travel. You go with me?"

"Now what's going on?" All my red alarm lights were flashing at once. Jeannana interrupted. "It's OK, Jackie, I will be going with Hasan to help him. We need to take a large van to carry food etc. and we will both be able to get special papers."

I searched Emin's face. He was quiet, but a solid family man. I respected and trusted him. The question flashed through my mind, "Lord, what could we be getting into?"

"Hasan I want to help you, but I do not want to help you with anything illegal." There were laughs and smirks round the room. Now I felt I should feel guilty for even having such a thought. Still I stood my ground.

"Tell me Hasan. What exactly do you want of us?"

"I need to get out of Bosnia. Me no go for six months. My people need food. They need me to go."

"I see that," I found myself saying. "Then I will come in van with you and Jeannana go in Bluebell with others, but please let's get one thing clear. I will not commit Paul or Jenny to take such a risk. I am only willing to make a personal commitment here, and that's only if Paul is in agreement."

I was acutely aware of Hasan's devastating charm and his expert way of getting his own way and, whilst I may have wanted to help him, I could see no reason for the others to be involved in extra dangers on their way out of Bosnia.

"Hasan what papers will you get?"

"I get good papers. I know many people. Nema Problema! Nema Problema!"

Everything is "No problem" in Bosnia. It's contagious. I smiled realising the reality behind his easy use of the expression.

"I'll tell you what we will do," I said, getting out the map. "Paul, Jenny and Jeannana will travel this way," pointing out the route they had already come, which I knew to be as safe as possible in the circumstances. "I will travel with you with my British passport…this way!" Pointing to the other side of Bosnia through the Mostar route where the UN wagon had been blown up. "Then we will meet here," pointing to the map. "But you need to know, the only way through is actually by the grace of God and prayer."

"Jackie, Nema Problema!" he was saying again. "Muslim man watch our way."

"Yes," I smiled, "but what about your enemies? Who tells them to let us through?" Trying to lighten the conversation.

Emin cut through my observations. "Jackie" he smiled. "You did right to make the decision not to help the army directly." He was being his usual sweet, supportive self.

"The truth is Emin, I had no idea I was not really conscious of our own mandate until I was pressed to clarify it in my own heart, but now I am satisfied having done so."

After lunch with the family, I made my way back to the school alone. The whole atmosphere was by now much more relaxed. The people knew Bluebell was completely empty. I knew if they bothered to talk with me now it was because they wanted to share and not for what they could get. This was my recreation time, and I was growing to love this part of the ministry.

Narjia had made some fish shaped pastry for our lunch. I had asked if she minded if I saved mine as I had a much better use for them. So after lunch with fish in hand, I happily made my way back to the school. I knew my time with the families would be blessed time. They were always so welcoming.

"Hi, Jackie!" "Jackie! Jackie!" The children would call out, some rushing up to hold my hand, others trying to get me to go into their room first.

Whenever I entered a room I did so in bare feet. This was their ground, sacred ground. These few feet per person represented everything they owned in the world. Each little area by each bunk bed was unique. There were some odd bits of curtain hanging up, suspended by string. A few metal pots and pans peeped out from under the beds. I notice a hand-drawn picture on the bottom of one bed. This picture had been brought from children in a school in England. But most of my pleasure came from the joy on the faces. Most were old and ingrained with hardship, but all lit up with smiles as I came to share some precious time with them.

In one room I was invited to sit on the only wooden chair. One lady rushed up with a hand-made pillow to put behind my back. She smiled, caught my hands in hers, put her head down and kissed them gently. The people all moved in closer, finding a little space on the floor or on the edge of a bed on which to sit. They gazed expectantly at me, wondering what might come out of the paper bag I was holding.

Proudly I produced the fish. I showed them it was to eat, but I had brought it to share with them. Now they were puzzled how could I make one small fish go round so many people?

"Where is Ricki? The tall boy!" I needed some help to communicate. Within a few minutes the young man appeared and offered his services again as interpreter.

"Ricki, please tell them I am very happy to be sharing this day with them. I would like to tell them a story about a small boy." They smiled in approval. I went on. "One day there was a big crowd gathered around Jesus as he taught the multitudes. The people had travelled many miles and had no food. Thankfully, in the crowd was one small boy. He had five loaves and three fishes, just like this one." I held up my pastry fish. "Of course, there was not enough to feed everybody, but Jesus prayed and then instructed his disciples to feed the people from the gift offered. All were fed, and, not only that, but there were many baskets full of food left over.
Do you remember when we first came here? We only had two bars of chocolate to share with you? Now, look what God has done!" Now triumphantly! "Seventeen tables full of food for you. Can you see how much He loves you? Can you see how much the people in England love you." Now, getting quite excited. "Do you know people have come to our door with bags of food. They ask us to bring this food to Bosnia with their love." Lowering my tones, "Will you please now see Paul and I are only the donkeys, carrying the gifts to you?" They smiled and I was happy. They had understood the point.

"Now Ricki, please tell them today is, what's called, Good Friday."

"What is this Good Friday, Jackie?" Ricki was asking.

"Good Friday was the day they crucified Jesus on the Cross. You are a Muslim. We worship the same God, Our Father in Heaven, but Jesus is his son, my Saviour. He died for all of us."

The message was relayed. “Please tell them I know I am a sinner. I have resented many things, hurt many people. Do you know Jesus Christ hung on the Cross for my sins, and what’s more He hung there for you… and the sins of the people who are still hurting your people?” Ricki wasted no time interpreting.

“Ricki, please tell them, Our Father God, only asks that we accept His Son Jesus Christ. Accept that He died for our sins. He died as payment for our sins.” Ricki spoke, the room was still. “He wants to forgive our sins and what’s more He wants us to forgive the sins of all those who have hurt us.”

“Jackie, we do forgive. We have no problem forgiving… if only,” he paused: “If only, they would stop killing us.”

I understood his point and looking back, although I did not realise it at the time, I now believe it was at that moment, God planted the seed of compassion in my heart for this young man. I believe to this day, at that moment this young man spoke his heart before God and God heard it and responded. He spoke his heart like a child with little religious teaching.

I continued more gently. “Ricki, What is the bottom line difference between Islam, Catholicism, and Orthodoxy as opposed to Christianity? It's the Holy Spirit that moves through us, that enlightens us to realise, that you can only die…not kill…for your faith."

"But Jackie how can you do that…how can you come here in the first place?"

"Well, you see Ricki, as I figure it…anybody can take my flesh life in a moment… but nobody can touch my Soul or my Spirit. I believe… as crazy as it may sound… it is better to be the one to be killed, than the one to do the killing. We don’t have to worry about this world, it’s the next we need to be concerned about. The Word of

God says: 'For God so loved the world, that He gave His the only begotten Son that who ever believes in Him shall not perish but have everlasting life'."

"So, are you saying Jackie that only Christians can have eternal life?"

"No, what I am saying is, what Jesus taught was everybody regardless of birth has to be born again. I am against the concept, which says that if you are born in England that automatically makes you a Christian or if you are born in Bosnia that you are automatically a Muslim. The first time we are born of the flesh from our mothers' wombs and then we need to be born of the spirit of God. Jesus taught that unless we are born again we cannot enter the Kingdom of God."

Silence fell across the room as the young man translated the message. The women nodded their heads in approval. They agreed. "Please, now let us pray together." They all stood up and we joined hands. My voice and heart went up to Heaven as I claimed these precious souls in Jesus' name. They in turn prayed their prayers to their God. We had the same Father. Now the Holy Spirit was moving. I simply became the bridge to His Son Jesus Christ.

The energy in the room was powerful. Words were not needed. We touched hands, smiled and nodded at each other. It mattered not that we did not speak the same language. We shared the same Father and for that moment, if only for that moment, we were one in Christ.

I made my way back towards the flats through the crowds of well wishers and dragged my weary body back up the long, dark flights of stairs. The higher I climbed the more creepy the darkness became. I hated the dark! I hated the gloom! And what's more I hated what these people were suffering!

Chapter 12

AN OASIS

It's hard for us in England to appreciate what it must be like: to be trapped in a small country surrounded by one's enemy; when you can't simply go and fetch food in to feed your family; when families are separated and one is unable to reach them. The agony and frustration is hard to imagine, and I certainly did not quite appreciate what it must have felt like for Hasan on this occasion.

He was a man used to getting things done and here he had to take the slenderest of chances to try and get out of his country, down roads probably used by him as a young man for courting. Most of the civilian population must be totally confused as to why they are being persecuted.

As Jeannana said. "What do they want us to do? Live on the moon?" So here was Hasan at this time, using his influence to get papers to travel through Bosnia and Croatia but with very little certainty, as a Muslim, he would not be slaughtered along the way.

Having visited "our families" in the school, and given our promise by the grace of God to return to the Hospital Director, we were now ready to leave.

Hasan drove a big, ugly, old van with me as passenger. Paul, Jenny and Jeannana followed in Bluebell since they had elected to travel the same route, under firm instructions, that if any of us were held up in any way, the others were to go on.

The whole atmosphere was tense, but I was heartened when the officials at the Muslim checkpoints seemed to have very genial conversations with Hasan. He was clearly a very popular person and used his personality to the full.

The whole journey ran remarkably smoothly. Hasan pointed out various landmarks along the way, including the convent where forty-two nuns had been murdered. The convent still showed the bullet holes and burnt remains of that dreadful night when the whole area was razed to the ground. It's hard to imagine what such a night would be like. Here was a whole nation where every person is scarred not only physically, but also with internal wounds.

The journey back across the mountains and through repeated scenes of devastation was no easier. We now had the added pressure of fighting our tiredness. I imagined Paul's natural cheerful nature in the vehicle behind would be a blessing, as we all continued to wrestle with the constant murmuring of our fears.

As we relentlessly ground our way down the mountain tracks, Hasan managed to work the vehicle dangerously close to the edge where there were many exposed, empty, crushed lorries, their occupants' fates probably sealed in an early grave.

Finally we approached the final Croatian border with understandable apprehension; Hasan was showing signs of mounting tension. He had increased his speed by fifty per cent and was chain smoking as his eyes darted continually from left to right. I checked in the wing mirror. Although Bluebell was still in sight, I was happy the old lady was still quite a safe distance away separated enough not to be associated with us.

Duly halting as the guards stood in front of the barrier, Hasan without a word handed over my passport. “Not enough!” they gesticulated, “Your papers!” With another deep puff on his cigarette, he complied and handed over the newly acquired “so called” pass. The guard looked him in the eye; every muscle in me went solid. Then as smoothly as possible he simply handed the papers back. We were through!

I didn’t know how Hasan contained himself but, as soon as we were out of sight of the border guards, he managed to fling his arms around me despite continuing to drive forward! He shouted almost at the top of his voice, “You Jackie! Big God!” How we rejoiced! Freedom never tasted so sweet!

We all shared in his elation by celebrating in a local coastline restaurant where Hasan ordered the best fish on the menu. To say we shared his joy is not quite accurate. Jeannana shared his joy. I however, squirmed in my chair as Jeannana held an octopus eye in her fingers, ready to let it slide down her long throat. “Don’t do it!” I screamed, completely letting myself go, I was ready to bale out of the window into the water, had I been sure I would have landed in the sea with the grace of Esther Williams, the movie swimming star. “If you eat that thing I will never let you use my lipstick again!” I threatened.

After a well-deserved break I joined Paul and Jenny in Bluebell. Hasan and Jeannana went their separate ways to attend to their own business.

After hours of concentrated driving we were relieved to be off the mountains, and travelling all together again. Paul began to enjoy the freedom of tarmac on Bluebell’s fine steering, and managed to underestimate his own tiredness on a tight bend. He simply missed a halt sign and pulled out, straight in front of a giant double tanker coming down hill at full speed towards us. Jenny and I screamed and hung on to each other. Paul, as usual, kept cool and accelerated harder, thus avoiding a horrible end for us all. The Grace of God had given him perfect timing.

"That was good wasn't it?" Paul proudly exclaimed. That did it! My frail nerves just snapped. "What are you doing Paul?" I protested. "Just cool it. Let's not repeat that exercise we may not be so lucky next time. You are driving like a maniac. I know you are tired. I know you just want to get this whole thing over with, but we are not going to get there if you continue in this way." I went on and on.

My words met hostile glances. His self-defence mechanism was in place nothing I was going to say would help. The dividing line was drawn. Things between us proceeded down the spiral fast and soon we were at each other's throats. The more my words were met with denials, the more I went for the jugular. I was still trying to give Paul a warning about his own tiredness, actions and reactions, but nothing I could say would, by this time, be taken on board.

"The fireworks in our cab are brighter than the Houses of Parliament on a Prime Ministers Question Time, or on a certain November day!" Paul quipped in his dry humorous way as a smoke screen rather than owning his own tiredness.

Poor Jenny must have thought she was right in the middle of World War Three! But bless her, unbeknown to me, Jenny had begun to trust my judgement, and measure it against her own instinct for survival. For the first time I sensed Jenny was in agreement with what I was trying, unsuccessfully, to communicate to Paul.

For Paul, that only made it ten times worse. He flipped completely and now driven by his own anger, drove faster and faster. I hung on in there, desperately thinking what to do, and at the same time trying to bite my tongue. There was nothing else for it. "Stop this vehicle!" I ordered. "We can't go on like this, we must stop!"

The abrupt silence was overbearing. One could cut the atmosphere with a knife. "Paul, you don't have the right to kill us, so please stop this lorry. We must stop and pray, we're all guilty, all at fault."

It was true to say nerves were shattered and bodies exhausted, so I asked Paul if he fancied a cup of tea as I reached for the flask of lukewarm water. I persisted more gently now. "Paul, why don't you pull over and drink this? The few minutes stop will do you good." For whatever reason, to this day I don't know why Paul had the grace to stop Bluebell. But stopping at that moment was to change the whole course of our lives. Silently, and without resentment, Paul pulled Bluebell over on to some ground just outside a small, local shop which happened to have a large forecourt. We had a short time of prayer, during which we asked our Heavenly Father to come into our hearts and forgive us, cleanse us, and fill us with His Spirit. Now our Heavenly Father could take over and really start to move in a miraculous way.

We sat quietly watching the world go by for a few moments, and refreshing ourselves on the cool liquid, which only half resembled the tea our taste buds knew. We watched with interest each person emerging from the shop, particularly a big, burly man with dark hair who was unshaven.

Despite his broad smile, his face portrayed the hardships and concern experienced by each individual family man at this time. By his side walked a very clear skinned, very gentle in demeanour, young girl. She seemed about fifteen years old and appeared to be his daughter. First he looked at Bluebell's registration plates then up to the cab. On seeing himself being looked up and down, he approached with a big, friendly smile.

That smile made a connection and was the catalyst for a whole new chain of events. It wasn't long before he was telling us the girl was, in fact his daughter, and he had three other children. He went on to explain it was most difficult to try and keep body and soul together during these times, as everything was in short supply.

It was difficult to listen to him attentively, because of his broken English, and excitable manner, but he communicated his anger about the cost of his purchase. The young girl was a lot easier to understand. She spoke much better English and tried to interpret for her father.

"My father says would you like to join us for tea at our home? It's not far away. We live up in that direction."
She pointed way up into the hills and mountains, beyond the rear of the shop. Maybe it was the sound of the word 'tea' or maybe because we had no more resistance in us, or maybe the purity of this young girl's face gained our trust, but we were ready to follow.

Before we could think it through, the father was approaching us with gifts he had fetched from his car, bags of lavender and a little bottle of pure lavender oil. He indicated to us that we should tie the bags on the light switch on Bluebell's dashboard.

"It is good," he was saying, gesticulating in a broad manner reflecting the fullness of his character. My base instinct and thought of English tea took over.

"Thank you, that would be most welcome. Shall we follow you?" I queried.

Paul laughed, "Do you know Jackie, listening to you trying to communicate with that man," he paused, "well you're to languages what Churchill was to Woodbines!" I picked up an imaginary flower. Now pulling off the petals, "He loves me, he loves me not, he loves me, he loves me not."

It wasn't long before we were following up a very steep hill, crawling at 6 mph round three hairpin bends on our way out into what seemed like Outer Mongolia! After about ten minutes climbing at Bluebell's slow pace, the road flattened out and revealed, on our left, about six gun turrets, all with heavy guns in place, and all pointing the same way over the mountains. "You know, if we hadn't just prayed and got right before God, I would say to follow a strange man all this way into this area, would be a ridiculous thing to do. I have to believe God is leading us here, because He has a real purpose for our coming." The other two agreed as we each smiled at our own child-like faith or utter stupidity!

At last we followed our guide, Dravco, round a right hand turn, opposite a cemetery, on to a dirt track and minutes later our host was pulling in between large boulders and two small trees which formed the gateway to his unique home.

It is unlikely that any home in the world is like this one. Firstly, it was almost totally built by this man's own hands and, whilst it did not have too much in common with suburbia, it had an unmistakable charm of its own. The children came running and lined up in order as Dravco proudly presented them one by one. They were all delightful, the sort of children who have lived all their lives in continuous love and hardship. They would be perfect actors for a T.V. series such as 'The Waltons.'

Then, much to our delight he presented his wife. This lady approached with great self-confidence and outstretched arms. I felt I could just fall into them and she would protect me forever. Maria, the wife, was Dutch. She could never be described as pretty but had a fascinating aura of sensuality. Her greying hair was very cleverly used to disguise one false eye. She was slim and attractive in a most unusual way.

It took only a few minutes conversation for me to know we were of the same ilk. She was my sort of woman. I could not believe this experience we were having. "One minute Paul and I are at each other's throats, then Lord, you bring us here!"

The children were quick to show Jenny, Bella the family dog and her three puppies, whilst Paul went out to find a box of sweets for them.

This home fascinated me. The woodwork, considering Dravco built it, was truly wonderful. There was a large fireplace surrounded by many shelves with books on everything from psychology, family health to homeopathy. On the far wall were two giant charts of the human body, exposing all the key organs. These I found intriguing, and went over to look at them, but I was led to the long, oak, family table that seated about eight people without crowding.

Soon jugs of tea and coffee were boiling on the wood burning stove in the chaotic, open plan kitchen. The design was not to my own ordered taste, but I loved the whole feel of the functional family home these interesting people had created.

It wasn't long before Dravco had asked if Paul, Jenny and I would like to stay the night and, although it was still only about 5 p.m., we willingly accepted the invitation.

We wanted to know more about this fascinating family who, we were by this time sure, God had allowed us to meet for His purpose. Before long every subject from the politics and hardships of the war to religion had been discussed. We were, of course, only getting the measure of each other, and whilst Dravco and I were soon to find we weren't always in agreement, Maria and I found we had much in common.

Nevertheless, Dravco and Maria were both fascinated by what we were doing. Dravco used every small incident we described as an excuse to cross himself in front of his imaginary altar! In a matter of two hours his moods had frequently swung fervently from one extreme to another. In my heart I registered a warning signal but, at the same time, had no trouble in immediately loving this extraordinary, eccentric character.

The evening passed without incident which was quite surprising as Dravco's gesticulations became more and more exaggerated with every glass of wine he drank. He was a man who clearly liked to be the king ruling his own family in a firm, explosive yet, I could see, loving way.

Whatever this man was bringing up in me, I was sure about two things. Firstly, he was a giant with a character that encompassed both the Lion and the Lamb. Secondly, behind every man there is a woman, and in Maria's case she had a full life's work offering her own gifts wisely and, at the same time keeping her place firmly behind him in support. I loved her for it. Before leaving for the ferry and after a most precious time of relaxation with the couple, they gave us a huge, hand made wooden rosary, a most beautiful gift.

The next chess piece came into our possession as we were on the ferry from Split travelling north to Rijeka the following day. Soon after we boarded, Paul, whilst up on deck, began to talk to some Irish aid workers, who said they were supported by some nuns back home in Ireland.

I thought it would be rather nice to acknowledge them by giving them the rather large wooden cross and oak beads which Maria and Dravco had given us. I felt such a gift should go into a convent, a worthy place for this work of art.

After explaining the personal value of the gift, I asked if they would like to take it back to the nuns as an acknowledgement from the people of Croatia.

The gift was graciously received and nothing more was thought about it until one of the same aid workers approached the group at the dining table much later. "We have a single mattress in the back of our van which we wondered, would you like it?" I was a little stunned by the question. "What a strange gift," I thought, "Well, Lord, if you think we need a single mattress, then we must need a single matteress. OK throw it on board!" Grateful, but without any understanding as to why it was given, the single mattress was loaded into the back of Bluebell. So pleased were we for a few hours of relative safety, we all proceeded to enjoy the deep red sunset over the harbour and celebrated by singing choruses seated in a quiet corner of the upper deck.

Before addressing any sleeping arrangements, Jenny took the initiative and simply curled up in her arctic weight sleeping bag in a small space under some stairs. We knew she could sleep on a clothesline but never the less in view of her sixty-nine years she often put us to shame in that respect.

Thankfully, Paul and I had become quite friendly with most of the crew and as there was a shortage of cabins, one of them asked if we would like to use his bunk for the night whist he was on duty. We felt like cats that had got the cream and, we even had completely clean sheets. So on waking early next morning, I was pleased to use the time to write our kind sailor friend a note of encouragement.

After disembarkation it took just another few hours to drive from the port back to Zagreb in Croatia where we were greeted with huge, warm hugs from Ljubica. Mascara now on, she looked a new woman and the flat was spick and span. She had a new, mischievous air about her, further enhancing her fun personality. I was seeing a new side to her and one I could fully appreciate. She seemed the type of woman few men would have the strength to resist, clearly in this mood she would get her way in most situations.

Hasan was expected in a few minutes, having completed his business and travelling by a different route for the last part of the journey. With his charismatic personality, it seemed a very full house when he arrived, yet at no time did I see his mantle slip. He seemed to remain distant, except where Haris was concerned. There was much discussion about Haris' future and a lot of talk as to whether, for his own safety he could go back to England with us. Ljubica clearly did not want to go, but there was nothing she wouldn't do for her sons.

I had perceived Haris's way of manipulating his mother into getting his needs met. As a young man Haris needed the lines of discipline to be made quite clear, any blurring of the lines left him insecure. Clearly Hasan had always been the authority and Haris respected and loved him. I also knew Haris would have done anything to protect his mother but, as he was not yet a man, there could still be playful friction between them. I committed in my heart to staying close to both of them simply trusting to be there when needed.

Deep in thought I became aware of strange music coming from the lounge. Popping my head round the door to enquire what it was, I saw Paul viewing the video made about our last trip to the Hospital. (The film the local T.V. crew in Zenica had given us). Suddenly horrific scenes appeared on the screen. The crew had spliced, in the centre of the film, pictures of some of the atrocities that had happened very recently in Central Bosnia.

I looked at the screen, hardly able to believe my eyes. Trays of men's genitals were being held up for all to see. They had been ripped off young men whilst others had been tortured in the equally horrendous ways. A pregnant woman had her womb cut open, so 'they' could bet on the sex of the unborn baby.

Feeling physically sick and horrified I left the room unable to control my emotions. "What are you doing walking away Jacqueline?" I berated myself. "This is reality. This is really happening. This is what is happening in Bosnia now, today! This is what it is all about." My heart was a mixture of anger and hurt, "Lord what is going on? Why did they give us this film? What is it you want us to see?" As usual there were more questions than answers.

Gingerly I returned to the room and forced myself to look again. Piles of broken bodies were shown on the screen, some, although their limbs were blown off, were still alive lying in pools of their own blood. These were the pictures the media in England were not showing. These people clearly wanted the true story to be told. "And, Lord, you wanted us to see the reality, but Lord, please show me what you would have us do to serve you and these people?"

I met Hasan in the hallway. “Jackie, you take Haris and Ljubica with you, your home?”

“That’s fine but will they come?” I asked. “And will our government allow it?” After a few phone calls to the Embassy to check, it appeared as they both had Croatian passports, they could go to England as guests.

We had yet to return to the hospital back in Central Bosnia, so it was agreed Ljubica and Haris would fly to England from Zagreb airport with a covering letter of guarantee, which I wrote and signed. Hasan would pay for Ljubica and I offered on behalf of us all, to pay for Haris. There had been a lot of soul searching by the family to decide what was the best thing for Haris, because of what seemed like his intent to get killed by going off and fighting for his country in this terrible war.

As I had just seen on the video what dreadful things they were doing to each other I had no doubt if Haris and Ljubica would go to our home in England it would probably save Haris finishing up in the army and eventually being killed. The decision was made! Tomorrow they would leave with just one suitcase.

“Isn’t it amazing,” I thought, shaking my head in despair. Dwight L Moody wrote: ‘A great many people are trying to make peace, but that has already been done. God has not left it for us to do: all we have to do is enter into it.’ So why don’t we?

With two good nights sleep behind us, we set off to find the warehouse in Zagreb to load the life saving food and drugs onto Bluebells back for the long arduous journey back to the hospital. The warehouse was full up to the ceiling with food and drugs, yet people were dying for lack of the life saving items getting through. After much discussion with the lady doctor in charge and wrangling with the customs officials, Bluebell was loaded for her most vital effort yet. Fully loaded, in the political climate, the journey if all goes well, could take anything up to a week.

We soon discovered the old lady was having some difficulty holding the road as the uneven distribution of weight in her load was causing her to be light on the steering. Paul was doing his best but, as the hours and miles began to mount, I realised the load would have to be re-packed if we were going to make it over those dreaded mountains again.

We didn't make the first UN base until about 2 p.m. the following day and to be safe we needed a top up of fuel as well. Having obtained special permission from the Commander we pulled over to the giant petrol tanker to refuel. Reluctantly, Paul agreed to stop and look at the weight distribution problem at the same time.

"Come on let's unload and reload Bluebell," was my hearty suggestion but, given the temperature was well into the eighties, the words from my mouth were understandably not received too enthusiastically by Paul. I felt that, given the difficulty of the fighting situation ahead, we should do all in our power to eliminate every unforeseen possibility and danger. This included looking at Bluebell's springs.

It turned out one of the rubber pads on her springs had completely worn away. This explained why she had been groaning under the excessive weight! Having tried, and failed, to get help from the 'top brass,' we did what we should have done in the first place. 'If you want any real help from the UN start at the bottom and work up,' was one of Paul's perceptions and usually he was right.

One young British soldier came to our assistance. His name was unknown as he laboured under Bluebell in the excessive heat. He may never realise the gift he gave that day, because many long arduous hours later, after we had battled again with the mountains and the heat, we were stopped at a checkpoint in a notorious bandit area.

I climbed stiffly out of the cab grateful to stretch my legs, but soon realised these checkpoint guards were high on drink and drugs. They looked at the paperwork and started to mime, "Hypodermic needle! Drugs to go in the arm." They were beckoning me to follow them into their wooden guardhouse.

Immediately, I became conscious of my vulnerability. I started to wave my arms making an exaggerated show of anger at their behaviour, whilst quickly making my way back to Paul in Bluebell. The leader followed.

"You no go through. You." pointing at me, "You! Come with me!"

"No way," I was gesticulating. Paul on seeing the danger was ready to move off quickly, and at that very moment three UN vehicles came to the other side of the metal barrier. The barrier was immediately raised for them without question. Quickly scrambling into the cab and ignoring the orders of the drunken guard, I shouted, "Paul, now! Let's go through, now!" Half way through we came alongside the first vehicle.

"OK ahead? Any trouble?" Paul was asking.

"No, It's a nice day, go and enjoy the sunshine!" the driver encouraged in a very casual manner. As the barrier lifted we moved rapidly through making the best of the opportunity afforded us, and sending a quick prayer of thanks 'upstairs.'

Thinking we were now over the last hurdle, we began to relax. I glanced casually into the wing mirror and was shocked to see two cars coming up swiftly behind us. Thankfully we were going downhill! Thankfully we were on tarmac! Thankfully that lone soldier had replaced Bluebell's rubber bush! Thankfully Paul had agreed to re-distribute the load.

I could by this time see four camouflaged, uniformed men in the first car, which had no registration plates. They had rifles. The second car was following close behind. "Paul, whatever you do, don't stop!" No sooner had the words left my mouth than the first car, blowing its horn, and flashing its lights, pulled past us on the narrow road, and stopped right in front of us. Its doors flew open. Paul somehow held onto the old girl's power steering and miraculously managed to just miss the bandit's car door as he skilfully wove around the hazard and avoided a potentially hideous situation. Again I looked in the wing mirror. The first car was backing up, but the second one was still coming.

Paul drove Bluebell for all he was worth. "Are they still coming?" He shouted desperately still trying to control the runaway mare. "Thank God we are going downhill. Thank God we are on tarmac."

Bluebell was, for eleven years old, absolutely superb. Nothing could touch her. The weight on board was working to our advantage. The old dear couldn't have stopped even if we had wanted her to.

The hunters backed off as Bluebell approached a town, which was under control of the pursuers' enemies. We, the hunted, eventually reached relative safety, most grateful to our dear old friend, and the unknown young soldier who replaced the rubber bush.

We arrived at the next UN base quite shaken up, but in our hearts we saw it as a warning to take, if possible more precautions in future.

The army provided a Warrior Escort, which escorted us through the dreaded pass where the Italians had been murdered. Now this was more than welcome but, to our dismay, we were escorted only a short distance and, for the first time, I was beginning to wish we could afford bullet-proof vests. We realised they were no protection against the AK47, a weapon that most of the armies used, but they would surely give a sense of protection.

On the next stretch we were all very subdued. I realised what a difference adrenaline pumping through the body makes towards survival. During a crisis normal functions like hunger and the need for the loo just don't exist. This is an advantage, after all this had been no time to stop and find a bush!

It was clear why the sixteen tonners, the professional UN aid lorries drove like 'bats out of hell,' but for us in Bluebell with such a low undercarriage, the most we could safely do was about 25 m.p.h. We were grateful to finish the next two-hour stretch unscathed. Even the recently burnt out buildings in Vitez seemed comforting habitation after the bleakness of the journey.

Chapter 13

IT WAS ... A MOMENT IN TIME

The final run into Zenica brought the usual mixture of excited emotions, disbelief that we were actually going to make it and hurt as we viewed the local population pulling old carts of wood miles along the dual carriageway. In addition there was inner excitement at the prospect of seeing the Hospital Director's face of welcome recognition, for the love and help we wanted to give to all his people. That for me was the actual purpose. Yes, we all had been willing to go back over these monster mountains just to see that smile.

This trip was no exception. The Director was so amazed, and grateful to see the tons of brown boxes being unloaded from Bluebell, that tears were streaming from his tired eyes. He, most of all, knew how much pain and discomfort this cargo would save. Looking up with his smiling tear-stained face, he held out both hands.

"Please Jackie, please tell everybody, please tell everybody in England. Thanks."

We each realise we are privileged to be the faces called, on behalf of everybody at home in England, without whom nothing could have been accomplished. To this very day we thank God for everybody who has touched this work and praise His name for every gift that has been given in His name.

The temperature outside must have been in the high eighties but for Paul, lifting heavy boxes inside Bluebell's womb and after such a gruelling week's drive, it was beyond measure. Every muscle rippled as the sweat ran down his entire body. Jenny's age was no barrier to her contribution to the unloading process. She was a tower of strength, even though shells were landing and exploding, killing, only a hundred meters away from us. Jenny continued working.

As the battle moved closer we all took shelter within the thick walls of the hospital corridor. The solid walls gave comfort, but what we most needed was a shower, something unheard of in this part of the world at this time. Water was measured by the cupful.

The gruelling task eventually finished, we all made our way to the Director's office, smelling of excessive perspiration mixed with an earthiness from the light brown dust. There was a small sink in the office to which we went in turn and sparingly splashed a few drops of water across our foreheads. I dared an extra thimble full under my arms.

Paul was desperately trying to get his hands clean with a small piece of soap, then struggling to wipe the dirt as best he could, down the tiny sink. Observing this the Director asked if we would like a shower; but in Bosnia at this time one did not like to say "yes," because one never knew whose share of anything one might be using. They will always give visitors their best.

Refreshed as well as possible, I sank down into an old well-worn settee wishing my body were not part of me. I ached from top to toe and my nerves felt like tight violin strings.

"That's it Lord I'm spent! I'm sorry, but if you want anything else doing, you will have to ask someone else! We are just finished. Please can we now go home to Old

Blighty?"

I should have known better than to say such a thing to my Heavenly Father. What a dreadful thing I had just done in the light of His Holiness.

After saying our emotional farewells we made our way back to the school opposite the flats to park Bluebell for her well earned rest. She seemed to purr as we reached the waiting crowd. Word soon spread around, and our faithful extended family wasted no time congregating round the back of the old girl.

Although the vehicle was now empty of aid, apart from a few packets of biscuits I had held back for the children, within seconds about fifty people had gathered mostly women with the children.

In the crowd to my left, I could feel the presence of Ricki by my side. Ricki's tall six foot four inch frame towered above me. This tall seventeen-year-old Muslim had helped us by acting as our interpreter. Paul, Jenny and I laughed and joked for a while with the crowd to relieve our tension.

Then amongst all the chattering that was going on, my attention was caught by a lady's face, deep in the expectant crowd. Looking at Ricki intently with all her body she seemed to be saying, "Go on! Go on! Ask her!"

For a moment, not sure what was happening, and not speaking a word of the language, I wondered if I was reading her body language correctly. The lady continued urging Ricki,

"Go on! Go on! Ask her!" she seemed to say. With a gift of knowledge I asked.

"Ricki, is that your mother?" I did not give him time to answer. "Is she asking you…to ask us… to take you back to England?"

Ricki bowed his head; a little ashamed anyone would ask such a thing. For he knew only too well the dangers for a Muslim refugee with no papers or passport.

"Ricki do you realise we only have a fifty - fifty chance of making it back to England? If you are with us we'll have something like ... about a four percent chance of getting out alive." Now, remembering the horror of the video, I added. "If they catch you... they won't waste bullets on you!"

He stood tall. His gentle countenance seemed to wave in the gentle breeze and now looked down into my eyes. "Jackie, what difference does it make? It makes no difference. I have no life."

Confused, I desperately panned the sea of anxious faces, searching to find direction as the battle raged within me. My heart, urgently wanting to help, full of compassion was telling me one thing, my mind telling me another. I could already see the headlines in the newspapers back in England. 'Christians Smuggle!'

My eyes were drawn like a magnet to the mother's face in the crowd; my gaze settled on a small, round, tear-stained face, entreating, and full of agony and desperation. Ricki's mother pleaded, without words, with all her being. A picture of my son, Richard, flashed into my mind.

Moments passed. Moments for both mothers. Moments of desperate conflict and inner struggle. By taking Ricki we could be saving his life, or hastening his death. For that moment I would have welcomed a committee to share the responsibility but was glad there wasn't one to prolong the agony.

Again my eyes were drawn, as if irresistibly compelled to the face in the crowd. Finding her gentle presence, our eyes locked, connected, pre-destined. Our mothers' hearts met. Our souls were at one. It was ... a moment in time!

Pushing my way through the crowd I reached out and firmly held the lady by her shoulders. Lowering my voice and fighting, for the mother's sake, to keep back my own tears, I gently, yet at the same time, bracing myself, said, "We will love him as our own." It was a moment of destiny for both us women, a moment of complete surrender.

Quietly I turned to Paul who was in the back of Bluebell starting to unload our personal belongings. My eyes fell on the mattress we had been given by the Irish men on the ferry.

"Paul, ... bring that mattress, ... bring your wire cutters," and, looking him straight in the eyes,

"and PLEASE! PLEASE! Don't ask me any questions why!" This is no time to have a debate!

Turning to Ricki I whispered, "Follow us into the flats. Please don't say goodbye to your mother now." As naturally as possible we made our way to the flat to figure out how to solve the next problem.

Once safely inside, we set about the difficult task of hollowing out the metal springs to make a space within the mattress. First I asked Ricki to lie diagonally across the mattress on the floor. The mattress was six feet long. Ricki is six feet four inches tall. We had to leave at least five inches of springs round the edge to help hold the shape.

For hours Paul, Jenny and Emin struggled tirelessly to cut out the thick, metal springs. They took it in turns until their swollen hands bled. The removal of the wadding caused a thick layer of dust to spread right through Nadja's home. There was no way she would complain!

The task completed, now was the moment of truth. Ricki crawled under the mattress. He wriggled and squirmed, struggling to fit his large body into the small dark space. At last he was in. "Oh! No! Look at that." There in the middle, undulating with the rhythm of Ricki's heavy breathing, was a big mound. We all looked at it despondently, hearts sinking. "There is nothing else for it," I exclaimed, delighted to have mentally solved the problem, "we will just have to throw all our dirty washing over him and trust the guards will not see the bump! Ricki lie diagonally under the mattress and let's test my theory." It was better.

The next problem was how were we going to get this young man, complete with mattress, into the back of Bluebell without anyone seeing us? "I've got it!" I cried, beaming once more. I again had a sense of victory much to everyone else's unease as to what I might come out with next! "We will have to meet Ricki on the motorway after curfew tonight." Now, imagining the darkness I added. "There is no petrol, no lights so there won't be or at least should not be, anyone about."

The tension and apprehension mounted at the mere thought of what I was suggesting. Sensing Paul's unease and disbelief, I challenged, "Well, what else can we do? Has anyone got any better ideas?" There was no response; everyone else only shuffled uneasily. "Then let's do it! Ricki, you go back to your family now and behave normally. Tell no one of the plan. Say goodbye to your mother, father and brother, but understand, you must do it in private. No one must know. We'll all be dead by this time tomorrow, if anyone finds out."

The thought of trying to take a young man three days journey through enemy territory, during the height of the war between the Muslims and the Croats at this dangerous time, sent shivers down my spine.

Refusing to even think about the consequences, we hurriedly ushered Ricki out of the flat to say his farewells to his family. “Paul, can you imagine, what it must feel like for him to have to say ‘Goodbye’ to his family under such dire circumstances.” Paul looked past me glassy eyed. I fancied his mind was somewhere else and, this time, not on food.

I was so disturbed for the pain which I knew his mother would be experiencing that I took the risk of sitting and writing her a note of comfort, trusting to be able to get someone to deliver it after we had left.

There was only about an hour to wait until curfew, and the whole family including Hasan who by this time had returned from Zagreb, gathered in the flat. Most of them were still shaking their heads in disbelief at the plan.

“What’s the problem with Hasan?” I asked Jeannana. She was reluctant to say. “It’s Ricki, isn’t it? He is a Muslim and Hasan thinks he should be fighting with the rest of his people doesn’t he?” I confronted. I knew I had hit the nail on the head.

“Yes, Jackie. He is not happy on two counts, you are right. He thinks Ricki should go to the front line, but also, he thinks you are taking too much of a risk for him. He doesn’t believe you can possibly get him through all those check points. You know they will search you.”

Hasan and I were very much the same breed, and I understood his sense of responsibility and concern. How could I answer him?

“Jeannana, ask Hasan what he would have me do if Ricki was HIS son?” Was I looking at double standards here? After all had not Hasan got both his boys out of the country very early on? He must see my point. In reply Hasan gave me one of those wry smiles, which says,

"Yes - you win! Check Mate!”

Now it was Emin's turn. He spoke about his fears for our safety. “Many people want to kill you Jackie, they think you are making money on the black market.”

“Are you serious Emin? I know you must be, or else you wouldn’t say such a wicked thing!” My body was hunched as if I had just received a direct body blow below the belt. Now I could feel my anger bubbling up. It was just as if someone had shaken the pop bottle.

“The trouble with these people, Emin, whoever they are, ‘they’ wouldn’t risk their lives or do anything without being paid, and they can’t understand it when someone else does. I imagine it doesn’t matter how many times we come, they will always judge us by themselves. Well we can live with that,” I added now thinking aloud.

“All that matters is, God knows. If only we could make them understand. If only they could see. If only we could communicate somehow to them, we come in the name of Jesus to just love them better. Why? Oh why! Can’t they see we come as an overflow of love for what Jesus has done for us on the cross?"

“But that’s the problem, Jackie. What’s changed since the beginning of time?” Paul was now in full flight. “The war in this country, like the wars within ourselves, they are judging us coming from their own guilt feelings. The problem is rebellion. Remember, it’s…because…of His forgiveness towards us that we can start loving our fellow man. Of course, they don’t understand us, Jackie you should know that!”

I knew Paul was right, but I responded in my usual determined manner. “Well we are available and are not going to respond in fear or by intimidation. We’re available, so however God wants to show His love for these people, and if He is still willing, He can do it through us.” Paul smiled and hugged me. He loved my childish determination, and anger against evil. He knew I hated sin, all that divides, all which causes us to hurt each other and, most of all, I hated it in myself. No wonder 'the enemy' would want to destroy us!

We now have to go and collect Ricki. "Jenny, I want you to stay here tonight. There is no point in you being involved in this risky task. After all, if we get caught out after curfew and they put us inside for the night, who will bring us a file to help us escape, if not you?" She understood, bless her. Making little fuss she just wished us well.

The concrete staircase was pitch black, even more creepy than usual. We used the bare minimum of light, making a cover to dim the torch. When we got outside a few refugees were still loitering around Bluebell, taking in the last of the cool night air before retiring into their stuffy overcrowded rooms in the school. As Paul put the key in the ignition Bluebell's engine suddenly sprang into life as if she had been woken from a deep sleep. She was very surprised to be going anywhere at this time of night. "Come on, old girl. It won't be long now. God willing, we will be going home tomorrow, then you can have a nice rest."

We drove through the deserted streets. The town was still. A stray dog sniffed the grass, no one had told him about the curfew! The throb of Bluebell's engine seemed to cut through the stillness.

It was only minutes to the motorway and, in the dark shadows; we could easily make out Ricki's tall frame silhouetted against the moonlight. Slowly we moved down the slip road and approached him. The air was motionless.

This whole area seemed deserted. It was as if the entire town had suddenly gone to bed. "Anyone out after curfew is probably up to no good," I thought. I remembered the words of my mother; "Anyone out after 10.30 is up to no good." Maybe not one hundred percent accurate, but I understood the essence of what she used to say. "My Lord, she would turn in her grave if she could see this now!"

Paul switched off the headlights and Bluebell purred to a gentle halt. Only the clicking of crickets interrupted the silence. Wasting no time Paul jumped out of the cab and briskly moved round to the lorry's back door. I heard the roller shutter go up. In fact the whole of Zenica probably heard the roller shutter door go up as the clatter reverberated around the empty streets.

"Come on Paul!" I was saying under my breath. Bluebell vibrated as Ricki jumped on board. down came the door again. "Let's get out of here Paul. Stop messing about!" Poor man he could not have done it any quicker if he had tried. Paul threw Bluebell's gears into position and promptly reversed her back up the slip road without using her lights.

"Oh! My Lord If anyone sees this now!" A car came towards us!

"Sausages! Let's see where they go. OK keep going!" By this time Bluebell was picking up speed.

"Which way?" Paul was asking. Suddenly everywhere looked unfamiliar. There was not a light anywhere and the moon must have gone behind some clouds. We did not recognise anywhere.

"Paul, I don't know. You know the way. You have been here often enough!" He made a left turn.

"No! This isn't it. Which way now?" he growled.

"Let's go left again here." I suggested. Dead-end. We were both getting frustrated and started snapping at each other angrily. The tension was clearly taking its toll. "Come on Paul, for goodness sake. It can't be far away. It only took minutes to get here. Where on earth are we?"

"This is it," Paul was saying, "I think this is the other end of the road. Yes, this is the right way." We had taken about twenty minutes for a two-minute journey. Poor Ricki must have thought we had changed our minds about leaving in the morning. Paul carefully manoeuvred Bluebell back into her sleeping place outside the school. Ricki was going to have to remain hidden in her all night. He would not even be able to go to the toilet in the bucket provided in case anyone should hear him.

The light clouds had cleared and the dark sky was as black as jet. Diamonds twinkled in a heavenly rest. After locking up the cab, Paul came over to where I waited for him on the pavement looking up at the bright, Bosnian moon. We started strolling back towards the flats. "Paul, I don't believe we are doing this. I don't believe it! I don't believe I'm a housewife from Barnsley and I am doing this! This is the sort of stuff films are made of. Paul what are we doing?"

He put his arm gently around my waist as we made our way across the deserted road, pulling me tenderly towards his body for protection.

"Jackie, you know I don't want to be famous, just effective for God. Anyway," he paused, speaking with a sense of triumph, "aren't you glad you're married to me? After all, no one else would be daft enough to do this with you!" I squeezed his arm, glad that whatever would happen; we were in it together.

In the early hours of the next morning, I rehearsed in my mind, the forthcoming scenes of our journey. Daylight brought us the opportunity to at least feel we were able to get on with the job at hand. The packing of our personal things was done efficiently and quickly, as the entire last minute organisation was something with which we had become very familiar. We had hundreds of letters to take back to England, vital links between the refugees and their families. People were always coming to us at the last moment and pressing yet another letter into our hands trusting it would bring the necessary help or comfort.

On this occasion we needed to slip out of the refugees' lives as smoothly and unobtrusively as possible. The plan was to go to the nearby UN distribution centre and tag on behind the big wagons gaining a sense of security from appearing to belong to the British Convoy. Having been told there was a convoy leaving at 8.30 a.m., we planned to arrive an hour before to give ourselves plenty of time to acquaint the other drivers with Bluebell's limitations.

By 7 a.m. having really savoured every mouthful of my final cuppa with Narjia and the girls, we all shuffled along a narrow passage to the front door, into the darkness and down the ten flights of concrete stairs. Working hard to keep our conversation normal in the torchlight we cautiously made our way into the early morning light and further into the unknown of a new day.

As we emerged out of the darkness into the bright, fresh, morning air, Hasan and Safet were waiting nervously, like expectant fathers.

Paul was bringing this now pregnant lady, Bluebell, right alongside us. It took only minutes to load our personal baggage into Bluebell, making sure we threw plenty of dirty washing over the mattress to disguise the tense, pulsating, body beneath.

Little contact with words or movement was made in case we alerted any prying eyes. Hasan paced the pavement, clearly disturbed about us leaving, maybe because he had first hand knowledge and experience of the atrocious treatment Ricki, or anyone who helped him, would suffer if we fell into enemy hands.

We didn't know it at the time, but this was the last time we would ever see Hasan. He was soon to meet a violent death about which there is still some mystery. It appears Hasan had been stopped at the checkpoint on the bridge only yards away from his flat in the early hours. Typically of him, he had decided to go and get the guards some cigarettes from his apartment nearby. That was the last gesture he was to make towards his fellow countryman.

Five days later he was found at the bottom of the lift shaft after falling or being pushed from the seventh floor. There were burn marks down his legs where he tried to save himself clinging onto the metal rope in a desperate last attempt to survive.

We are told his gun was found at his side, one bullet being fired but having not left the barrel. He had either tried to defend himself or tried to attract attention, being still alive when he had hit the bottom of the shaft sustaining bad injuries to his hip.

As his own hair was found under his fingernails it would appear the latter theory is most likely, but whatever is to be said of this man one can only testify by ones own experience of him.

For me, whilst I realise he was anything but a saint, I admired the man. He was a leader among men, a strong yet loving father and disciplinarian, the fruit of his life accounted towards 'His people.' Thousands of which do not realise they have received help as a direct response to his original request for his son to go and get help from the 'English people.' For me he was a proud patriarch of his people, but one like the rest of us mortals who suffer greatly through our own personal weaknesses.

Chapter 14

THE GREAT ESCAPE

Only yards from Hasan's concrete tomb Narjia and the girls were doing their best to be cheerful, but it was obvious this lovely lady was having great difficulty in controlling her emotions. Emin bowed and shook his head, almost unable to accept we might never get through again. After all, we had become their and the refugees' only link with the outside world. Losing connection with us would leave Emin and his family feeling more helpless and destitute than ever. We all experienced the bond of love between us ripping away at our hearts, as we prepared for what could be the final 'Goodbye.'

"How Ricki's family must be suffering at this time," I thought, "and Ricki, in the darkness of Bluebell's womb, will need to muster every bit of courage to stay put." Quickly I pushed those thoughts aside. "Come on Paul, let's get out of here."

Cracking my imaginary whip, John Wayne style, I shouted, "Wagons Ho! Let's roll." For a moment there were smiles, and feeble waves as Bluebell slowly but firmly pulled away for the start of the long difficult labour which would have to be endured if there was ever to be a birth into freedom.

The sun was already high in the sky as we arrived at the UN base. Pulling in behind some Land Rover type vehicles I was pleased to see the familiar, black smiling face of the convoy leader.

"How are you doing? What time are you leaving?" I asked.

"Probably about 11.30."

"11.30! What happened to 8.30?"

"There's been some trouble ahead, and we're hanging on a bit until we get confirmation we can proceed."

Already feeling the heat of the day and realising the temperature would be well into the eighties by mid-morning, I looked up at the clear blue sky shook my head and slowly walked back towards the cab.

" Paul, it looks like we're going to have something like a five-hour wait. Can you, in a minute, go to the back and very quietly communicate to Ricki? You'll have to go in and pull the roller shutter door down after you so no one sees the activity. Before you do Paul, let's just pull over to that spot over there, it's a bit quieter."

I pointed to an eight-foot high wire fence situated near the beginning of the convoy. "If we wait there, then when the convoy pulls out, we'll be well positioned to tag on without too much trouble."

Paul rolled the old lady into position. As soon as we had parked, Jenny immediately tried to jump out of the cab.

"No Jenny! Stay here with me and let Paul deal with it," I requested firmly.

"But I could be getting something out of my bags!" she protested.

"No Jenny! We're all experiencing a lot of tension and we need to calm ourselves a lot more or else they'll wonder what's up. I know you are worried about Ricki but I think you'll have difficulty in behaving naturally. I know you want to give him support, which I understand, but we are already very conspicuous." Jenny tried to protest again. I cut her short, spelling out the obvious.

"Do you realise Jenny we are the only blue lorry in the compound and the only one with two females on board. These men have nothing better to do than to glue their eyes on Bluebell and our sylph like figures"

Jenny stayed where she was, quite frustrated but willing to concede and whilst we waited, we amused ourselves by watching the soldiers throwing a few apples to the children gathered at the fence. They seemed to be cheerful, chirp little souls at least until the apples landed the other side of the fence. Then they became tyrants, the bigger ones exerting their strength over the younger ones to grab all the bounty for their own use.

The nearer the time moved to the 11.30 departure time the greater the anxiety of our trio. "Paul, when this convoy starts off, whatever you do keep well up to them! Don't leave any spaces because you know in this first section there are a lot of refugees waiting outside those gates and if we get separated at the beginning we'll never be able to catch up!"

One Warrior led the convoy, followed by nine sixteen-tonne giant lorries. Pregnant Bluebell brought up the rear. Paul wasted no time in leaving the compound. The sun was hot and we were grateful to feel some air blowing through the cab.

Paul and I were both on high alert. One wrong move could jeopardise our chances of getting through the checkpoint between the end of the motorway and the beginning of the mountains about six miles further on.

"Paul, it looks as if they'll drive straight through this checkpoint. Come on! Keep closer then we'll get through with them!" By this time we were well into our top speed for the conditions, about 45-mph and hugging the bends as best we could.

Jenny and I were hanging on to Bluebell's sides like warbles, flies under the skin of a horse. Bluebell was clearly enjoying herself. She was like a young mare released from her cramped stable. Paul rode uncompromisingly round every bend and Bluebell bounced over every bump. "Paul, we'll never make it at this rate! If she hits any of those boulders, we'll be finished!"

"Jackie! Shut up! I'm not losing them now!" Bluebell was now like a thoroughbred pulling at the bit. Paul used his gear stick as a whip to encourage her to go faster. She tried her best to work with him, but a cloud of dust from the vehicle in front, which blew up like a dense fog was blinding us. Paul and Bluebell were running with blinkers on.

"Back off Paul! You must back off! She can never keep this pace up for six hours!"

Actually I could have saved my breath because the further we climbed up to the mountains, the more the convoy pulled out of sight, until it became only a cloud of dust somewhere in the distance.

We were again trundling along on our own at a mere trot instead of a gallop. There was solid rock to our left, a sheer drop to a river on our right with a dense wood spreading into a green backdrop.

We were all beginning to feel a little more comfortable as the sun was now shining and the visibility had improved considerably, when all of a sudden, we heard a sharp hiss, quickly followed by a blue flash darting across the front of the windscreen.

"Sniper fire! Sniper fire!" I shouted. "Drive! Drive! Drive!" We heard the second bullet hit the top of Bluebell and, in a sudden silence as if in slow motion, the window on Paul's side shattered into a million pieces.

"Get down! Jackie." Paul was shouting at me. "Get down!"

"Get down Jenny!" Jenny and I were shouting simultaneously.

Down on my haunches, my head just appearing over the bottom of the windscreen, I was shouting directions for all I was worth.

"Right! Left! Paul, Right! Right! Drive! Drive Drive! Keep driving!" Paul, anticipating death, expecting the next bullet to be his, was driving with his head and torso flat down over the steering wheel.

"Lord, don't let us die here! Lord! Don't let us die in this dirt!" I continued to pray out loud, now in tongues, the words came tumbling from my lips. Words I had not heard before. The sound of machine gunfire continued, 'Tat - tat - tat.'

Totally immobilised by fear all I could do was to think, "if Paul gets shot now I won't have the courage to move across into the driver's seat!" I could see the scene in the film where the co-driver on the stagecoach gets hold of the reins and saves the day. At that moment I knew I lacked the bottom line courage.

"Keep going Paul, please keep going!"

Our lives depended on Paul keeping his nerve and driving fiercely forward. Bluebell was being whipped and lashed for all she was worth!

Without moving I visualised myself cowering in the corner on the cab floor waiting helplessly for our assailants to come and cut our throats. 'Tat - Tat - Tat-Tat!'

"I don't believe... it's still coming!" The continuous sound that echoed through the valley, felt like there was no getting away from the demons of hell. I had always imagined sniper fire to be a single, deliberate shot from a lone figure looking through a telescopic lens.

To my relief, Paul was still driving, still with his head and torso flat across the steering wheel. We turned another bend and, apart from the roar of Bluebell's engine and the pounding of our heartbeats, there was an unreal silence, but we still hurtled along at top speed in case more snipers were waiting around the next bend.

I glanced across at Paul; blood was trickling down the side of his face and running into the hairs on his chest. There was no doubting the courage of this man who had just saved all our lives!

Taking a deep breath both Jenny and I struggled apprehensively, and very tentatively, back up on to the seats. As soon as we had recovered our composure, Jenny pointed to the scorch marks of a bullet hole in the doorframe on the near side of Bluebell, only millimetres from a picture of Jesus.

"That bullet must have come through your side of the window Paul, across in front of our chests and straight through the opposite doorframe on Jenny's side." Stunned into silence, we were all unable to take in the reality we had just experienced. We had just narrowly escaped death.

Within a matter of yards we came to the end of this treacherous section of the route. This was the exact place where the Italians had been killed. There, by the grace of God, we had made it! It must have been by the flutter of an angel's wing. We were all quite unable to take it in.

Now, seemingly enjoying the scenery, sat one British UN Warrior! Two soldiers perched out of the top of the turret complete with guns in hand. Slowly because she was still in shock and wounded, Bluebell limped by in front of the large dusty tank. Paul pushed his elbow straight through the remaining shattered glass on his side window and shouted quite deliberately. "Where the bloody hell were you when we needed you?" My usually mild, kind husband clearly was not amused.

Already my mind was racing ahead. "What if Ricki is dead in the back? Shall we turn right and go to the base? What should we do if we have a dead body on board? Should we just go to the UN and say, excuse me we have a dead Muslim on board, what shall we do next?"

I looked ahead; "There's the dust of the convoy ahead. Look we can just see them. We're on tarmac for these few miles, let's see if we can catch them up before the next mountain road."

Realising that the bullet holes and the smashed window might draw unwanted attention to our vehicle, I changed my instruction. "No, slow down Paul! Let's drive through here as if all is fine!"

"What about Ricki?" Jenny was asking.

The truth was, I dare not let my mind even address this question let alone answer it, but I knew I had to. I felt like a cow.

"I'm sorry Jenny, he's either dead or alive but, we definitely can't stop to check now we are still in bandit country. What time is it?"

"It's a quarter to twelve," Paul replied. Looking across at him, I was grateful to see his wounds were only superficial!

"It's a quarter to twelve on a Monday morning," I continued still trying to get hold of the situation. "Goodness, Jenny, what are we normally doing at a quarter to twelve on a Monday morning? I'll tell you this, if we get out of this little lot, then I'll be happy to do just the washing on a Monday morning for the rest of my life."

Jenny quite understandably was still worrying about Ricki. "Jenny, we'll stop as soon as we dare, but for the moment we are going to have to trust that God has looked after Ricki."

I allowed my mind just a little space to imagine what it must have been like for him in Bluebell. "Can you imagine being in the dark under that mattress, on bare wood, with those metal springs sticking in you and hearing all that machine gun fire? Can you imagine what it must have been like being tossed over all those bumps at top speed? How could he have survived?" My heart sank...but I was still unwilling to panic.

We journeyed on, still in shock, still unable to absorb the reality of our escape but still desperately trying to gain some composure.

"When you think of it, when you think we were probably travelling forward at about 40 mph when that bullet came sideways across our chests, then you realise God must have had an angel deflecting that piece of metal!"

These thoughts were still racing around in my head when Bluebell was halted, at the beginning of the next mountain pass, by a line of stationary vehicles. It appeared one of the lorries of the original convoy had blown a tyre, and nobody could get past.

Jenny was quite taken with a bright yellow lorry parked to our left. A lady standing by a vehicle bearing the words, 'Edinburgh Direct Aid' smiled a big warm open smile and waved in acknowledgement of fellow citizens. "A British convoy. Thank God for them. Let's pray they have an easier time going through that stretch then we did." Jenny waved, and again the warmth of that lady's smile seemed to move in empathy towards our trembling hearts.

We were able to move up a few yards and halted practically alongside Martin Bell, the BBC news reporter who was inside an armoured Land Rover travelling in the opposite direction.

Trying to block out our frightening experience with light-hearted banter, we chatted with the crew about everything except our deadly secret.

One of the crewmembers was kindness itself and offered us a couple of oranges and an apple. Unobtrusively I went round to the back of Bluebell, and lifted the roller shutter door enough to allow space to roll the fruit along the floor, trusting it would refresh Ricki, should he still be alive!

Martin Bell stomped around and complained to Paul how annoyed he was to be held up. I kept quiet wanting to say, "how lucky he was, able to travel in his bullet proof land Rover. I was glad that was all he had to complain about." Instead, I pondered in my heart on how very close Mr. Bell was to a headline story, but kept further quiet, also knowing we were not out of trouble yet. When at last we were able to move forward the convoy in front was within a few minutes, well out of sight again.

"If we keep going we will soon be able to find a quiet place to stop." Paul said breaking into my thoughts. Still blocking what I did not want to know about Ricki, I took from that remark that he himself was needing some care and attention.

Within about half an hour we came across a small group of French Canadian troops 'dug in' at a rather large clearing, at the side of the road.

"Stop here, Paul, let's see what's what." Paul took little persuading.

As soon as he jumped out of Bluebell, the soldiers, seeing blood on his head and down his front, quickly carted him off to their small first aid post. Jenny wasted no time in getting out to search, unsuccessfully, for a toilet. The soldiers, with great amusement, offered her a bedpan and politely turned their backs whilst she used it.

A big burly Sergeant strode over to the driver's side of the cab. On seeing me, who must have looked less than my usual manicured self, roared in a jovial voice, hands on hips, "And now, what can I do for you, Lady?" I hesitated momentarily, then, from a child within, dropped from the height of the cab above, straight into his strong, long arms.

"Please give me a hug?" He held me tightly and for a moment, I felt secure and safe. "Thank you. I needed that!" Then, professional till the last, and as an after thought, I added "Oh! Incidentally, have you got any diesel?"

Jenny, having used the bedpan in the back of the army truck, joined me standing alongside Bluebell's petrol tank. Simultaneously we looked down, our eyes drawn to a large bullet hole exactly where the mattress would have lain. Stomachs churning, heads motionless, our eyes fell to the ground. Was there any blood dripping through the floorboards? It was essential we acted as normally as possible. We couldn't admit to ourselves that Ricki was either dead or injured. Was there anything we could do or say to help him at that moment without inhibiting his chances of getting out?

I was relieved the tense atmosphere was broken when Paul returned quite happy after receiving the tender, loving care of the soldiers who had removed fragments of glass from his scalp, whilst other soldiers took a video of this strange blue vehicle sporting a new type of ventilation.

Desperately needing to find a place where we could be on our own to check on Ricki's situation, we had to drive along for about ten further minutes before feeling secure enough to pull over behind some giant rocks away from prying eyes.

Now was the time to face the truth. I stayed in the cab, unwilling to face the possibility I could have been responsible for killing Ricki. Paul and Jenny walked swiftly around to the back of Bluebell.

I sat there, too scared to go and look, motionless, every sense alert. The roller shutter door went up.

"Ricki! Are you there?" No response.

"Ricki! Ricki! Are you there?" Paul's voice was getting more urgent. A loud "Alleluia" rang out from the back of the vehicle. Ricki must have responded! I could scarcely contain my delight. Praises were swelling up to Heaven. Hearts were overflowing with praise and thanksgiving.

"What a Mighty Father we have. Alleluia! Alleluia! And Lord! Would you mind if Bluebell becomes Saint Bluebell from now on?"

It took many more hours to travel over the rest of the mountains. We were aware we had peace in our hearts knowing that, despite one of the bullets coming within millimetres of Ricki's head, another passing through St. Bluebell's side and coming out just behind our backs, we undoubtedly had been protected by the grace of God.

If we had been protected this far we felt much more confident about the rest of the journey. At least we felt confident until we came to the border checkpoint between Bosnia and Croatia!

Stopping to show the papers, our eyes moved apprehensively along a line of armed men standing in true 'Rambo' style.

"These papers, no good!" I reached for the next layer.

"We go back to England. Empty."

Rambo looked again then beckoned to Paul. "Open! Open!" he ordered. My heart sank, "Not now! They can't find him now!"

"Open!" Rambo repeated pointing to the back of St. Bluebell.

Paul slowly, reluctantly, taking as long as he possibly could, dismounted from the cab. It took him exactly five paces to reach the back of St. Bluebell. Watching in the wing mirror I counted every one.

"One...two...three...four...five!" Six men, complete with machine guns, moved with Paul around to the back of St. Bluebell out of sight.

"Pray in tongues, Jenny!" I encouraged.

"This could be the last time I see my husband alive!" I thought.

I am sure Jenny was praying for all she was worth. I was sure we were all hardly able to contemplate the next few moments. The roller shutter door went up, slowly. I felt the whole of St. Bluebell bounce as the guards jumped inside.

One, two, three we could feel the vibrations! They must now be standing right next to the mattress. "Lord! Put a hedge around that boy! Blind their eyes! In fact do whatever you have to do…but Lord do it now!" Helplessly I threw my hands in the air. I hoped the washing still covered the bump.

Silence!…Then the sound of the door closing. It reverberated like a drum roll bringing down the final curtain at the end of a theatre scene. Jenny and I waited.

In the wing mirror I could see Paul swaggering back, hardly able to restrain the smile from bursting through on to his ashen face. He entered the cab.

"I don't believe it! They stood only two feet, two feet away from the mattress and saw nothing!"

We couldn't believe we had been only feet away from, whatever? It seemed incredible we could have had another such narrow escape again.

We were relieved to realise we were only a short distance from a house where we had rested on previous journeys. We wasted no time in heading there! This home was right in the middle of a town and had always been safe for us but, now we had a shot up lorry and we were carrying a Muslim in Croat territory, would it still be safe?

By the time we arrived I had already worked out a master plan.

"Wait here you guys. Let me go and see if I can get some help." The household was surprised to see my tall silhouette through their glass door. Welcoming me enabled the family to release the tension and quell the anxiety they had been feeling about us all since we last met.

"If it's all right with you. Can we stay and rest here with a friend? We need to get him unobtrusively out of St. Bluebell and into the house!" My mind was already actively engaged in the logistics.

I mustered up six assorted sized males. "Come on you boys. I've got a job for you. Come on, Paul! Let's get you men inside St. Bluebell to help unload our bags."

Paul said nothing and I am sure that he could not understand my logic. Six men boarded St. Bluebell and seven emerged into the bright sunlight, heading straight for the welcoming home.

The signs of strain on Ricki's face were beyond imagination. He had been in the back of St. Bluebell for twenty-two hours. What it have been like for him being bounced on bare floor boards, alone, in the dark, under the dusty mattress, sharp metal spikes sticking into him, through twenty odd check points was beyond my imagination. He had not dared to breathe when the guards had entered the lorry not knowing if the next breath would be his last.

Once inside we all relaxed, hugging each other lovingly and cheerfully. The mother of the house quickly produced a clean, white tee shirt to replace Ricki's dusty, sweaty one. He was offered a warm shower and needed little persuasion to enjoy what must have been one of the biggest gifts anyone could have given him at that time. This was the love of God in operation. Not Croats and Muslims, but brothers and sisters.

I imagined Eternity and wondered how God would re-pay our host's kindness in Eternity. Surely He would give these people a Crown of Jewels, surely they were princes amongst princes.

Refreshed, and unwilling to put the family at unnecessary risk, we were keen to get Ricki safely back on board. This was achieved by merely reversing the original strategy, seven men boarded, six emerged.

The next part of the run to the ferry should only take two to three hours but it was now late in the day, and Paul was deeply concerned about us being on the road after dark and especially in our shot up state.

We would have to take a chance on staying at another house we knew, but would Dravco a Croat, give sanctuary to Ricki and St. Bluebell? There would be a welcome for the Brits but I was not so sure about one for Ricki, a Muslim, or St. Bluebell in her damaged state. There was nothing for it, we would have to risk it as the ferry was not due to depart for another seventeen hours, and we certainly couldn't be on the streets for that length of time.

Very wearily and quite reluctantly, we headed towards what we hoped would be an 'oasis in the middle of the desert.' I thought of the scripture. 'When you receive one of mine, you receive me' for I knew this particular family had hearts of gold but could they find it in their hearts to receive an angel without knowing it?

When we arrived at the house I decided to test the ground. "Wait here. Let me go in first and explain the situation. We must not compromise these people. They must freely make their choice."

Before I reached the door the children had spotted the holes in the vehicle.

"Come and see this!" they called to their father. The sight of a bullet ridden St. Bluebell in any of our front gardens would cause some curiosity!

"Mama Mia! Oh! My God! Oh! My God!"

By this time Dravco's hands were way up in the air. "Oh! My God! What has happened to you?"

"Dravco, we need your help. We need to park the lorry here over night, but do not want to put your family at risk."

"Come in. Come in. You people my friends."

"Wait," I was saying, holding him by the arm. "You do not know the whole picture yet. Let me first explain before you make your decision."

It is fair to say Dravco was rightly very apprehensive when he learnt of Ricki's presence in the back of St. Bluebell. He needed time to consider, and withheld his decision until after refreshment. Having eaten and drunk plenty he suddenly commanded, "Fetch the boy. He sleeps upstairs." Decision made. We could all stay.

Paul went to fetch Ricki. Jenny and I witnessed the beautiful way in which his oldest daughter sweetly and lovingly tuned into Ricki's situation. Her heart was reaching out to him in total compassion. 'A child shall lead them.' One could see she was imagining what he must have been through.

It was not the easiest of nights. Paul and I were thankful to be offered the bed settee facing the front door. I watched that door most of the night, worried in case our dear host had a change of heart and went to phone the authorities from the phone box at the corner of his lane.

I need not have worried. To this day the whole family have been most faithful, and I could see why our Heavenly Father had led us to this home on that first occasion. God is the master of the chess game and we are the pieces.

Thinking about the journey ahead, I realised we still had a long way to travel, and I was continually mentally working though the logistics of the forthcoming ferry journey. I could see many potential dangers, and we all spent much time before our Father surrendering the situation unto His care.

By the following day we had to wait before boarding the ferry and stress levels were greatly heightened.

At last we were ready to load, and watched as the ferry company's staff instructed everyone where to position our vehicles on board. The heat in the hold was tremendous and hit us like a warm, tidal wave, and this was even before the main entrance doors were closed.

"Ricki can't possibly survive the night in this heat and breathing in these fumes there's no fresh air whatsoever." No sooner had the thought entered my head than I saw a lorry pull up only inches behind St. Bluebell's rear door. This would prevent any means of escape into fresh air.

In a moment of panic. "Stop! Stop! I need my toothbrush out of the back."

"Yes!" Jenny agreed, "I need my bag as well." Bless her, just waking up to the fact she really did need it. Between us we created such a commotion, the poor staff working to get the last vehicle on board behind us signalled for the lorry parked directly behind us to move back a few feet.

"What on earth are you two girls doing?" Paul asked getting annoyed. "What are you messing about at?"

"Paul, we need our bags for the night. We must be able to get into the back of St. Bluebell. One cannot breath down here!" I was hoping he was reading my double meaning. Dutifully he opened up the old girl's back. First lowering the hydraulic ramp, then slowly pushing up the roller door just enough to enable him to get inside and slowly get out our bags. I stood watching and praying. "What now Lord? What are we going to do?" To my absolute amazement, the lorry behind did not bother to close the gap, and there were three feet to spare for later manoeuvres when all was quiet.

We could do nothing more for the time being so made our way up to our cabin, one small three berth. There was not enough room to swing a cat and the heat was overpowering. We fiddled with the air conditioning, but it made no difference. This was not going to be a comfortable night.

To kill time and relieve some of the tension we went for a meal and hoped no one would guess our secret. Jenny began talking to an aid worker returning home to England who seemed to want to attach himself to us.

"Get Jenny away from that man," I was instructing Paul, unable to deal with the situation calmly myself. I was worried Jenny, in her generosity of spirit would give the game away.

"Let's just all go back into the cabin," thinking we wouldn't make any mistakes there. I was probably the one who would make the mistakes now as my nerves had completely gone. I was only just hanging in there.

Once inside the comparative safety of the cabin, I put an Alan Pimlot tape on my little recorder. Paul and I had shared many peaceful and joy filled hours worshipping with this anointed singer. The gentle sound of his melodic voice brought down the calm of the Holy Spirit.

We rested, prayed and worshipped, enjoying as best we could the less than perfect situation. "Paul, its 10.30. That boy's been down there five hours. He must be nearly suffocating by now. We can't leave him down there any longer."

"Jackie, we can't risk bringing him up."

"Paul, we will have to. Will you please go down and see if you can get him up here?"

"I'll go too!" Jenny said, excited at the prospect of seeing Ricki again. "No, Jenny, you stay here. Paul will be better off on his own." Clearly hurt but willing to accept that none of us had the strength to argue.

Jenny made the best of the time by joining me in prayer for deliverance from the immediate dangers. Maybe only seven or eight minutes later there was a quiet tap on the door. We held our breath. It was Paul and Ricki. "Praise God! for now all was well!"

After our initial relief that Ricki was with us, we all tried to sleep a near impossibility in the stifling heat. Four bodies in such a small space made it difficult for us to rest and we gained no relief for our physical tiredness. Jenny tried waving the door back and forth to create some movement of air. It helped a little. When she finally settled down, I found myself keeping door watch. I tried to sleep with one eye and two ears open, and comforted myself with the thought Ricki was at least with us and not still in St. Bluebell's burning womb.

By 6 a.m. we were still as tired as we were when we first lay down. Paul escorted Ricki back down into the bowels of the ship. Jenny and I kept a prayer covering over the situation, and were relieved when Paul returned, mission safely accomplished.

The usual hustle and bustle started as lorry drivers and families returned to their vehicles ready to disembark. As the doors of the ferry opened up, everyone was relieved to be getting their first taste of fresh air for twelve hours. St. Bluebell rolled out, a bit like Jonah coming out of the mouth of a giant whale.

After what we'd been through getting out of Bosnia the Croatian, Slovenian and Austrian border crossings were all taken in our stride. Our main problem now would be on arrival in England.

How were we going to get Ricki into England? Were we going to declare him? Would the authorities send him back? I wrestled with all these worries throughout the whole of Germany and Belgium. So decided to write a full statement to have ready for whatever situation came up. Not wishing in my heart to deceive anyone or to flout the law of the land, I wished to be open as to how our Heavenly Father had moved the chess pieces in this situation.

In case we became separated when we arrived on British soil, we made sure Ricki had, in his possession, money, various phone numbers and our addresses. Following the lorry in front we passed through customs and on to passport control with three passports ready at hand.

When replacing the shattered glass, Dravco, Bless him, had completely sealed the window. This meant Paul had to open St. Bluebell's door to show the passports, which slowed down the queue. To save time the officer in charge waved Paul straight through.

We could not believe our luck! What were we experiencing? I soon became conscious of the speed ramps and remembered we had passed over them on our way into the docks.

"Well, if we passed over them on the way in, then we must by now be well on our way out! We're through! We're in England. Lord, can you imagine? We've made it!" My hand punched the air. Excitement welled up, so elated were we; the cab was too small to hold our explosion of exhilaration.

"Come on you guys. It's four o'clock on a Saturday afternoon. The sun is shining. Let's park Bluebell and show Ricki the ferry he has just come off!"

Overflowing with thankfulness just to be alive, all four of us were like spring lambs skipping with light hearts arm-in-arm, along the cliff path as we surveyed the beautiful shimmering sea, which separated our treasured little island from the vastness of Europe. It was a moment to savour. I remembered my school song, *'This Royal Throne of Kings, This Sceptred Isle, This Earth of Majesty, This Seat of Ours...This Precious Stone set in the Silver Sea. This Earth. This Realm. This England.'*

Although it would take another eight hours to reach home, nothing could dampen our high spirits. The journey up the M1 seemed to last forever. We were about to discover how powerfully God had moved in Ricki's life, how many similarities there were to Joseph in the Old Testament times.

Here was a young man who had been plucked from his mother's arms and transported by complete strangers across the other side of the continent. Here was Jenny sharing with him Joseph's story so he could get just a glimpse of how much God was in his situation. Ricki told how he used to live with his close-knit family in a five-bedroom house, set in five acres of ground.

Then, simply because they were Muslims, life changed horrifically over night. First his father and mother were both sacked from their jobs. Suddenly their world went crazy as their fellow neighbours and school friends started a systematic 'cleansing process' of all Muslims from the area. For two weeks they slept in the woods which surrounded their home. Other Serbs (their very neighbours) were setting their homes alight. Their world went crazy and nothing made any sense any more. The situation of war meant someone from his class at school would quite happily shoot him. Not for who he was but for what he was.

There was no one to turn to, no one to tell 'them' to stop. Then they had to sign a paper saying it was not their home any more. If they did not sign they were shot. Eventually hundreds of Muslims were herded together like animals on to cattle wagons and taken to a camp, but not before 'they' opened fire and killed some of their fellow Muslims and one school friend. The family had looked on horrified. There was nothing they could do, they were helpless.

In the camp they slept on the floor, all four were surviving on one small tin of beans. Ricki and his brother were lucky, they found some manual work for nine hours a day which gave them enough money to supplement the family diet to buy one piece of bread a day. Ricki told us that, despite the deprivation, the lack of sanitation, electricity or running water, "I would have stayed with my family had it not been for the fact all the young men were rounded up and sent to the Bosnian army front line to be used as 'cannon fodder.' We would have to kill our own people or be killed. It was then that I knew I would risk death to escape. Somehow they missed me, but I was due to go into the army in five days time and I would have been sent to die for the people who took everything from us."

"At least that is what would have happened, if you guys had not come along. The worst bit for me was when I was cowering inside the cramped mattress, parked outside the school, when I heard my mother's voice. It was then I cried, but I cried quietly."

'Us guys' sat in stunned silence, trying to grasp the enormity of what God had done with our simple faith and obedience. We travelled on in silence, each lost in our own thoughts.

Eventually Jenny, complete with all her worldly goods, was safely returned into the welcome embrace of her closest available family member, Marco Polo, her cat. He rubbed his smooth, furry body along her gamely, ageing frame. They were together again.

Paul and I still had a few more miles to travel before our reunions. Radiant with happiness, glowing with joy, yet with no real comprehension of what God had done through us, we turned the last corner into our own road.

The yellow streetlights and warmth from friendly homes welcomed us into the bosom of our estate family. We drew up slowly, St Bluebell's engine purred almost regally, outside our own front door. The lights of home shone, welcoming us back into a safe harbour.

As St. Bluebell's engine gave her final, gentle groan, Ljubica emerged from our front door. Her arms opened wide. Warmth, love and comfort poured out through every pore of this lady from Bosnia. We could hardly contain our excitement, amongst the entire bustle of greetings, hugging and kissing. Ricki crossed the threshold into a safe family home.

Excited chatter bubbled as we enjoyed a welcome cuppa. "Come on Ricki, you can sleep in Richard's big double bed tonight. You can really stretch out and even watch television if you want."

Leaving him to adjust to his new surroundings, I filled a bath with pure, clear, hot water before releasing oils to create a sea of perfumed froth.

"Ricki, have a bath," I invited, handing him a large warm towel. "When you've finished jump into bed and I will bring you a lovely mug of hot chocolate."

It wasn't long before this young man was sitting up wrapped in the warmth and comfort of a cosy, soft duvet. I sat on the edge of the bed, leaned back against the fresh, cotton pillow and put my arm around his broad shoulders. He responded instinctively by gently resting his weary head against me. I tenderly, lovingly stroked his forehead, kissed his thick, black hair, "You're safe! You're home! Sleep well! Good Night! God Bless! Now we must look to God for your family!"

The headlines reported: The Great Escape,
Bosnian teenager who escaped inside this mattress.

Chapter 15

NEWS AT TEN

It wasn't long after we returned home with Ricki before the bullet holes in Saint Bluebell were being noticed. We realised a decision would have to be made regarding the declaration and legalisation of him. Further I needed to test what my own instincts were telling me, so I took counsel from a minister friend a few miles away.

"Well I know what I would do," the friend said.

"Tell me" I encouraged, believing what he was about to advise would tie up exactly with my own thoughts. "Declare it the way it happened and do it now."

Delighted his advise merely confirmed my own thoughts and not worrying about the consequences, given we knew imprisonment was a possibility, my next concern was how exactly to go about it?

Immediately after the receiver was replaced, the phone rang.

"This is Caroline Kerr, from News at Ten. We are doing a programme about people from Bosnia in this country. Do you mind if we interview you about the situation out there?"

I was quite used to my Heavenly Father working fast. "But Lord, is this the way you really want it? Do you really want this to hit the headlines?" Before I could gather my thoughts there I was verbally reliving the whole story.

From that moment on, for the next few days our home resembled Piccadilly Circus. Within an hour there were television cameras and wires everywhere. At one time there was a television crew in the lounge, another in the kitchen, and our garden playing host to yet a third. Ricki remained calm and composed in the middle of these entire proceedings. After all, we could do nothing other than tell the truth and trust we would come out of this situation as safely as possible.

Much to our embarrassment, the headlines appeared as 'The Great Escape.' We were all heralded (however reluctantly) as heroes. At no time then or now did we ever believe ourselves to be brave. Deep down we all knew, without any shadow of doubt, our own nothingness in the situation. Each one of us had known the moment of naked danger, real terror. We had looked death squarely in the face and we could all remember the moments of fear and dread when the bullets came. We could each still feel and re-experience in every quiet moment, a gripping all consuming fear which confirmed for each of us over and over again, we were anything but brave. With nerves still raw I recorded how it felt at the time.

"There is a sense of being on hold. Not being able to start life again.
Waiting...waiting for what?...Permission to start to live again?
Can we give ourselves that permission?

There seems to be no relief, a sense of unreality prevails.
The world is moving fast yet we are on hold...unable to get back in touch with living.

We need space to recharge...We are not able to recharge because we are holding the fear, the responsibility, and it's awesome. It's as if our eyes are on the job, which still needs to be completed,...yet we are held...suspended.

We have life, but...don't seem to be able to give ourselves permission to live it.
What should we do? Wait? No! Paul, needs help... he is suffering.
I feel his pain...I hear it ... behind the jokes and the smiles when he closes his eyes
... the dreams, the screams.
We must break the cycle. We must get back in touch with reality.

We trust the fear will lessen. It will subside.
We must allow time to become the welcome healer.

We know inside, there is no escape.
We know inside...we must go back...we must continue.
The risks are great and we know there could be persecution.
Everyone will view what we have done differently.
In Bosnia it will be viewed one way...in Croatia another...
the authorities will view it another...the Church will see it yet another.

We feel alone. So what next? ... The nightmares will have to continue.
We know they will subside.
The dreams for us are worse than reality, but not so for the people of Bosnia.
Their reality is worse than any of our dreams.

Ricki was also burdened. He was holding the fear as well. Carrying the horror for his family and his people. They were still in the living hell. Then graciously and lovingly like a precious gem, God cast a healing gift into his morass of uncertainty and pain. The News at Ten film was sold on the world network and shown in Zagreb. It was immediately picked up by an amateur radio ham, who promptly radioed the news into Central Bosnia. Within three weeks of Ricki leaving Bosnia, his family, by the grace of God, had heard he had made it to England. They knew he was alive, safe and well. For Ricki this was yet another unbelievable gift.

He was declared to the authorities and was given exceptional leave to remain and permission to start his studies at university.

Over the months we began to share our story in schools and churches, in an attempt to raise the on-going funds to continue the work, but it took a couple of years before our intense fear began to subside and eventually dissipate.

It was very clear if we were going to continue we needed to replace dear old Bluebell with another vehicle more able to cope with the terrain. This we did with an even older and very masculine looking ex-army, 4 wheel drive, Bedford MK lorry. On principle I was not going to like him. He was big, crude and ugly, and resembled a giant green camouflaged snail sitting in our drive, hence ... Sidney Snail was born.

By the end of 1993, we lived daily with the worsening situation in Bosnia. Besides the continuing resolve of the Serb forces to take and re-take land whilst at the same time cleansing the Balkans of as many civilian Muslims as possible, the Croats and the Muslims, were now fighting each other. Guerrilla warfare was waged over every pocket of land and every village. The savage enemy was doing its worst claiming the title deeds of each heart and home with each impending assault.

This may have been a simplistic way of looking at the conflict, but the way I saw it; three different sides were now fighting for the same territory. One side fought for power, one for perceived rights, and the third for sheer survival.

The worsening situation made the need to help even greater, so when Paul announced he was willing to try again with a new co-driver, I was exalted in my spirit yet at the same time relieved the work could continue without me for a while. I had no trouble calculating that the odds of our personal survival ratio were getting shorter. If we continued returning, who was to say we would always come out alive. It was simple mathematics, and last time had been in my opinion, too close for comfort. I simply needed more time to recover.

One Saturday morning in November 1993 found Paul, Ricki and I enjoying a family breakfast. Paul and John were due to leave for Bosnia that particular night. It was Ricki's l9th. Birthday and our kitchen resembled a fairground after the carnival was over! We had just shared a breakfast of pancakes and toast, the lemon on the pancakes had excited our gastric juices. 'Sounds of the 60's' was on the radio, taking Paul further back down memory lane to recapture his 'flower power day's' of youth. We were all trying to pretend we were part of a normal family on an average Saturday morning.

It was as if there was a snowball rolling down a hill, gathering speed and soon it would roll out of sight. Shortly Paul and John would be on that snowball.

The real problem being, at that moment...I knew...Paul knew what it was like ahead. In the early hours of the morning I had felt the child in him move towards the mother in me for comfort and protection. I heard cries from his pictorial sleep. I could see his pain but was unable to help.

The music again came into focus. More laughter around the breakfast table. Was this really happening? I knew the fear Paul was living with. He didn't want to go to Bosnia again without me. Yet, after the last time, he didn't want me to go either. I knew the snowball had gained a momentum, which I could try to stop, but should I?

John, bless him, was fired up with the great adventure, boys together, happy to be serving. They were both aware they might have to pay the ultimate price, the only difference being Paul knew what that terror felt like John had yet to discover his limits. Maybe, later that day, Paul and I would be able to find some space together, to really share where we were, instead of just playing the game of 'happy families and it's O.K!'

Once more the music came into focus and this time it was much softer. The phone rang to draw me further out of my thoughts. Someone wanted them to help bring a loved one out of Bosnia. The wife pleaded down the phone ... I sank back into my chair. Didn't they know we would bring the whole population out to safety if we could? Didn't they know our hearts were breaking and bleeding with them? How could we bring hope where Governments had failed? Where was the voice of the Church?

By 1 a.m. the combination of the early hour, physical tiredness from loading the lorry and all the last minute briefing, were taking their toll on Paul who was understandably quite exhausted. His body language spoke volumes. How anybody with the prospect of driving through the night, completing a channel crossing, and expecting to drive on through France and Belgium without sleep, could still smile ... was beyond me. Such is Paul's disposition and I love him for it.

Silently, Ricki and I wandered outside to observe the final departure, each immersed in our own private thoughts and trepidations about the trip. The men were doing their last minute, personal loading on to the lorry. Space was at a premium. Two flasks of hot water, bedding and clothing for freezing temperatures, maps, files and paperwork left little sitting room in Sidney. I could see Paul was not happy. Knowing the need for uncluttered exits, I was confident he would re-organise at the first pit stop.

Wondering how Paul was keeping his cool, I turned away and walked slowly ahead of them up the road into the clear still night, glad of the opportunity to explore my own thoughts and feelings.

Sidney's engine roared like thunder into life with clouds of vapour pouring from his exhaust. I was sure He would wake up the whole neighbourhood as he crawled with ungainly awkwardness, out of the narrow drive. The Monster rolled towards Ricki and I. There was a certain comfort in the ugliness of size and heaviness of those huge wheels slowly rolling past in what had been the quiet silent night.

As neighbours slept unaware of the departure, the boys flashed the lorry's big, white eyes in salute. The Snail was happy to crawl back into service, doing the job for which he had been built.

I struggled to give a reassuring smile and a last minute wave as they passed. We stood silent and still, starring into the distant horizon until the last traces of the ungainly silhouette vanished out of sight. The night sky was suddenly cold and empty of the metal monster. Ricki's arm gently enfolded my shoulders in reassurance and comfort. Slowly and silently we walked back into an empty home. Now it was my turn to learn what if felt like to be left at home in the supporting role.

At the height of the war- November, 1993.
Paul and John leave with the lorry's
original canvas back cover.

Chapter 16

BON BON ALLEY

A few days after leaving, the boys put a message on my answer machine to say there were torrential storms in Metkovic, on the Croatian/Bosnian border where they were waiting until Monday morning for clearance. This meant sleeping in the cramped cab for three days and nights. In their wisdom they thought they would go to the local 'flea pit' for a change of scenery! They would phone me on their return from the cinema.

Early the following morning I was definitely beginning to feel very uneasy. I thought they were mad to even consider sitting in a dark cinema in bandit land, wearing moneybags. Weren't they asking to be mugged? Why hadn't they phoned? Was Sidney still parked up or had they gone through to 'dead man's land' trying not to worry me? I knew worry was a waste of time and energy - it doesn't accomplish anything, so taking authority over my own thinking I told myself to practice what I preached.

"Get ready Jacqueline and go to church. This afternoon you will have ample time to bite your finger nails."

By six in the evening the tension was telling on me and I felt a kinship with the refugee families in England. That day there had been many phone calls from all over the country asking for news of the lorry. I heard the hope in the callers' voices when they came to the phone, then I heard the disappointment when all I could tell them was, "The lorry is still in Metkovic, trying to get through." I had expected a call all day, but what I didn't want to hear was they'd been unable to get the necessary papers to continue so I kept telling myself, 'No news is good news.'

The truth was I wanted to be there with them. I wanted to put the might of my determination behind theirs. I wanted them to be able to go forward, yet dreaded the thought of them going on because I knew the evil of the most monstrous tyranny that lurked around every corner.

Impatiently I tried to occupy myself. I did some ironing and then tried to watch a film on television, concentrating on neither. I read a letter, which was sitting on my desk, it simply said "Thank you for letting me look into your garden." Although this brought a moment's pleasure, which I appreciated, my thoughts were soon back with Paul and John in Bosnia. I prayed and waited unable to do anything else.

I really could align with the pain of the refugees' families. No one could really communicate the tension in which those people lived on a daily basis, knowing their loved ones were living in permanent danger. In some small way I could be part of their pain, and most of all I wanted them to know, *'God knows and He cares,'* after all, wasn't that why he had called us?

When the men subsequently were unable to get through, I wrote to the families telling of their frustrations and sense of helplessness.

Dear Friends,

"Paul and John are disappointed at not getting to their destination in Central Bosnia for the first time in our history. We don't have to tell you the situation is bad at the moment. Three days ago two Danish Aid workers were killed and seven injured in a U.N.H.C.R. convoy. Hence all movement in Central Bosnia and all operations

are suspended!

Please understand the men did their best. We are still very small and ill equipped, but still willing to try to do a big job. With the weight onboard, John and Paul could only travel at 10 miles per hour up the steep mountain tracks and would have been a sitting target. Their solitary situation would have left them exposed through the front lines for over several hours.

As for the future, for the first part of this week I spent time in prayer, trying to arrive at the place of being willing to go back myself. Last Monday, a man from the Ministry of Defence advised that there is only about three weeks before the snow will prevent any aid getting through so maybe you can see our absolute frustration. We share your sense of desperation.

As many of us will know, when we come to the end of ourselves there is still only one place to go, and its back to the power source. So here I am again back before my Father, knowing He is able to guide us forward safely.".

As I saw it then, there was a whole nation surrounded by 'the enemy.' Here in Britain we had thousands of the Bosnian refugees living in trepidation, listening to every radio report, hoping against hope that the next village to come under attack would not make their loved ones, the next victims in the contemptible catalogue of human crime.

Such was the climate of the time, which led me to surrender yet again to be willing with Paul to try once more to reach our refugee friends. Many thousands were going to die in Central Bosnia that winter and we felt the need to try to feed the least of these, so again I prayed. "Lord we just stand before you in total helplessness and look only to you to open the doors of the way forward." If Nothingness was a prerequisite of missionary work then we were beginning to understand a further dimension of our calling.

By the 26th of January 1994 we felt the need to send this newsletter.

Dear Friends,

I have just been on a Political Radio programme where the question was asked, 'Should the UN pull out of Bosnia?' We are not politicians but we ask what would Jesus do? Jesus would go and save the one lost sheep. He would feed the people with loaves and fishes, and he would be angry against passivity.

We need a parting of the Red Sea. We need a corridor from the sea, through to Central Bosnia so wounded civilians can get out and food can get in. I believe if the UN pulls out in the spring, there will be an almighty battle when hundreds and thousands more civilian lives will be lost.

I know if I were cut off in such a way, I would hope that, the good in the world out there, would care enough to send in the 'Cavalry.' Friends, we are the Cavalry: Each one of us who have been moved in our hearts to the needs in Bosnia. We must continue to minister to the sick and hungry. We have all been called.

We have received many letters regarding the dangers and asking us not to go, but we need to listen only to His voice. When I go to God's Word for our own situation and safety, I see when St. Paul was going to Jerusalem, the Holy Spirit warned him as to the suffering he may endure. His answer can be found in Acts 21 verse 3: "What do you mean to weep and to break my heart?

For I am ready not only to be bound but also to die for the name of Jesus Christ."

Our prayer is, God will always give us His Courage and Grace to go forward wherever He may lead. When I go to His Word for Bosnia I read in Lamentations Ch.4 verse 17 "As for us, our eyes have watched for a Nation that could not help us." Verse 18 "Our persecutors are swifter than the Eagles of Heaven, they pursued us upon the mountains, they lay in wait for us in the wilderness." So the question remained for us, not should we go, but rather when?

Because of the heavy snows of the season in January 1994, the next mission found us in Central Bosnia taking a whole week to do what in normal times would be a days journey. In what I think was our hardest journey ever, there were times when we found ourselves with a fully laden lorry, sliding broadside, completely out of control down a mountain track with hair pin bends looming.

My unreasonable shrieks for more concentration from Paul were in direct competition with the roar from the engine, the spinning wheels and crunching gears, as he wrestled relentlessly, needing to double de-clutch at every bend. Those days I would have done anything rather than face those mountain tracks in snow, but I can recall with thankfulness a miracle relating to snow chains a few days later.

We were at a British UN base and had been to the evening briefing when the Officer in Charge stated all aid lorries intending to go over the mountain tracks the following day, would need four snow chains. We would not be allowed to go any further without them. This put us into a flat spin as the usual chain quota for Europeans was two. Where were we going to get two more snow chains from in the middle of Bosnia?

Because of the late hour and his exhaustion Paul was not interested in the problem. He simply found himself a spare patch of floor up on a filthy congested balcony overlooking the gymnasium, and promptly curled up and slept like a baby. I on the other hand, spent most of the night waiting for an incoming convoy in the hope of maybe borrowing snow chains. By 3 a.m. my hope had expired and reluctantly, I gave in to the cold and tiredness.

I lay down on the main floor in the gymnasium amongst three hundred snoring British soldiers who were 'in transit' to Sarajevo. They all looked so comfortable and cosy in their Arctic sleeping bags and I could see I must have looked positively ridiculous in a white towelling dressing gown, white towelling slippers, trying to get comfortable under a white duvet on a hard wooden floor. I couldn't make up my mind whether it was the snoring, lack of my man, or the cold floor, which prevented sleep. Eventually in desperation, I picked up my bedding and found a corner under a radiator in the ladies shower, where I spent the rest of the sleepless night praying about the much needed snow chains.

The following morning the intensely cold atmosphere, deep snow and lack of sleep heightened my desperation to solve the pressing problem. We drove into every compound only to be disheartened even further, by seeing UN drivers routinely using hydraulic lifting gear, to fit brand new, gleaming snow chains with little effort.

We felt small and demoralised. Here we were, Mr. and Mrs. Joe Bloggs, in the middle of Bosnia with one battered old lorry, trying to do what super equipped, highly professional regiments were doing in sophisticated armoured monsters. To make maters worse, if that were possible we were in addition soaked to the skin.

I had fallen through some ice into a deep hole, which left me standing in eighteen inches of iced water. "Lord…What are we going to do?" I wailed in utter dismay, feeling we were getting nowhere fast. Where could we get snow chains when there were no garages open and no AA? "Lord... if you want those incubators to get to that hospital, then Lord we need a miracle, and Lord we need it now!" There was no finesse in my praying.

"Paul let's go over there. It seems to be some sort of factory. You never know and we have to try something, we can't just give up and go home."

To our amazement the building was where the British regiment did their laundry. It looked like a scene out of M.A.S.H. the American television programme. There were washing machines, huge commercial dryers and an eighteen-foot sign, which read 'Beaver's Laundry.'

Very tentatively I approached the Sergeant in Charge who was standing behind an ordinary metal table. He stood tall and straight, waiting for me to explain why we had entered the building uninvited. "We need a Miracle..." I dared to say, very sheepishly.

"Try me!"... He dared to respond with an expressionless face. I felt that now I was being asked to walk on water in faith believing that our God was able to give us the miracle we so desperately needed.

"No, we really do need a Miracle! I lamented on like a child. This is our ninth trip into Bosnia. We have drugs and incubators for the hospital, and we need to get through" I went on, gaining momentum. "You see we have a Bedford MK and only two snow chains. We are not allowed over the mountain unless we have four... We have tried everything...we really do need a miracle."

Without a word, and without losing eye contact, he picked up a big bunch of keys from the table in front of him...slowly turned and reached towards the metal cabinets behind him, bent down and pulled out a sack of clanging metal.

"Did you say...a Bedford MK lady?" He asked with a

big grin on his face. My mouth dropped open....he slowly but firmly pulled out a pair of snow chains to fit our...20 year old obsolete ex-army lorry.

"Now, if you and your driver would like to get your wet clothes into the dryers we can also make you more comfortable."

It took little persuasion for both of us to strip off down to our undies. Modesty was thrown to the wind as we gathered round the table with the soldiers to share a laugh as I stood there, wrapped only in a black shawl, cutting a precious home made cake, saved especially for such a celebration. However much my vision can extend too, I didn't expect to share the cake in partial nudity amongst the British Army.

Warm and comfortable we drove back to the base, me prescribing a hot meal and a nice long rest for the afternoon. Paul, anticipating the prospect, jumped out of the cab with his usual exuberance at the thought of hot food. "Oh No! ...In Bosnia nothing is easy! What is the worst thing that can happen to us now?"

"Don't tell me ... we have a puncture!"

"You've got it in one!" Paul growled. We could do nothing other than crawl slowly and sheepishly back to the Sargent for help. Paul's rest was cruelly snatched from him and, to add to his discomfort, we were about to get another soaking to the skin.

By grace we had acquired snow chains, now all we needed were new tyres to fit them. Despite the concern Sidney Snail's 'rubber shoes' were giving us, we were up at 5 a.m. the next morning boots blacked and mentally ready to complete the most hazardous part of the journey. We were about to drive once more, through the very same mountain stretch where we had been fired upon whilst travelling with Ricki and Jenny. To say we were not looking forward to it was an understatement, we did not even want to admit this to ourselves.

Sidney's windscreen was solid with ice. We tried

to peer through the 'letter box' of an opening in the improvised metal shields but visibility was down to five percent. The shields had been made for us in England and were a loving attempt to aid our safety. As we were now into 'helmet and flak jacket land' it was all I could do to hoist myself into the cab, wearing the protective clothing.

Paul turned the key ... no response. Sidney was frozen and he just didn't want to move. Paul sprayed every moving part of the engine with some foul smelling stuff, which took our breath away. We waited.

"Nothing Jackie! All that effort yesterday and we still can't make it!" Paul for the first time was nearly in tears.

"Come on lover try again! Try again!" Sidney was adamant; he didn't want to pull his load up those mountains any more than we wanted to go.

I radioed the main operations room. "This is the British Aid lorry. We have a flat battery and could do with a quick tow."

"Sorry Ma'am, all our men are about to leave. No can do." The line went dead. Incensed and hurting for Paul, I baled out of the cab, marched to the best of my ability, and confronted the young soldiers who were all manoeuvring their armour plated Warriors.

"Come on you guys, get this lorry out of here, at...the...double!' I commanded. To our absolute amazement they jumped to attention and within a matter of minutes had towed Sidney the few yards necessary for him to roar into action.

"Terrific, now all we have to do is keep the engine running for the next twelve hours," moaned Paul quite uncharacteristically.

"You are never satisfied. If you can think of, or do, anything better, then fair enough. At least we can be on our way now, so if you don't mind, let's get this lorry out of here and follow that monster in front. You're in the army now."

I didn't like 5 a.m. starts in Arctic conditions at the best of times, and liked them even less when we had achieved nothing. Considering Paul wore only a normal anorak and was without Long John's and vest, it was a testament to his commitment that he was still willing to go forward at all. Nothing he could have said at that time would have quelled my admiration for him, it was beyond measure. Just to let him know I gave him a quick smile and planted a kiss on his cold cheek trying to avoid his frosted whiskers.

We followed for hours and hours through the most hideous conditions, which my mind will not allow me readily to recall. By mid afternoon we were on our own. The vehicles behind had fallen back because of a breakdown, and Sidney simply could not keep up with the ones in front.

The snow crunched beneath the tyres and the cold metal chains hit the undercarriage of the lorry with every revolution of the wheels. We were about to pass along the dreaded section where we had nearly died. We knew we would have to face this moment at some stage and as we travelled closer the tension mounted.

"Jackie... it looks as if we are on our own again." Paul was expressing the sense of helplessness we both felt. Determined to offer my dear husband some support, I ferreted around our bags to find an unopened card, which had been given to us in England by a beautiful couple, Molly and Bob Logan. Inside was a picture of two owls with halos above their heads. Baby owl under the wing of Daddy owl. I turned to the inside of the card. Psalm 91. Verse ll. *'For He shall give his angels charge over you, and keep you in all your ways.'*

"Imagine that Paul! God will send ten thousand angels to guard us in all our ways. Do we need to fear? Let's sing 'Jesus Name above all names' then, if we are shot at again, at least we will die singing the Name of Jesus."

I was not sure Paul liked my logic, but we sang anyway and yes it did help; in fact it made all the difference. We weren't exactly blasé... but we knew we had been given the courage to overcome that part of the journey, which we had both been dreading for months.

All we could see ahead were mountains of white snow but as we passed a thicket in a wooded area about fifty people came running over towards us from the under-growth, waving, shouting and screaming. We spotted a lone British Warrior surrounded by locals begging for anything they could get. One cigarette was worth a fortune in these times. The Warrior waved us down.

"Sorry you will not be able to go any further. You'll have to wait here until the rest of the convoy catches up, there's trouble ahead in 'Bon Bon Alley.'"

We were to learn from the soldiers that the latest desperate action 'game plan' by the starving locals was to try to hijack a lorry by slowing down the vehicle. Women and children would throw themselves in front of the thundering wheels as the wagons turned a bend. This enabled the men to jump on board with Stanley Knives and steal whatever they could.

Immediately we could sense the extra vulnerability of the aid, protected only by Sidney's new canvas covering. This weakness would present no problem for the locals in their efforts to steal from us. Although we did not begrudge them the food as they were starving, we knew that if people were so desperate in that part of the country, the desperation was likely to increase the further we went?

We waited as the young soldier had instructed us, Paul automatically turned off the engine to save diesel forgetting the old lorry would need another tow to get it started again.

Within seconds the locals had swarmed to Sidney's doors. We gave them all we had in the cab in the way of sweets and drinks, even the batteries out of our little tape recorder.

"Lady…it is my girl friend's birthday on the 21st. of

next month. Have you, maybe, perfume or something you can give me for her? Immediately I thought of the giant bottle of precious Estee Lauder perfume, which I had been given as a gift at Christmas. I hesitated briefly, as this was a particular perfume I had waited a long time to own. "Sorry…I have broken the top but, if you would like to give this to her…please tell her, London, Paris, New York." I tried to communicate its value. He smiled graciously, and quickly tucked it inside his coat, away from prying eyes.

As we shivered in the below zero temperatures, there came a knock at the door. The same young man re-appeared. "Lady, this for you." He held out a penknife with a carved wooden handle.

"Why ... thank you," I spluttered, quite taken aback. "But I can't take it. Don't you think it will be of more use to you than to me? You might need it to help you one day," I protested, not meaning to be ungracious.

"No, lady, you must take, and please always think of me."

The convoy behind never did catch up and after a three hour wait in sub zero temperatures, the Warrior gave us a gentle push to get us going back to base. The Sidney receiving a gentle push from a Warrior is like an ant being pushed by an elephant!

The next morning 'Bon Bon Alley' was as ugly as it was reputed to be. We had heard horrendous tales from other aid drivers, many having turned back, refusing to risk travelling further forward. We knew we were extra vulnerable with Sidney the Snail because he moved so slowly.

Battening down everything we could, we made sure our Jerry cans of diesel were securely padlocked. Once Sidney was made as safe as possible, we set off in convoy following armoured vehicles. All went well until we came to a crowd gathered by the road. Jeers permeated the crisp cold air as the desperately hungry hoards surged to barricade our way. The instinct to accelerate and thrust a way through was compelling.

"They'll not realise we are trying to get through to people even more desperate than they are, if that's possible. They will just see us as 'the enemy' ignoring their needs."

As we approached a narrow bend the frenzied crowd of women and children seemed to be propelled into the path of each lorry. Fearing the children might be caught up under the massive wheels, the convoy was forced to slow down. We felt helpless as dozens of youths jumped on the back of our friend Sidney and started hacking and slashing away at his tarpaulin.

Within seconds boxes of Hospital Aid were being thrown out onto the narrow, snow covered road. "What a waste" I found myself screaming, as I put the sirens on full blast as a means of trying to distract them for a moment.

"Why the blazes doesn't that UN armour plated vehicle close ranks and drive on our bumper?" I bellowed quite exasperated. The Snail trundled over bricks and branches, which had been thrown into his path. In the wing mirror I could see groups of men fighting over our spoils. Boxes of plastic tubes only fit for operating theatres were strewn in the road.

"What are we doing? What a waste!" The drive along this section of road only took about ten minutes, but it was ten minutes of concentrated rape as the Snail's canvas back was left slashed to ribbons. Mentally battered and bruised little did we realise the worst was yet to come.

The view through our metal shields made us feel like sardines trapped in a tin.

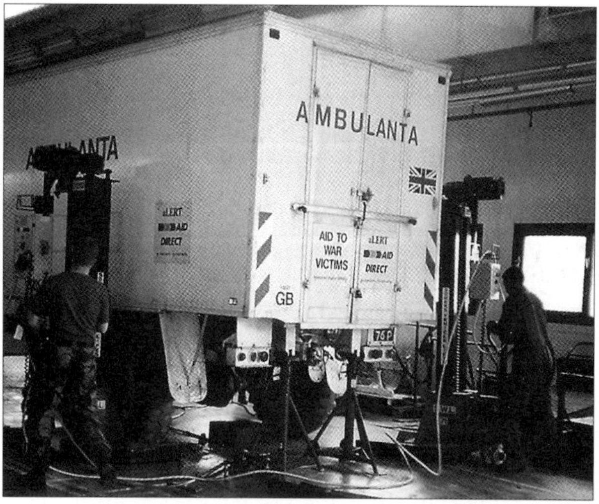

We will be eternally grateful for the assistance we received on many occasions from the various regiments.

Chapter 17

THE WEASEL

We almost made it to our destination that day in spite of the thick snow, but ... at the very last checkpoint manned by Bosnian Croats we were confronted by a short, wiry man with a demeanour that reminded me of a weasel. The guards cocked their rifles.

"Papers!" They ordered. "You! You come!" One of them indicated we should follow him inside a small, wooden hut. An unshaven guard, his face heavy with stubble, pointed with his rifle to a long, wooden bench running the full length of the hut.

"Sit!" he commanded.

I was grateful to see a small iron, wood-burning stove in which freshly placed logs crackled and spat in time with the 'Weasel's' tongue. The Weasel moved forward, standing only inches away from me, pointing his finger so that it almost touched the end of my nose. His penetrating glare stung me into immobility.

"SERBIAN S-H-I-T ... MUSLIM S-H-I-T." The words rolled off his thin wet tongue ... down his long pointed finger ... on to the end of my nose, clearly intending to hit me straight between the eyes. Those words were meant to cut deep, as deep as a knife plunging with full force way up to the handle. My defences came up. Immediately I tried to block his evil, penetrating gaze.

"Lord, put a hedge around me. Don't let any of this filth get in."

The Weasel continued, repeating again and again "SERBIAN S-H-I-T ... MUSLIM S-H-I-T." Saliva poured from the corners of his mouth as he struggled to offload his venom. Frustrated by our lack of response, he tried a new tack.

"You ENGLISH, why you here?" With all the disdain he could muster, he drew a map on his hand.

"My people here ...MUSLIM all around," he indicated. "You want me ... let you go ...?" His eyes narrowed. "To help that S-H-I-T?"

I could see the Weasel's point, but his politics were not ours. He wanted revenge. He wanted to chew up his prey and spit them out into the gutter. We wanted to reach out and smooth away the pain of all those souls in the gutter. Our objectives were clearly different. We could not be at one.

Our continued lack of response made him even more frustrated. I was trying hard not to let him notice my trembling bottom lip, determined not to give him any pleasure. His eyes flashed. He turned, swished his body like a scorpion, addressing me straight between the eyes again, sneering.

"You! How much money you make ... coming here?" This was now the perfect insult. We had taken enough. Enough was enough.

Slowly I stood up, pulling myself to my full height, towering above him, full of cold indignation and pointedly but slowly looking down at my watch.

"Ten past eleven on a Saturday night. Ten past eleven on a Saturday night, minus twenty seven degrees and here I am ... with you ... on the side of a mountain ... fifteen hundred miles away from home." I paused.

"Do you know what I'd be doing in England on a Saturday night in our warm, centrally heated home?" I paused again, this time to let him take it in.

"Well I'll tell you ... I'd be in bed with my husband, … and ... probably enjoying sex! Do you really think I would do THIS ... for ... MONEY?"

His own men began to snigger, trying to muffle their sneers behind their hands.

"No doubt you need help for your people." I went on, more lightly.

"You give me papers to get through, then we'll have the same papers to come and help your people. If you have wounded ... show us your wounded, then we can help your wounded also." I made a clear distinction between helping his people and helping him.

Again his eyes narrowed. "You think you clever lady. I can do what I like with you. I am king around here! I very important man!" Now eyeball to eyeball with him.

"Yes, you very important man in the eyes of the ones who need your special talents." I could imagine this evil man's special talents being used to run his prison. I could imagine him doing that job very well. "Lord, you have told us to love our enemies, but I am having a bit of trouble loving this man!"

I tried desperately to see some good in him. "Maybe he is a good family man, but somehow that mantle just doesn't seem to fit. He looks more like one of those worldly wise types who might be seen wearing a greasy Trilby hat and a grubby leather jacket, hanging around tick tack men, probably acting as a bookie's runner."

I could feel my nervous system struggling to hold control of my body. The pains in my limbs were now transferred to my mind. I began to imagine all sorts of things which might happen to us.

"Stop being silly," I challenged myself. "Come on Jacqueline! You can do better than this! It's time this whole exercise finished one way or another." I was beginning to lose patience with my own weakness. It was time to dig in. "Lord, show me how to handle this situation in Your Name."

The guards were getting agitated, some stroking their rifles, some fingering the triggers. The Weasel was pacing rapidly backwards and forwards across the limited floor space, trying to decide his next move.

"Well, maybe I will help him with his next move," I thought.

"You need drugs for your wounded? No problem." Now I was talking his language. "Your men have guns. You know what you want from our lorry, you know you can take everything and we can't stop you, we are small people, nobody will miss us, you can do just what you want with us."

His mind seemed to like these new thoughts.

"You have the power to do just what you like, and we can't stop you, so please go ahead and do what you will." I was tired and getting fed up with this situation, but instead of letting him rest on these new tempting thoughts, I continued. "We could give you all the bandages etc. you need for your wounded. OR you could take everything from our lorry and we wouldn't be able to do a single thing about it but I tell you this Sir, God will know ...and one day you are going to have to stand at the Judgement Seat and answer for tonight and every night! The choice is up to you!"

There was a deathly silence. The Weasel needed time to consider these new thoughts. He gave me a sly look momentarily still not quite sure which way to jump. I on the other hand was giving a quick look across the room towards two wooden beds only feet away, which had not escaped my notice. By this time even the bare mattresses looked quite inviting and I was having trouble keeping at bay the pain in my body. The tension was eating into my bones.

It was almost 2 a.m. and Paul exhausted from the harrowing driving was beginning to show signs of loosing patience. Even the soldiers were getting fed up, as we had all been going round this same interminable circle for no less than ten hours. The Weasel was in a corner and didn't quite know how to get out, in order to retain credibility.

We imagined the Weasel needed to keep well in with the UN. Questions would be asked about us whether he liked it or not. He paced the floor, stroking his imaginary beard and adjusting over and over again the position of his dark brown , grease stained Trilby. There had to be compromise. There had to be a way out and the way out came in quite an amazing way…

"I will call upon the Lord" came the sound of Paul's singing ... "Who is worthy to be praised." I joined him in singing and we started harmonising like never before. Usually we couldn't even find the same key! Yet, this time we sounded like the choir of Heaven.

"The Lord liveth, so blessed be the Rock" ... On and on we went in complete harmony.

"This is impressive stuff!" I thought. It even sounded good to our own ears. All the guards started to clap enthusiastically. Even the Weasel half smiled. At last! The negative cycle was broken. The Weasel had nowhere to go, his own men were now applauding his captures.

He needed to regain control quickly to re-establish his authority.

"You ... go!" Paul and I could hardly believe our ears! Were we dreaming? Was this man now calmly telling us to go?

"Go where?" interrupted Paul ... "Where would you like us to go? There are shells falling in Vitez behind us, bandits on the mountain roads in front of us, and the lorry is frozen solid!"

"You sleep lorry!" was the reply. Now Paul was really getting annoyed.

"I have not slept in that truck so far this trip, and I don't intend to start now in minus twenty-seven degrees!" He stood up and cast his eyes over to the two grubby, navy blue and white, striped mattresses, lodged temptingly on the splintered, wooden bed frames.

"Your men can move over. My wife and I are having one of these beds. With that Paul proceeded to stride over to the grubby bare mattress and lie down! Within minutes he was sound asleep. The soldiers all stood with mouths open in absolute amazement. That confirmed it for the Weasel. The English were unequivocally MAD!

His tone of voice changed. It became smooth and smarmy. My flesh crawled as he reached out to touch.

"Maybe you have gift for me lady? Maybe Whiskey? Cigarettes?"

"Sorry, no," but delving into my pocket, desperate to find something of my choice to give him, I produced a little book which dear Jenny had given me for the trip. I carefully wrote on the flyleaf, "I pray that one day we will be one in Christ Jesus," signed it and gave it to him. To my amazement he accepted respectfully and graciously.

There was now nothing for me to do but join Paul, who, by this time was snoring in complete harmony to the music of the logs crackling and spitting on the freshly made fire.

At 6 a.m. we woke stiff and cold. Using my hand to clear the condensation, I looked through the small, dirty, cracked window. The snow was about three-foot deep. "This could be difficult," desperately crossing my legs realising I had not seen a toilet anywhere in the last fourteen hours. "And where are we going to clean our teeth?"

By this time Paul, with hands already turning blue with the frost had a blowtorch on the lock of the Sidney's cab. Almost crawling out of the cabin into the snow, I heaved myself up and climbed inside the lorry to retrieve a flagon of almost totally frozen water, then dug deeply into my make-up bag for toothbrushes. Leaning over a wall to clean my own teeth I decided to spread the toothpaste on Paul's brush, leaving it ready for his use.

"There you are Paul." pointing to the wall, which was now substituting as an en suite! Before I could do my hair for the day with my portable curling tongs, Paul was standing hands on hips, full of hurt indignation.

"Jackie, my toothpaste is frozen!"

"Oh my Lord! What a terrible wife I am!" I feigned exasperation in mock surrender.

Could one begin to imagine the thoughts of the British soldiers, as they passed a few minutes later. Imagine them seeing a woman with blonde hair, sitting in the front of a frozen cab on the side of a mountain, in minus twenty-seven degrees, curling her hair and putting on her lipstick?

We didn't realise the significance of this seemingly trivial act until several months later when I wrote to Alan Witcutt, the husband of Christine, the lady who had waved to us after we had been fired upon. A single, sniper bullet had killed her instantly, two-days later in Sarajevo, July 1993. Alan's reply reduced us both to tears, especially when we read the title of Christine's book, 'Flak Jacket and Lipstick.'

Paul had always been amused when we approached a difficult situation in life, that I had always, as an utmost priority, put on my lipstick! It was so good to know I was normal, and my twin female aid worker responded in exactly the same way. Somehow this common instinct had brought us closer.

With Alan's permission and as a tribute to Christine we would like to share his letter with you, as it illustrates the beauty in the hearts, and genuine love and concern of so many people in England for the people of Bosnia and Croatia.

Alan and Christine Witcutt return from their first successful convoy to Bosnia - April, 1993.

A simple marker built in August, 1994 on the Aonach Eagoch, 3000ft. mountain in Scotland where Christine requested her ashes be scattered in the event of her death in Bosnia.

Dear Jackie and Paul,

I was delighted to receive your letter. I am catching up with answering many letters I still get from caring people, also being closely with the radio, TV. And the printed word, public speaking, means I get a lot of correspondence to deal with.

Most of my trips to Bosnia have remained sharp in my memory, and well I remember the cheery wave and smile we also received from your group heading back down towards Split.

I am still totally involved with E.D.A and our trucks go out every 4/5 weeks and radiate out from Vitez.

The Serbs have denied Sarajevo to us, since Christine and I were there in July. If peace spreads, I will be going back before the summer ends. There are so many people that I want to see again and a hospital is going to be named in Christine's name in Sarajevo.

If it had not been for the many caring people who have gone out of their way to help us, I would have perhaps fallen by the wayside.

Since that day in Sarajevo, my world of normality has been destroyed. The realizations that someone did not care who they killed, even aid workers were fair game for their mortars and bullets. And this horror perpetrated on our family has also been the lot of thousands and thousands like us.

In the mean time I will continue doing what I can along with the caring people in E.D.A. to show we will not walk by on the other side.

After observing the live and let live attitude in Sarajevo, my involvement is my way of protesting at the obscenity of ethnic nationalism.

It is what my wife would not only expect of me, but would demand of me. I hope I do not let the people of Bosnia, especially Sarajevo down.

Christmas for us as a family, along with many thousands of others, was a time we would have gladly cancelled. So in closing Jackie and Paul, thank you for your kind thoughts and prayers for this family.

I continually pray for the strength to carry on this work and more so for a lasting peace and to again a living harmony of all peoples involved.

Sincerely, Alan.

P. S. I enclose photo of a lady whose smile you remember. Christine's picture sits in my study still giving encouragement by the warmth of her continuing smile.

Alan and His family have gone on paying the price long after peace has begun its work in Bosnia. They can take great comfort in the scripture: "*All thing work for good for those who are called according to His Purpose.*" Romans 8v28. In the Kingdom of Heaven, nothing is wasted.

Chapter 18

A TOUCH OF THE EMOTIONS

There are many thousands of people in England who have given of their 'Widows mite' in support of making our missions possible. We know their 'love gifts' without doubt have saved lives.

There is no person in Central Bosnia with whom we have spoken, who is not carrying a deep pain etched within. Each has an ache, where their heart has been ripped apart, savaged by loss and broken in two. The pain is so deep; words cannot describe the intensity.

There is a grief, which cuts like a knife and has a stranglehold, which stretches human endurance and daily survival to the limits. Death at times would be a welcome relief.

There is a hopelessness, which can consume the human spirit in a pit of despair. There is an Evil, which is so corrupt, and dark, from which we all try to run, which eats away at the very souls of mankind.

The people in the Balkans have experienced all of this. They have been raped, tortured but worst of all ... at times ignored.

"Don't they care?" is the continued cry from within the broken heart." Governments have made and sold the landmines ... then sent food to help the child with the blown off leg. Man's inhumanity to man is incomprehensible and these people have learned, however sharp or long the ordeal within the human soul, there can be no terms of compromise. Peace within is the only real peace.

Paul and I become used to carrying the pain of these people in our hearts, but never more than when Ricki had been living with us in England for nine months, did we attempt to action a mission with so much forethought and prayerful deliberation. For the first time we found ourselves more personally involved emotionally.

During this period he had been one of God's great blessings to us. There are no words to describe our love towards him and many more of 'our Boys'. Anyone visiting our home has much difficulty in distinguishing, which of 'the boys' is our own son.

Richard has been fantastic and we are really proud of the way he opened up his own heart to receive Ricki and Haris as instant brothers. Over the months we had been carefully photographing every 'normal' activity for Ricki's parents, believing one day we would have the pleasure of being able to reassure them of his well being.

So, by the end of January 1994 after surviving, yet again four arduous weeks to reach Zenica, we were delighted when at last we were going to meet Ricki's family once more. What I was not looking forward to experiencing was the anticipated emotional part of the reunion. Both Paul and I had been a witness to some very emotional situations and somehow whilst in the midst of it, in order to have been of service, we had managed to keep our own emotions battened down. Now finding ourselves in this situation, I wasn't sure if I could handle being in the middle of this highly charged atmosphere.

When we were finally united with the people of Central Bosnia again, we were totally unprepared for the great changes since the last time we met. People, who six months ago were able to keep afloat, were now sinking in a sea of despair. An air of desperation hung over the town. Our lovely hospital director gazed at us with a glazed look emanating from his gaunt face. He was like a candle, which had been snuffed out. The light had gone out of him and he was only a shadow of his former self.

Sarajevo - under siege.

As we unloaded sacks of flour and rice for the Hospital, we noticed an elderly man carefully gather up the grains of rice that had been spilt and gently, place the precious morsels in his pocket.

We moved apprehensively on to the school where the large crowds swamped us, pushing and shoving in desperate attempts to obtain food. People begged and pleaded frantically, some stealing whatever they could as we pretended not to notice. We were emotionally distressed by our inability to meet the needs of all. How inadequate we felt. We could never be satisfied with the little we were able to offer and shared the people's sense of panic.

We did however know we were bringing some hope, the fact that we were still getting through seemed little consolation at the time but, it did reinforce what they saw as their only hope. For Paul and I the hardest part was always feeling we were not doing enough when measured by the need, but one thing I have learnt is, if we will do our best then we can rely on a 'just God' to honour our offerings.

I remember well one time we parked Sidney just outside a Muslim/Serb front line. It was clear snipers, at a two-mile distance, would have picked off our British lorry. So we loaded a few boxes of bandages and dressings, which we had perceived to be a pittance, into the boot of an old car and took the risk of speeding them into one small town, a few miles just out of Sarajevo, where Hasan had advised of great need.

We were taken to the Commander of the troops and were amazed to discover the only medical facilities for a whole regiment were three crepe bandages, which had been used several times. I remember whipping myself for the pittance that we had brought thinking that maybe we were insulting the whole army.

I was comforted by my own reply to my eldest son Michael's questions that asked, "Mum, why are you going again? Aren't there plenty of men much stronger than you, does you going… really make a difference?" On hearing his apprehension and the emotional cost to our family who continually waited for news of us, I found all I could do was answer.

"Maybe you are right, but if it makes a difference to one mother's son, then I think… that could be my son!"

Imagine therefore our joy when a few months later, we received a letter from a young man who had escaped from Sarajevo and whom we were able to help to safety during the war. He wrote from America. "You people gave me hope. For three years I had lived, having given up all hope and belief that there was any goodness left in the world, with the exception of my parents, but you two came along and I have changed in my heart. Through your faith in action you have given me hope and a new life."

Four years later, I remember meeting his mother and father. They proudly showed us a photograph of their son, being met at an American airport, I just burst into uncontrollable tears of gratitude and thanks to God. I had no idea that I was still carrying this young man in my heart, who but for the grace of God, I realise could have been my son. He remains…one of 'our boys'

Now we were in Central Bosnia again, one of the few aid lorries to get through and I was heading straight for Ricki's parents. Paul was doing some last minute deliveries of food parcels sent by refugees' families in England. We were their 'Postman Pat,' their only bridge. Encouraged by a file full of letters from relatives expressing deep appreciation we were compelled to continue the missions long after sense or reason told us to stop.

I made my way to the upper classroom at the end of the corridor. It had been Ricki's parents and brothers' home, along with twenty others for over a year. I soon tuned into Ricki's mother's gentle, calm way and was anxious to give her the carefully prepared photo album of Ricki's new life. Within the pages were scenes of unimaginable joy, in direct contrast to the family's gloomy depravation. I had been able to appreciate the sordid conditions and daily fears, which had led Ricki's mother to literally entrust her son's life into the hands of complete strangers. These photos were meant to bring her pleasure so that she would know her trust in God's providence had been well placed.

We could now both share the fruit of her courage. Smiling I gently offered her the gift, miming the actions of taking photos and at the same time pointing to my watch, hoping she would open the gift at a later time as emotions were running high. We women were only just hanging onto any sense of decorum when Ricki's father pushed his son's sheepskin coat towards me. Ricki had already told me about his favourite coat, which had been the only possession he had been able to save when they fled their home at gunpoint. I felt I knew it well.

"No problem" I smiled receiving the coat with hands outstretched. His mother indicated a gift for me personally. The gentle lady had lovingly crocheted a white, lace tablecloth and if that was not remarkable enough I was later to discover that she had made it by crocheting with a bent wire.

Then trying to express her eternal gratitude further, Ricki's mother took the ring from her own finger and forced it onto mine. The tears were beginning to well up to near overflowing ... but neither of us would let go. I turned to the interpreter nearby. "Please tell her ... Thank you, but I will only wear the ring until the day Ricki gets married, then I will give it to his bride."

This remark opened the floodgates of tears and pent up emotions; despite my determination, I could hold out no longer and in the heat of the moment turned myself away only to be caught in the arms of Ricki's six foot handsome youngest brother. Instinctively his strong arms opened, he smiled a broad open smile and I could do no more than collapse, caught securely in his young compassionate arms. Weeks of tension came flooding out in deep unfettered sobs; mascara ran in a torrent of tears over my flushed cheeks as I tried to hide my embarrassment.

"Oh good gracious this will never do! Look at me, this is ridiculous!" I hastily wiped my face on the back of my hand and struggled to regain my composure as the beautiful family joined me crying and smiling.

I poked in my pockets but never a tissue when one really needs one. I tried desperately to wipe away the mascara, but the father's arms reached out, also wanting to hug this person few ever get to see. His thick dark rimmed glasses held together with brown tape, did nothing to hide his love and compassion and in the middle of a war I was totally safe and secure.

Sidney - with his new modified container being transported along the Neretva river in 1994.

Chapter 19

NEAR FATAL MISTAKE

Back in England by July 1994 we could stand Ricki's pain no more Paul and I knew that the next Mission we were planning could cost us everything. It was a choice we made independently of any other persons; in fact, Ricki was the last to know of our intentions.

The journey into Central Bosnia had been one of our easiest. The hot sun and the fact that Sidney was being towed along the river by the UN on a huge raft because the bridges had been blown up, almost gave our journey a holiday feeling. For a short time it was hard to believe there was even a war still going on, so we made the best of this time together and enjoyed the company of the British soldiers who invited us into the launch on our improvised maritime excursion.

Given it was the height of the summer and I loved the extra sense of well being provided through the heavenly rays it was a little disconcerting to have Emin call a conference round the table in Zenica to warn us of his fears. We knew we were regarded as part of the family, so anything he wanted to bring to us he would do so in a right and proper way.

Firstly he raised his concerns about our safety. "Please we love you, and you will always be part of our family but, we really do fear for your lives. You may not understand how things are done out here and I have heard there are many people who want to kill you." What he was saying of course, was contrary to what we were experiencing giving out aid, and yet we had every reason to trust Emin, and certainly did trust his judgement.

When I questioned him further, he went on to say that Britain was openly supporting the Serbs and, given we were British, we were considered to be part of the British Government. We were simply being looked upon as a potential enemy. Certain people could not believe we were there unpaid, of our own free will so, as far fetched as it may seem, they would rather believe we were there for some sinister reason, for what we did not know.

Secondly, there were many people in refugee camps for whom we had brought private parcels, from relatives in England. For every parcel we were able to deliver, we made ten enemies; jealousy was well in play. Clearly we were in a 'no win' situation. Isn't it a fact that Christians, who take the call of discipleship seriously, and are being used in a positive way, are in the frontline battlefield of spiritual warfare? Of course, the enemy wants to destroy us at all costs. I have learnt that 'old spikey' will stop at nothing. If he misses us physically he will go for our reputations and witness, very often using our weaknesses or those of the people closest to us.

Ricki had no idea about the plan formulated in our hearts. It wasn't until the night before our return trip, when he was giving me a telling off over the phone, for not keeping in contact, did I even begin to share our preconceived plans.

"Where have you been? What have you been doing? Why didn't you phone me?"

In my efforts to reassure him I said, "Look Ricki, everything is fine, we start back tomorrow, Sunday, and we will try, God willing to bring three special packages out for you."

There was a long pause. The silence lasted for ages. In the silence there was a shared, very real understanding of being totally at one. I will never forget his simple words of response, "I just want you guys to know…that what ever happens…I will still love you.

Take the packages anywhere in the world but please just get them out of Bosnia."

Relieved and grateful, his words freed us to know in a really wonderful way, we were free to do our best, in fact, free to follow however we were being led. His gift of trust made all the difference. He was with us in spirit. There was no separation at all. We knew he was there with us…hoping…yet like us, daring not to hope that the ones he loved could be liberated from the trauma of their living hell.

The following day the atmosphere was very tense as we drove out of Zenica. The temperatures on previous days had been very, very hot although that day at 5 a.m. a dry haze seemed to hang about in the air. "Thank you Lord, you have settled the dust on these mountain tracks for us before we have reached them."

The first couple of hours went reasonably well. We weren't expecting an easy ride so were feeling quite pleased with ourselves when we reached our first couple of towns. Simply following a straight route south out of Bosnia, somehow, we missed a right hand turn. There was no reason to make that turn at all. At that point it was a good road and we drove straight on at the junction, totally oblivious that we were heading right into Sarajevo.

We came upon a Croat checkpoint and they were quite cheerful with us. The guards looked at our paperwork and questioned us. They were laughing and shrugging their shoulders saying, "Yes, fine. Go if you want to." In addition they seemed to be saying, "you crazy people" but still we did not pick up the implications.

Within fifty yards we slowly approached another checkpoint. We were rather surprised, but nevertheless took it rather as a matter of fact. At this checkpoint there was a woman, it was the first time we had encountered a woman guard. She was wearing a navy blue uniform and looked more like a policeman than a soldier. In fact she looked more like a character out of a James Bond film.

She was heavily built, wore thick red lipstick and sturdy black shoes. One imagined a dagger would shoot out from the toes of the shoes.

Because the barrier was Paul's side of the cab, I leaned across him with the paperwork, handing it over quite confidently, it never occurred to us there would be a problem. Suddenly, there was a sense of something not quite right. We could not put our finger on it.

"I don't remember seeing that uniform before. I haven't seen those badges before." Paul was questioning his own thinking out loud.

"Papers!" the Gestapo like woman announced. "These papers no good."

"What do you mean, no good! Don't be ridiculous, we have been all over Central Bosnia with these papers and you are telling us, that they are no good?" I carried on digging a hole.

"We've been driving around for two weeks, no problem. What do you mean, these papers are no good?" Again, I gave no space for contradiction because in our experience, these papers were excellent and well in order. In addition we were empty of aid and as far as we were concerned, we were on our way back to England. Why should there be a problem?

"You wait here! I go see my commander." Our James Bond character marched into the office and we could see her gesticulating on the telephone, obviously taking instructions.

The other guards had moved closer and were now, stroking their rifles.

"You stay here! My commander say…you stay here!" I think by this time we had read the clues, but I kept on the attack relentlessly.

"What do you mean? Go no further…How can we stay in Bosnia for the rest of our lives? Don't be so ridiculous, we're on our way back to England." Now even the lady guard seemed as confused as I did.

"This no Bosanski…This Serbska!"

The sound of clashing cymbals reverberated in our inner ears. We dissolved into nothing! Words would not come out of our mouths. Finally, Paul said somewhat more coherently than I could have managed.

"Sorry…It's our mistake! I see it is our mistake! No problem! Sorry to have troubled you with our presence, we go back…we go!"

Never before had Paul manoeuvred that lorry to do a three-point turn so quickly in such a small space, whilst I reeled under the enormity of where we were at that very point in time. With three Muslims on board, and only an eighth of an inch of metal between us we were staring almost certain death in the face.

We had now seen the implications of our situation and could not believe we had been so stupid. At that moment, we had no idea how we had got there. All we knew was, I had been stupid enough to argue when we had endangered ourselves by driving straight into the hands of 'the enemy' Whether we had intended it or not…we had most definitely been in…Serbska! Of all the times to make that particular mistake, this was not a good one! We were stunned into silence as we drove for the next couple of hours.

When eventually we arrived at the UN ferry point, which we hoped, would transport our lorry back down river. We pulled up behind four other dusty civilian vehicles.

"Sorry, no ferry today. In fact there hasn't been one for four days and we aren't expecting the water level to rise for another two days at least," quoted a sergeant obviously following orders. My mouth dropped open. Here we were, in blazing hot sun with temperatures well up in the eighties, with three people who could cook to death in the vehicle if we didn't move within the next two hours!

"Lord what are you doing? You control the tides! What on earth do you want us to learn from this situation? What is your purpose?" I sank back into the seat unable to compute the situation in my brain.

"Paul, I'm going up as far as the bridge to see the Commander in that Warrior Tank sitting there."

Bracing myself, I marched along wearing what were dusty 'whites' carrying an official UN map. Without looking up at him, I proceeded to unroll the map resting it on the armoured vehicle. Pointing out the position of the bridge on the map, I said, "if we cross this bridge here and go over those mountains there, I think we will land up eventually in Mostar?"

"Yes, that is so," agreed the Commander, "but it is only open to UN personnel."

"Right! Good! So if we keep on this route here, and follow along there," I continued moving my fingers over the map, avoiding eye contact, "then we will come out in Mostar?"

"Yes, you are right." He agreed again. "There's already one convoy coming this way, so, if you wait about twenty minutes, we will be able to give you clearance." I couldn't believe my ears! It would seem he had moved according to my affirmations.

Back at the lorry we sat for twenty minutes with the hot sun blazing through the windscreen. Twenty…long…tense…minutes until we were given the signal to roll.

"Stop!" Ordered the soldier at the bridge. We held our breath.

"Our Commander wants to know if you can give this man a lift? He is a Muslim with papers who has been living in Sarajevo for four years. He's been sleeping under those lorries for four nights and he is trying to get back to Spain to be with his wife and child."

Relieved that was all he wanted, I hastened a reply.

"Paul, will you put our bags in the back? He can sit on the engine. It's a bit hot but he must be in the front with us." I said hoping, he would read between the lines. Thankfully, Paul was just happy that we were on our way to get some moving air into the cab so, without questioning, responded positively to my request. We could not afford for our new passenger or the UN to be anywhere near the back of the lorry.

It seemed the God of all creation who created the tides was this day very much ahead of our situation. The UN even phoned ahead to every checkpoint along the bumpy, four-hour route, that consequently every barrier was in the 'up position' on our approach. Again our way had miraculously been cleared.

"Mama Mia! Mama Mia! You lady, you my Mother, you save me! Mama Mia!" Our travelling companion went on and on, unable to believe his luck.

"Actually friend," I interjected putting the record straight. "Actually, God in Heaven sent you two rather grubby angels today, I know you wont believe me, but He loves you so much He sent two willing angels just for you…oh and incidentally, you have no idea just how much we appreciate Him sending you to us!"

All four of our charges were eventually deposited into relatively safe areas. Our 'Mama Mia friend' did make it back to Spain and Ricki was eventually re-united with his parents and his brother Denis. Ricki went on to graduate from Sheffield University having studied Mechanical Engineering.

Chapter 20

THE RETURN

By March 1996 Ljubica had decided to return to her former town Ilijas, a half-hour drive from Sarajevo which had been liberated from the Serbs under the Dayton agreement. Neither Paul nor I were happy with her decision and whilst we understood her reasons, we had grave concerns about her well being. The only thing, which gave us some comfort, was that she had well measured the teachings of Islam and Christianity and had made a commitment in her own heart to open herself in favour of recognising her need of a Saviour.

The whole experience had happened un-beknown to us in the back of a taxi one evening in Bradford. She had gone to the bus station to meet her two nephews who had been in hiding at her brother's home, whom we had met at the early part of the war. On hearing that the two young men were from Bosnia the taxi driver assumed that they must be Muslims. He then went on to describe the very calculating way in which he hoped that Islam would gradually infiltrate and overcome our 'Christian' society in England. Quite simply Ljubica measured the motives of his heart against what she had found were the motives of our hearts, and firmly decided that she wanted and was indeed, now ready to invite Jesus Christ into her own heart. By the following Sunday, she had come to our church and made a public confession of her testimony and faith.

Russ, her eldest son, was still in America having just graduated from Wittenberg University and Haris, the original boy at the fence whom we first met in 1992, stayed in England moving into our home. Along with our son Richard, the two boys brought much cheerful banter and joy into our lives as they teased Paul and I unmercifully most meal times. However, within a year of Ljubica's return both sons chose to follow her back to Bosnia as they felt the need to 'be there' to protect their mother after Hasan's tragic death.

With the little car piled high with personal luggage and three women, we safely arrived in Central Bosnia. The journey back to Sarajevo would necessitate Ljubica, Elaine and myself driving for nearly two more days over snow covered mountain tracks from Petrovac in our little old Polo. With lack of wisdom on my part, we had started the journey far too late in the day, the snow was still falling in soft flakes and we were soon to realise there was no way back over the treacherous single-track path.

More or less at the summit there was a Muslim checkpoint and we were confronted with the familiar words, "You go no further." We were inclined to agree, but knew we could not have turned the car around in the snow even if we wanted to and reversing with my spinal problem was out of the question. Ljubica to the rescue, turned on the charm.

"My friend's from England" she seemed to say, much to their delight.

"We big friend in England. Riad Terzic," was their enthusiastic response. Immediately we were home and dry, the boy under our mattress had been their school friend, and his fame had gone before us. God had again placed His angels in position, and we were allowed to take a route that was banned to all civilians at this time.

After two days travel we eventually arrived in what at best can only be described, as a scene of desolation, a town from a horror movie. The whole town

The views from the fully loaded Polo as Ljubica and Elaine, with Jackie driving, climbed the mountain track in order to reach Sarajevo.

was just a haunted concrete shell. Ljubica insisted on walking up the main street on her own as we followed in the car, trying to negotiate at snail's pace the holes left in the tarmac from exploding shells and grenades. Household rubbish was piled at least ten-foot high. Everything from pots and pans and broken dolls lay amongst the rotting, rain sodden personal effects. Every shop building on both sides of the main street was ransacked, burned or completely blown up. The further we followed the lady's footsteps the more one could feel her heart sink amongst the devastation. Were these the same streets, once lined with rose bushes where she had previously walked?

A little further on we were all delighted to find just one small coffee shop open. For the first time in my life I welcomed going into a smoke filled atmosphere, to meet the only inhabitants of the town. Ljubica clearly knew all the men present as personal friends. As befitting her status, she was being treated with due respect but, could these men stay close enough to protect her? Was this to be her home for the rest of her life? She had just left the security and relative comfort of England, to return to a town where she trusted she could make a real difference as a schoolteacher, in the rebuilding of the lives of the future children. But where could one woman start, with no income, and only the covering of her late husband's good name and memory?

It had been Hasan who had first instigated Haris and Safet asking for help from the English people. Now how could the English people be part of the rebuilding process?

Having absorbed the devastation and conferred with the men of the town, Ljubica was ready to face the fateful time of returning to what had been her own apartment home.

Elaine and I crawled out of the cramped car to join our friend on the grass verge outside her flat; only then, without her realising it we saw Ljubica was standing next to an unexploded shell. None of us panicked, taking the view that the shell had remained safe until we arrived and there was no reason to suppose our presence would activate it now. Elaine and I made eye contact. Were we already beginning to catch the 'that's just the way it is' disease?

In trepidation we climbed the filthy, urine soaked cold concrete steps. Although it was out of context Ljubica's front door was still in place and still on its hinges. The flat even had a claim of ownership in Hasan's name, by order of the town's Police pinned to the door. Slowly we dared to enter. The whole place was desecrated. Every piece of furniture had either been destroyed or used as a toilet. Her kitchen had been completely ripped out, and every piece of sanitary ware in her bathroom had been smashed to pieces. Even the water pipes had been ripped out, with every electric switch ripped from the walls along with all connected wiring.

We moved in a state of shock into the second bedroom. The scene was made all the more personal as we spotted Haris's school report from five years earlier, still on the windowsill. The only possession left from what had been a comfortable home and affluent life style.

How could we leave our friend here? But leave her we must. All her bridges back to England had been burned. This was to be her new life. No man to protect her, no real home, no income, her only comfort the comfort of the Saviour within her own heart. If ever she needed a friend in Jesus, she needed him now.

It ripped us apart to leave her in such circumstances, but if we were to be of any help to her and the other thousands who may return, then we knew the work needed to go on.

The area when Ljubica returned to start her new life in Bosnia.

Chapter 21

THE FORMATION OF THE HOLY GROUND MISSION

For nearly a year and a half I had been writing and re writing the Ricki part of this story, whilst at the same time Paul and I had continued our 3,000 mile round trips, made possible by the support of an ever growing body of people back home.

There was a stage when I thought the book was finished until a lady in Ireland said on reading the draft manuscript, "Well yes, but what has happened since? Come on Jackie, there must be more, I have an instinct that you haven't even begun to tell the real story yet."

How could I answer the Irish lady's question since the story was still being lived?

Paul and I believe, it is not enough to play ones part at a time when the war situation is high profile. Indeed, it takes the extra quality of endurance to continue in the long term rebuilding process long after the media hype has ceased.

I know that I am not in a position in 1999 to write the final chapter of the work which Paul and I have been privileged to pioneer. I expect somewhere in the future we can only live it. So instead, I'll try and bring this very small portion of God's story up to date with the events from March 1996.

At least for the moment, gone is the emergency work of those war years and gradually over a period of time, we found ourselves more and more moved towards strengthening our support base in order to extend the arm of our calling.

For two years Eileen, my prayer partner, and latterly Elaine, a retired school teacher, had spent much time spiritually listening and working through the 'inner nudges' until we believed that we had understood many of the lessons we were being taught. We carefully measured our experiences and then checked them through with the word of God.

Given we needed to return to England to raise the necessary help, it was there we quite simply told of the need and trusted God to move hearts in support.

Thanks to the ongoing financial gifts from all manner of people within our neighbourhood, schools and local churches, within two months we were able to return to Ljubica and her people.

Again we completed the fifteen hundred miles over land and sea, and this time with two full lorries, seven other vehicles, and twenty-one people all armed with paintbrushes, school equipment, food, general aid and a lot of talent and energy, willing to give generously.

In the following four-week period, ten rooms were painted in the maternity block of the hospital at Petrovac. Three large rooms in the secondary school at Ilijas, and five rooms in a small school where Ljubica was about to start teaching. Today in that same town there are approximately 2,000 children and 7,000 people mostly refugees from Srebrenicia and Zepa towns which saw unbelievable atrocities. These people may look normal, but each person has their own inner scars, which are unlikely to heal until a climate of forgiveness comes into play. Given the political history of the country, that could be centuries away, which makes the need for witnessing with our lives the gospel message, so much more important.

To that end little did we realise that another piece on the chessboard was coming into play. At the time of distributing food, clothes and shoes from the back of our lorry, I managed to pull a child on board who was being crushed in the surge of excitement. To my shame, I became conscious of taking a pace backwards, as the smell from the little one hit me. Immediately I looked around for clean clothes to fit him, but everything we had on board was too small. In passing a food box outside we discovered the child was with his elderly grandfather who had been doing his best to look after him since all three of his sons had been separated in the war.

The following day, after much reconnaissance, Ljubica, Elaine and I were at the the Mayor's office.

"Please give us that building for God's work." I was referring to a building, which had been a Medical Centre before the war. Although badly damaged, in my mind's eye, I could already see the building fitted ready for children. In fact it would provide a home for one particular child and his grandfather, who I definitely knew needing bathing.

The eighteen-roomed building had neither windows nor doors, no water pipes or electricity; all the wiring had been ripped out. It had no toilets or sanitation of any kind, yet still I could see its wonderful potential. "How can I give you that building?" The small sincere man protested against my onslaught.

"Who else will bathe that child if we don't?" I continued with no punches spared. The poor man had his finger to the temple of his head, trying to make sense of what was being asked, so he enquired further. "What makes you people tick? I hear many good things about you, but I don't understand you." Now scratching his head trying to work through his own thoughts. "Before the war I was a Godly man." the Mayor continued. "My wife died in my arms, then the war came, and I went to the front line.... and killed many. Now," bowing his head with tears in his eyes…in repentance. "Now I don't know what to do."

The mission building in Ilijas: before and after refurbishment.

Immediately my tone changed; gently and quietly I continued to speak: "Thankfully God knew your heart and we have come to bring you and the people of your town good news." I began to speak with an anointing that could only have come from the Holy Spirit. Elaine began to pray in support. The presence of God began to fill the ugly room.

"You are not proud of what you have done. You have a humble heart. Well, the Jesus we serve has died on the cross for all our sins and our Heavenly Father wants only for us to accept him into our hearts to receive complete forgiveness. Would you like us to pray with you?" I dared to ask. Ljubica interpreting took a big breath. I could see she found the whole conversation quite an unequivocal experience to be happening right in the heart of Islam. We continued as the Spirit of God gave utterance as the humble man opened his heart and prayed for forgiveness. He asked Jesus Christ to become his personal Saviour. We were to learn later that this man had been one of the chief leaders in the local mosque before the war.

Eventually the Mayor came to learn that we were the English people whom he had heard about, who had driven an ambulance to the front line, as a gift to his regiment. He also discovered it was Paul and I who had brought bandages in the boot of a car, right in the middle of the fighting. Apparently the Mayor knew first hand that those few bandages had served to save many of his friends lives. We also came to see that those two simple acts, would become the cement in the foundations, for us to serve in the town. Six months later we were leased the building.

Paul and I became the founder members of the Holy Ground Mission. A pioneering Missionary Society, which would give lay people like us, the opportunity to discover and work out our own faith, whilst at the same time serving within a structure, which is seeking to be faithful to the new testament pattern.

We each began to develop in new ways through the work and witness, and as usual all growth was painful. One of the first battles we needed to confront was our own unworthiness as leaders. We needed to look carefully at our own personal call in discipleship and balance that with the perceived understanding within the structured church of how leaders are ordained. The question of administering communion out in the mission field was an area I needed personally to feel comfortable with before the Lord. It was then, that I heard about a candidate for ordination who was asked by the credentials committee, "Would you be disappointed if we did not ordain you this year?" He replied. "Oh no, God has already ordained me, he's just waiting for you guys to get the paperwork done."

With that point settled and our commissioning service behind us, we decided to send out an edited version of the writings of C.T.Studd 1861-1931 founder of the World Evangelisation Crusade.

Whilst we in the Mission were **not** making an attack on the Established Church we were certainly moved at the time against the apathy which we "Christians" sometimes give out as spiritual confetti. The cliché's help us to sit more comfortably unmoved against Satan's negative, thought provoking attack within ourselves, our families, our marriages they perpetuate the constant evil which we continually label as somebody else's fault. We are our society and we can so easily be tools in Satan's hands. If as missionaries and Co-workers we are to be effective in our calling then we need to be vigilant first in confession of our own sin. Sin is first about ownership, taking responsibility and accountability. There can be no escape against the final judgement.

Charles wrote:-

Christ's call is to feed the hungry, not the full: To save the lost not the stiff-necked; not to call scoffers but sinners to repentance.

Not to build and furnish comfortable churches in which to rock Christian professors to sleep, by means of stereotyped prayers and artistic musical performances, but to raise up living churches of souls from amongst the destitute.

To capture men from the devil's clutches and snatch them from the very jaws of hell, to enlist them into an Almighty Army of God.

This can only be accomplished by a red-hot Holy Ghost religion where neither Church, State or traditions are worshiped or preached but only Christ and Him Crucified.

It's experience not preaching that hurts the devil and confounds the world.

The training is not that of the schools but of the market place.

It's the hot free heart that knocks the devil out. Nothing than fork-lightening

Christians will count. A lost reputation is the best degree for Christ's sake.

The difficulty is to believe that God can use scallywags as us, but of cause he wants faith and fools rather than talents and culture.

All God wants is a heart any old turnip will do for a head, so long as we are empty for then He fills us with the Holy Ghost.

Nail your colours of Christ to the mast and do it now! For the sake of the work He has given us to do, the evangelisation of the unevangelised.

Christ does not want nibblers of the possible... but grabbers of the impossible by faith and wisdom from the Almighty Saviour who gave the command.

Is there a wall in our path?...Then leap over it.
Are there loins and scorpions in our way?...We will trample them underfoot!
Soldiers of Jesus! Never surrender! Nail your colours to the mast!

Can we listen to these words of an African pastor and will we make them ours?

"I'm part of the fellowship of the unashamed. The die has been cast because I've already stepped over the line. I'm a disciple of His and won't look back, let up, slow down, back away or be still.

My past is redeemed, my present makes sense and my future is secure. I am finished with low living, sight walking, small planning, colourless dreams, and cheap living with dwarfed goals.

I no longer need pre-eminence, plaudits or popularity. I don't have to be right, first, tops, praised, regarded or rewarded. I now live by faith, walk by patience, lift my prayers and labour in His power.

I wont give up, shut up, let up, until I have stayed up, stored up, prayed up, paid up and preached up the cause of Christ. I must go till He comes, give till I drop. Preach till all know, and work till He stops me. And when he comes for His own, He'll have no problem recognising me-for my banner will be clear.

Today the Mission Centre is an oasis in the middle of a spiritual desert. It is a home for many children who are fed and clothed daily. It is a Humanitarian Aid Distribution Centre for over two thousand of the town's inhabitants, hardly any of whom have work. In addition, it is a home for the dying where the Gospel message is preached through our daily lives.

Even today it still seems an impossible task that so few people could have established a Mission Centre in Ilijas, whilst at the same time continuing to commute back to England, in order to raise the financial support for the ongoing work. With no Government or official funding, the missions' work is still run on faith. We know every gift given to keep the work of the mission operational, is a direct result of God moving the hearts of *His* people… and for that we continue to praise *Him!*

Continuously over the years, one cry would always be heard from our lips. "Lord send us your people with hearts like Lions, who are sold out for Jesus." We realise that the gospel message can only be brought alive as the Spirit of God moves through the faith of *His* people in action.

However we must be vigilant. One of the dangers is that we become distracted from our first call of taking the gospel message, by endeavouring to fulfil the physical work with too few hands; we could become a blunt sword.

The daily work has been, and no doubt will continue to be, extremely exacting. These extracts from our Day Logs show why we need 'sold out' long-term missionaries:

Friday, May 16, 1997. JR

The physical work on the building is hard, mostly for the men. Paul and Frank have spent their first weeks in this building, without windows or doors, battling against the cold. They wash their paintbrushes in the melted snow off the side of the hill. However, there is no greater battle than trying to get through the oppressing bureaucracy. The customs officials want the weight of every knife, fork and spoon recording and considering the lorry's six ton load, there is no way we are prepared to play that game.

The whole system has a root of fear, a few keeping control over the masses. It seems nobody will take final responsibility for saying yes. The goal posts are constantly moved, and it seems, the game is to send a person from one department to another until one is worn down into complete submission, and simply gives up.

I'm confident that if we can get established, the work of the mission can come into its own. It is desperately needed for the 'little people' at the bottom of the line where little free help ever penetrates.

We must keep alert to the wiles of the enemy because right from the start we are challenging Satan's stronghold. It is easy to buckle under the pressure of a lot of people who think they have the right to demand their needs be met. Victory can only be won through prayer, patience and endurance. It is a time to dig in and hold the line.

Saturday, May 17, 1997. JR

It's 2. 30 a.m. Having slept, I continue to lie on my bed wrestling with the demons of darkness. With this machine writing has become my emotional outlet. It's where I can lay down all my thoughts as if on an open table.

Afternoon: *One very thin lady along with a 10 ten-year-old boy has come for any help she can get. I suspect she has come for money. Both are riddled with fleas. She is like someone out of Belson and I suspect with a drink problem, which is confirmed later. I invite them both for a meal, she indicates all she eats comes back up. I know she is right. How can we help? I feel a million miles away, but in a moment our eyes meet and she senses my heart. Tears are softly shed; new warmth permeates the whole building, she is much loved.*

Monday, May 19, 1997. JR

To our real joy two, grubby children appear for the second time. They are happy to be washed and fitted with new socks and shoes, and receive a second dose of vitamins. We are in desperate need of flea powder for them. I don't think the customs will allow me back into England unless we get this problem solved or I spend six months in quarantine. As the shower is not yet fitted we bath them outside in the sun. They have faces of Angels and I love them already.

Meho is one of those children who, when he gives you a smile speaks volumes. In just two days I have seen him blossom from a frightened little mouse into an impish happy child. He is already established well into all our affections.

Meho -with his new bicycle from England.

May 21, 1997. JR

I have discovered a British Police officer. What a joy to meet the people who are doing the real work at ground floor level. He is going to have a word with a Gunman counterpart. He told me to expect Flea powder at 9 a.m. tomorrow. I would not have believed I could have got excited about anything so mundane.

July 8, 1997 On Duty Pete and JR

Pete has taken glasses up the hill to complete yesterday's commitment. His morning was a great success. He went on a visit to take shoes, bread, and tomatoes. Boots for another man and glasses for Tomo the man with the stroke. Just a few pairs of glasses tucked in my personal luggage have gone a long way. Pete also had a good time of ministry with the man in the wheelchair. I thank God for him.

It is raining and we are besieged with about 40 children. Ladies from yesterday are insisting on receiving everything. They hover. I am sad to say greed not need, exists. I openly pray in front of them. Tongues are a powerful gift in such situations. I feel I need six pairs of hands.

We are asked to visit a lady who is near to death. She has open wounds; I clean them and do my best. We are pleased to see she is much loved by her family.

Afternoon. *We visit a camp fifty miles away, of refugees whom we have been looking after for three years. Just to see their faces was a joy. By the time we return we are very tired and decide on light food.*

10 p.m. *Ljubica arrives in heavy rain to say she has been trying to calm her neighbour and can we help. The lady is a Serb. She claims someone is trying to kill her. (Not surprising she is frightened. She is one of only a handful of Serbs in town.) She says she wants to see her children just once before she dies. We have contacted* *both children. Neither are prepared to come. She stayed in the mission last night; I sat in her room quietly singing until the early hours.*

August 3, 1997. Tina.

A Soldier from the Bosnia Army came to thank Paul and the Mission for helping the children in Ilijas, especially his sister's daughter who is now ill in hospital. He was on the front line during the war and despite all the horrors, he came across as a gentle good-hearted man. A deep thinker, not bitter but philosophical. He feels the soldiers have recovered very quickly from their experiences of war and the recovery would be even quicker if the economy was in a better state. He expressed the view that during the war they had a focus to survive, now there is no focus, no goals, and no purpose. Living here is like walking constantly on a rumbling earthquake.

December 19, 1997. JR

What an unbelievable morning. After a very deep time of communion with our Precious Lord it was as if the gates of Heaven opened. People flooded in for help, yet in an uncharacteristically ordered way. They had so many varied needs yet the Holy Spirit totally ministered His wonderful grace and presence. So much deep healing. If this were my only day here in the Mission Centre for the rest of my life, then I would be satisfied. It was just as if all I had to do was raise my hands in adoration of Him and He sent down the rivers of healing love.

Tina, one of our missionaries, with Meho helping at the Mission desk.

At one time there must have been 12 people in the room all waiting expectantly and no one went away wanting or disappointed. The Holy Spirit ministered in full power. His presence was confirmed by the fact that at the same time of ministry there must have been over 40 children playing happily feet away and another 19 adults came in for spectacles.

One lady came for pills for anxiety, depression and the like. I refused saying I would not give her a plaster to cover the blockage within. Everyone else sat around stunned. Some nodded in agreement, especially one very young lady, whom I am told is an alcoholic. For two hours she has just sat here and fed off the teaching, which I was able to share. Silver and gold have I none but in the name of Jesus Christ ... receive.

The wonderful thing about this work is; one does not have to be wise, wealthy or clever, anyone can step out in whatever amount of faith they possess and be channels of blessing for his neighbour.

Monday, January 12, 1998. JR

A slow start to the day because of the black smog, which hangs over the town, like a thick blanket. The cold, grey day is brightened by the children's laughter coming from our playroom. I am pleased that one mother has remembered to bring her daughter for her second dose of worm medicine.

The people begin to be drawn into the warmth of this building, most gathering around my desk as if it were a magnet. Some come just to sit and absorb the atmosphere, others come to lay just a little more of their grief out to be heard and held. Some come with hope that this place may be the answer to their prayers.

One old man wait's about an hour for the opportunity to show me a photograph of his son whom he lost in the war. An average good-looking 14-year-old boy in his blue and white football strip. It's easy to be with him.

A young couple came with their year old son trusting they could have ongoing help. The Mother is nine months pregnant yet looks only six months because of malnutrition. I give them a cot, blankets, sheets, nappies, pins, rubber pants, baby clothes, talc, vaseline, shampoo all their Christmases at once, but before they leave, I lift a pair of scissors and mime to the young husband a certain operation. The ladies gathered... smile in agreement.

A well-dressed young lady asks for some help for a certain problem. I take a breath and count age on my side as an asset. In the middle of it all a tidy middle aged man comes in quite urgently wanting to be seen. We take him in to our little medical room where we discover his back badly burned. He says he had a fit and fell onto an electric fire a week ago. The whole area of flesh is charred and by this time well infected. The name Jesus comes out of my lips as I quietly wonder about the pain he has already been through without help.

"You must go to doctors I advise." He laughs a soft laugh at my stupidity.

"No money, no doctor" he replies embarrassed. We do our best.

In five hours I have witnessed the varied spectrum of colourful human nature. It is here to be discovered, experienced and tenderly carried each morning of the week.

"Jackie, cuppa tea?"

"Yes please" is my natural response as I wonder why I am feeling so drained when it's only two o' clock.

Chapter 22

THE BIRTH OF HOSPICE CARE IN BOSNIA

By March 1998 a doctor from the local medical centre was asking if we would take in two cancer patients for care. I knew right from the very beginning, we would all be in for a steep new learning curve, and I would probably be called upon to walk the extra mile, but I also knew
... *'His grace would be sufficient.'*

Immediately the local paid staff went into revolt from their fears and prejudices. If I would dare to take these people into the mission, they certainly would not go into the same room and clean. Regardless of the verbal pressure from the local staff, beds were moved and prepared for the new arrivals, everything was well in place.

By mid-afternoon we were ready to receive our first patients. The first was half way up the path on a stretcher before my attention was called to supervise the blanket covered lump that was to reveal an emaciated skeleton, curled up in the foetal position. I took a deep breath to find the inner strength and authority, which went into action straight away. The hospital staff were delighted and most reassured, which in turn gave me the much-needed encouragement.

The second man Shefco, walked in wearing his Sunday suit with a huge lump on the side of his neck. Immediately I knew him. He had been in before and I recognised him as the man who waited to show me the photograph of one of his sons. I had seen his inner dignity and respected the way he had quietly observed life around him. This man runs deep and I was sure we would get on well together.

Ljubica was quite rightly concerned as to how I would cope alone at night and urged me to find a trained nurse to help.

"No Ljubica, I need to discover what is needed first. Give me just one night, then I will know so very much more and will be able to decide which way to move."

I instinctively knew the first thing I needed to do was to make some real contact with the first soul who had come in on the stretcher. I knelt on my knees by his bed to be at his level, so I could make eye contact. As I stroked his face he opened his eyes; a way out look at first, then it happened, we connected and he knew he was safe. I saw the twinkle in his eye.

We need twice as many pillows in the building, I thought, and if we had backrests, then that would make things a lot easier. Thankfully I knew just the right man in England. I was sure Mr. Todd, one of our staunch supporters, would soon make some designed like deck chairs.

The town's chief nurse came to fit the drips trying to use our overhead heating pipes instead of a medical stand, but with the collapsed veins she finally had to give in and fetch a precious stand from their meagre level of equipment. Next came the catheter for the urine and I have to say I was more than delighted to have to empty a bag, rather than sleep next to what I knew was the special smell reserved to take away man's dignity.

The whole exercise seemed to take hours before our new arrivals were a little more comfortable and it looked safe enough for me to dare try for some sleep in the next room.

The next three nights became an education. No one interested in human nature should be without these experiences. I already knew that within most male bodies there is a little boy still trying to get his mother's attention. It was truly amazing to me, how even when one was at death's door, racked with pain, unable to move off a bed, one could find so many ways of testing the love of a complete stranger. But test it he did, systematically over the next three nights.

I soon discovered I needed to lay down all my stuff about hospital corners on sheets. The smooth sheets were pulled straight off along with the protective rubber by the patient. I decided to give in gracefully and wrap the skeleton covered with skin in a duvet and pretend I had been that wise in the first place. At the same time, I removed the lighter, which had been hidden under the pillow to accompany the much-needed national drug. Yet, by 2 a.m. my suspicions were well founded as I followed my nose. Yes, between them they had managed to beat the system. Four dog ends had been stubbed out onto the bedside cabinet.

"You naughty boy," came out of my mouth almost like a verbal torrent of gushing water, but in a flash I knew it was only a game, and I had better let them win.

"I'll have your tail off for you if you don't watch out," knowing full well neither could understand a word I was saying, but I was sure they both knew something I didn't.

All through the night, at a rate of every 15 minutes, I continued to stumble out of bed in the dark, trying to find the elusive slipper and the sleeve of the dressing gown, which always seemed to get inside out.

Morning brought perfect sleep to the two babes and strangely enough I was not at all tired, which is what I had expected of my nature.

As one particular member of Bosnian staff arrived, I knew I was headed for trouble the moment she came in through the door. She did not see why she should have to look after old men and proceeded to carry the rest of the team with her.

"What's your real problem?" I tried to encourage getting at the truth.

"I don't want to be near them. We could catch what they have. I'm scared" she blurted.

"Now, that's understandable. However, tell me, what would you have me do with these men, let them die alone?" I confronted, as gently as I could but without compromise, I knew however, the balance had been lost in the routine. I chose to understand her fears but, why was I not surprised when the doctor came and the infusions would not go in through the veins?

All along I could sense the anger in our second patient. Anger he was well justified in feeling having witnessed his wife being burnt alive by his neighbour along with his two cows and home. How could we not love him and comfort him as best we were able?

I believed the ladies would rise to the new situation. I had seen their hearts, and somehow, I was going to pick them up and carry them for a while, at least until the dust settled.

Saturday night brought very much the same pattern from the men. Constant groaning from one in deep pain and a continual need for the spittoon from the other. Meanwhile, in the dark I tried my best to rustle the sheets over my ears at the appointed moments of release.

Next, from my bed I could hear strange ripping sounds coming from the sick room. Quietly I waited hoping for a clue as to the new test that was being set before me. The sounds from the room quietened; I crept in to see if I could guess the new game. In the dark I could clearly see something, white? The little Tyke had systematically pulled fifty rubber gloves out of a new box, and I presume, joyfully scattered them over the floor as far as his strength would allow. I could not believe anybody in that condition could be so mischievous. No, I would not blow. This was only a test, a mere game.

Smiling inside I snuggled down into my small bed for prayer. I claimed every inch of ground in Jesus name. God rained his grace down from heaven and gave me such an overflowing love for these men. Victoriously I claimed them for the Kingdom of Heaven for all eternity. Nothing would break my love for them, regardless of how much they tried to set me up.

Sunday was physically hard and the constant night duty after long days was beginning to take its toll. I did the best I could with a Sunday service in between constant sick room duty and wondered where the rest of the churches were.

Early Monday morning I was beckoned over to the bed. My little boy was hungry. Could I believe, at 4.20 in the morning and almost without a breath in his body,… he wanted… bread? I fetched the manna and sat and watched as he ate like someone half starved to death on earth but who was now at the banquet of heaven.

"Have I just seen what I have seen?" I was sure this was the supernatural strength, which comes before death. Rather like a pregnant woman getting a burst of energy and cleaning the house just before labour pains begin. I could of course be wrong, so I listened astutely for the rest of the night.

Morning brought the usual constant stream of people needing food and medical help. By 11.30 a.m. I had dealt with twenty-four requests for food to everybody's complete satisfaction.

Then a social worker came to check upon our patients. Shamefully both Ljubica and I bloomed with pride at how strong our first soul was getting, describing some of the antics of the previous night. Still with pride and satisfaction, we walked confidently into the room.

"Come on treasure. What are you doing down in the bed like that?" I moved to straighten him up. His hand was on the side rail as if he was trying to get up. I stopped in my tracks as Ljubica's words penetrated my skull.

"He's dead."

She's right, I thought, but disbelieved my own eyes. Slowly I moved to stroke his forehead, then fell to my knees to look at him from a different angle in the hope that with a change of direction, the view might reveal a different picture. Then as if programmed, I walked quietly around to the other side of the bed and put on rubber gloves without even thinking. I straightened him up whilst at the same time beckoning to the other patient to leave the room and against my principles, go and have a cigarette.

We closed down the reception and made sure the children were all safely out of view to all the comings and goings. One of the ladies immediately came forward and helped me lay out the body in the nice clean sheet, which we had put on the bed only half an hour before.

"I'm so glad we had put a lovely new shirt on him. Didn't he look sweet?" I rejoiced that my little boy was going home looking smart.

Alone, I said my farewells. Again, I claimed his Soul entreating the Father's mercy in Jesus name. I did not know what else to do except take time for a silent personal tear.

Bedtime brought a flood of loneliness for me. In much physical pain, I climb into bed. Where was Paul? Fifteen hundred miles away. The best I could do was to get his dressing gown off the back of the door, put it around my back and pull the sleeve over my shoulder for a bit of comfort at the end of the day. The one thing of which I was sure, the little Tyke did know something I didn't know. He had succeeded to get right under my skin, and he had made his way straight into this old heart, that Jesus gave.

By August 1998 we had an urgent call from Bosnia because our second cancer patient was in the final stages and desperately needed pain relief. We are ever thankful at the wonderful way in which our mighty God moved at that dreadful time.

I sat in front of my open Bible with my heart tumbling out thoughts not whether knowing if I could even put together words that could convey the need out in Bosnia for that one poor man and many thousands like him.

My own logic and torrents of thoughts felt irresponsible at the least. My brain was telling me... "You can't just up sticks and fly to the other side of the world in response to every need." Yet, I knew deep in my heart the sin would be... not to take some action.

At that moment I could only do as I had done in the past, that was to lay out the problem openly, then trust the Father to move the chess pieces in that current situation.

By eight o' clock that night I had an unprecedented urge to go and collect some work from a lady who had previously offered help, but who had been restricted because she had needed to nurse her brother who had just died of cancer.

Paul suggested that we eat first but I knew that I would be weak enough not to want to bother to respond to the quickening in my spirit if I dared to sit down and relax.

When we arrived, without either of us saying a single word about Bosnia or Shefco's situation, the lady in question went up stairs to fetch a big bag. To our amazement she began to lay out boxes of Morphine onto the coffee table in front of us. We both knew that in six years of taking hundreds of tons of medical aid, nobody had ever given us any Morphine. Only God in His infinite mercy could have brought this urgent help into our hands.

The following morning I checked with the police and then acquired the relevant clearance from the Home Office. By mid morning one of our missionaries Hilary, who had been on compassionate leave awaiting an operation, had phoned to say she had discovered that she had been missed off the waiting list, and that she had

Shefco on her heart over the last week. She had wondered why this should be. When I was able to share the current situation with her, straight away she made herself available. (Hilary was the only one amongst us at that time, who was qualified to administer the relevant drugs.)

That same night four of us moved into the presence of our Heavenly Father in prayer. We all agreed that as God had provided the morphine without us telling anybody of the need, then we could trust Him to provide the cost of the airfare to get Hillary with it, out to Shefco.

Having been challenged (tongue in cheek) by Paul the previous night for my lack of faith, I actually decided to book the ticket by phone first thing the following morning. While I still had the receiver in my hand, Paul having opened the mail rushed up the stairs to my desk with an air of excitement and triumph. He calmly put a cheque in front of me received from a blessed lady in Sheffield who knew nothing about the situation. She had been moved in her heart to give the mission half of her holiday money because she had not felt the need to go away.

Such blessedness! Such love!

What can we say but, "Lord we love you... you blow our minds, your love is more precious than silver or gold?" Can you imagine a God who cares that much about just one man in the middle of Bosnia? A God who thinks that man is precious enough to move heaven and earth to show His love for him and then in His grace to do it through people like us? Can we help but love Him?

I write this next testimony to share that no situation is impossible for a God who cares:

By mid summer 1998 we were sent a 'minder' in the form of a gentle giant who had been born in Sarajevo thirty-six years previously. He could speak German and English. His mother had taken him to Germany when he was eight years old, after his father had been killed on a railway line.

He hadn't been in Germany long before the eight-year-old found himself in bad company. Over the twenty-eight years he started taking drugs and eventually as an adult found he was waking up from a drug overdose in prison.

The German authorities decided to deport him back to Bosnia as he only had a Bosnian passport. He found himself with all his worldly possessions, in two cardboard boxes under his arms, standing at Sarajevo airport in shock, unable to believe the devastation before him.

In time he was given a room and a mattress by the authorities, but he soon became hungry. Again he went to the authorities for help and a social worker told him to go and steal if he needed food.

Back in his room he looked out of the window onto the market place below and was tempted to go and steal food. Instead, he prayed to the God who gave him life, to take it from him and let him die. Not realising God had heard his cry he went for a walk around the town, passed the mission building, and noticed Paul coming out whistling a song of praise. Approaching Paul, he asked for work. Paul, sensing a deep need, asked him to knock a small hole in a wall to make a hatch between the kitchen and a proposed new Hospice unit. Paul then paid the gentle giant, by giving him sugar, coffee, milk and a tin of corned beef to take home and prayed with him.

A week later I arrived and naturally invited the gentle giant for a meal where both Paul and I were able to share how he could have a clean slate and be forgiven of

Juso - dealing with some of our mothers who visit the Mission for help.

all his past sin. Tenderly he wept like a babe, spewing out all his pain until exhausted. Very gently we were able to pick him up and stand him on Holy Ground. Our friend Juso, now works in the mission and is fast becoming a great man of God serving whoever he is able in the name of Jesus.

We don't know who gave us that corned beef but we do know God used it in a mighty way.

One day our regular taxi driver came to ask if we would consider taking in his recently widowed neighbour. Apparently the man had suffered a stroke six weeks earlier and although paralysed down one side, had just been returned home to an empty flat, after six weeks in hospital. The taxi driver heard him crying for two nights and came to the mission for help.

For a further three weeks we cared for and nursed the neighbour until he died in peace. The dying man said to one of the staff, "I knew I was safe when they wiped the tears from my eyes."

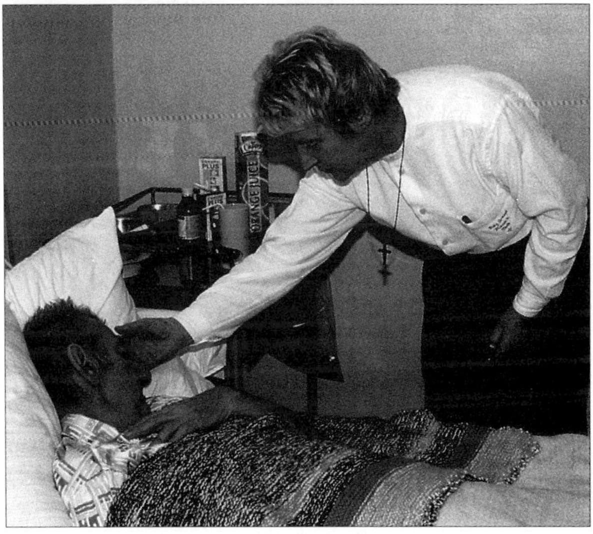

Checking on a patient in the Mission's Hospice Unit.

We took in a lady with a brain tumour, who was screaming in pain because of the lack of suitable medication. Another eighteen stone lady was only with us six days before she died, and an elderly, frail Nanna, who was on the streets with nowhere to live says, she hopes she will never have to leave the mission....unless it is in a wooden box!

In contrast, I looked into the face of a man one day who was beaming with joy.

"Would you mind if I took your photograph?" I enquired, as I wanted to record his beauty.

"Go and tell the world what God has done for me." He pleaded with a smile, so big it would have thawed an iceberg.

God's healing touch encouraged us all in the Mission.

"No problem, you can do as you want as long as you tell the world just what God has done for me." For two years this man had attended hospital, his body racked with pain, his hands and arms covered in sores. He said he felt like a leper when the doctors told him they could do nothing more to help.

"Tell me how far do you walk to come here each day for prayer care?"

"Six miles, but I would willingly walk twenty."

Such was the delight of the humble man sitting in front of me. As I looked into his face I could see the obvious joy. This man had been without hope when he stumbled into the mission building. But when God chose to heal him as encouragement to all of us, He did not take into account our lack of medical experience. He only proved faithful to His own word through faith in the name of Jesus Christ. *'The Spirit of the Lord is upon me. Because the Lord has anointed me; He has sent me to heal the broken hearted; to proclaim liberty to the captives; and the opening of the prison to those who are bound, to proclaim the acceptable year of the Lord.'*

We have since received a 9-year-old refugee boy, from Kosovo into the Hospice unit. This young child along with his family was homeless living in a refugee camp. The young boy one-day went outside the compound and had a car accident, which sadly put him in a coma with the need to be drip-fed. After a time in hospital the medical profession said they could do no more for him. Their prognosis was; the child would not live much more than a further couple of months, so he was brought to the mission for care.

At the time of publishing this book it is six months later and we are praising God that the child is going on from strength to strength. So for all who send financial gifts, please know your sacrifice is really appreciated, needed and goes direct to actually keeping the 'House of Love' in Bosnia operational for all these people.

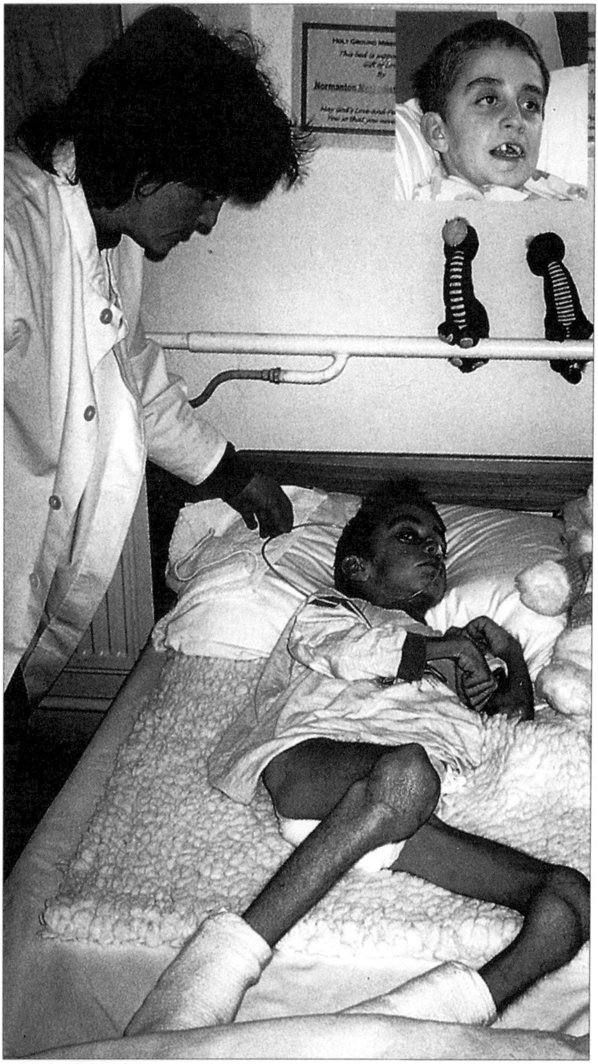

This Kosovar refugee came to the Mission in a coma, having been given only two months to live.

Praise be to God that he left a few months later with a smile on his face again.

Today in 1999 the phone calls come in.

"How is the work going on out there?" That seems like a simple enough question, but I wish the answer were as easy.

I believe the whole area of the Balkans is probably one of the greatest mission challenges of our time. With the vacuum left after the breakdown of Communism, and various political and religious groups fighting for power, it is not surprising the whole area of the Balkans has become one of the world's toughest spiritual battlefields.

Bosnia is a bit like an iceberg. There are more dangers lurking under the water than one can first see. This bureaucratic, legalistic pool is the home of some of the world's most damaged people. These people are not only war victims still nursing deep unhealed scars but they are also social victims trapped in a power struggle between extreme nationalism and the mighty advance of unseen darkness.

The average man in the street, is trying to survive in this furtive breading ground where control is gained by using one of Satan's greatest tools...fear. Fear coupled with a sense of hopelessness can totally control or immobilise the strongest of men. Add to that a nation, where the largest percentage of families relies on a small social payment. One can then begin to understand why people still walk around in a demonic stupor, using every available means possible to survive, regardless of whom else they are depriving.

Missionaries, planting the seeds of forgiveness in the name of Jesus Christ are teaching the Holy Word of God right in the midst of the lion's den, whilst at the same time trying to chip away at the mountain of poverty.

Our calling does not win popularity, because it challenges the strongholds of the powers of darkness. It is without doubt front line spiritual warfare all the way.

Sadly, we often need to pass through the valley of grief before our hearts are pliable enough to become the channels of healing unto the nations.

It is easy to see that this handful of worn out workers in the "Holy Ground Mission" needs your ongoing prayer support. We want you to know how vital the part, you who pray, play in this mission's work. You may find yourself one day asking:

"When did we feed you...clothe you...visit you...Lord?" And Jesus will answer. "When you did it unto the least of mine...you did it unto me."

Can you imagine how heartened I was during one Sunday service? After I had, as simply as possible, given a gospel message, I asked the children to draw a picture about what they had heard. One little boy Dennis drew a cross, with people positioned around the base of it, and a big bag hanging from off the cross members.

"What's that big bag hanging on the cross Dennis?"

"It's a bag of sin," he said triumphantly.

"Well that's a big bag of sin for one small boy." I gently teased.

"Jackie don't be silly. It's not all my sin." My eyes filled.

I turned to the second boy and his picture. Again the picture was of a cross but this time there was a wreath of flowers draped over it.

"Please tell me what does your picture mean?"

"Well Jackie. The flowers are a 'thank you' for what Jesus did for all of us."

Finally the highlight came for Paul, Juso and I when we responded to a request by the Mayor of the town, to visit a man in the final stages of cancer. His grown up Muslim sons were in denial of his impending death, unwilling to be open on the subject. I could see this denial was holding the father in a further place of pain.

After weeks of daily visits, we eventually grasped the opportunity and asked for the privilege of praying with the father. He was delighted.

"Heavenly Father we thank you and praise you for this man's life." "Amen," he interjected.

"Lord we thank you for giving him the blessing of wonderful children and grandchildren." "Amen," he responded for the second time.

"And Lord, we want to ask that you will send the comfort of your Holy Spirit to his wife, giving her strength at this time." "Amen." He was now getting quite excited as the presence of God filled the room.

"And Lord, Heavenly Father, we really want to thank you, that you loved us so much, that you stood by as your only son was crucified on the cross for all our sins." With that his voice resounded in a mighty, "Amen!"

I don't know how close that came to a sinner's prayer but I do know the peace and happiness, which filled that home.

Just in case all the blessings mentioned in this book are not enough, and as a postscript to *'His story'* we would like to share with you our own Cinderella story.

Last year a lovely girl called Rachelle volunteered three months of time to serve in the Mission's 'House of Love' near Sarajevo. There in the town she met and fell in love with Haris our 'boy at the fence.'

This August 1999 just as this book will be going to print, God willing Paul and I will have the great privilege and joy, to stand with Ljubica in England to witness what for us will be the wedding of the year.

Isn't our Heavenly Father wonderful? Only He could have written such a perfect script confirming, Gods word…

Rachelle and Haris on their wedding day in England,
August, 1999.
Only a loving heavenly Father could have written the script.

"I know the plans I have for you."

...and then came Kosovo.

The Bridegroom

Oh love to Jesus, love divine,
to thee I give this heart of mine.
Why should it be,
I cannot see why you
suffered pain for me.
You hung there on that
cross of mine,
bleeding, breaking that I
should shine.

O master come and be with me,
I have such awful need of thee.
Come and give me peace within,
cleansc my heart from my own sin.
Let me live and love thee more,
together victory to store.
Until that day when angels call me home,
to live forever in thy love. JR.

Penned in the garden in the summer of 1992 before the call of God on our lives.
One does not have to be wise, wealthy or clever, anyone can step out with whatever amount of faith they possess.
May our steps be ordered by the.

Holy Ground Mission

(An interdenominational Missionary Society)

tick here

.... I am moved in my heart and wish to become part of this work by sending a donation of £.......

To Tax Payers in England only. (Where a gift is over £250 and you would like the Mission to get the benifit of the Tax relief please fill in a Gift Aid Form, available from the Mission)

.... I would like to invite one of the missionaries to come and share with our church or group the up-to-date position of the work, of how God is moving in the hearts of His people.

.... I would like to receive.........further copies of the book "**A time to live, a time to die**," in support of the Mission's ongoing work.
I am sending a cheque for £........having added an extra £1 per book to include post and packing.

.... I would like to receive............further copies of the book "**A time to live, a time to die**," to sell within our church as our way of supporting the work of the Mission. Please contact the Mission by Phone on 01226 200 133.

.... I would like to become a co-worker in my area to raise funding in support of the Mission's work.
My name and address is...
....
....
My Phone number is...

.... I am moved in my heart and will fill in the **Standing Order Mandate** in order to make a monthly gift towards the Mission's work.

The Mission will send to your bank:
STANDING ORDER MANDATE

To the Manager of...bank.

Address...

....

Please debit from my account, by the sum of:-

(in words).........................Every 4 weeks, (Quarter) (Year)

Account No............................Sort code............................

commencing...............; to the credit of the account, of the

Holy Ground Mission.
Account No. 28171183. Sort code 05-08-23
Yorkshire Bank, 12 Loundside, Chapeltown, Sheffield.

Signed ....

My Name is....................................Mr/Mrs/Other...........

My Address is...

....

Post Code......................Phone No....................................

Please Post to the **Holy Ground Mission.**
P.O. Box No. 275. Barnsley, S75-3YE. England.
Phone: (0044) International code. 01226 200133.

Only if you are a Tax Payer in England and you wish the Mission to get the benifit of Tax Relief on your Standing Order gift - please fill in the **Deed of Covenant** Form.

DEED OF COVENANT

To the **Holy Ground Mission.**

I promise to pay for......years, *(covenant gifts need to be for a minimum of four years)* or until I die if earlier, such sum as after deduction of income tax at the basic rate amounts of:- £...................

Every 4 weeks.(Quarter) (Year) for the benifit of the work done in Bosnia by the **Holy Ground Mission.**

From the date below

................................(This date must correspond with the date of signing and witnessing.)

Signed and delivered in the presence of a witness:-

....

Date........................

Full Name..

Address..

....

....

Witnessed by:- Signed...

Full Name..

Address..

....

Bless you and thank you!

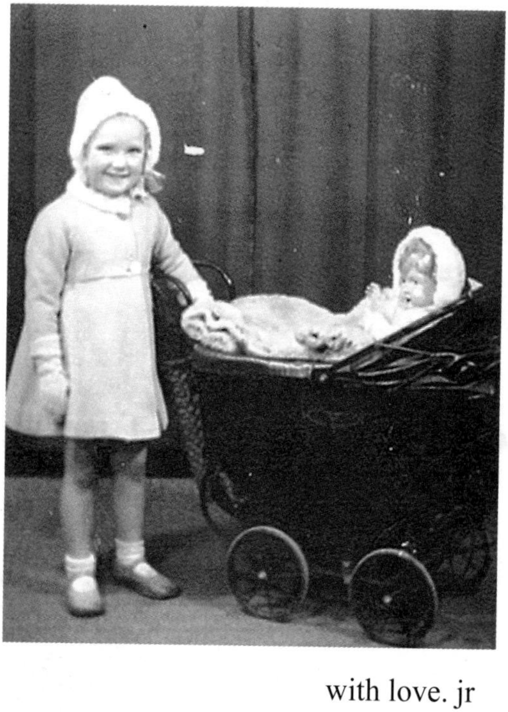

with love. jr